WHERE MOUNTAINS
ARE NAMELESS

Also by Jonathan Waterman

Arctic Crossing
The Quotable Climber (editor)
A Most Hostile Mountain
Kayaking the Vermilion Sea
Cloud Dancers (editor)
In the Shadow of Denali
High Alaska
Surviving Denali

WHERE MOUNTAINS ARE NAMELESS

Passion and Politics in the
Arctic National Wildlife Refuge

Including the Story of Olaus and Mardy Murie

JONATHAN WATERMAN

W. W. NORTON & COMPANY
New York London

Excerpts from "The Spell of the Yukon" by Robert Service and "Hey Mom, What Does Refuge Mean?" by Laurie Kutchins reprinted with permission. Olaus and Mardy Murie photos (first photo insert) courtesy NCTC Archives, Murie Collection. Arctic Refuge and wildlife photos (second photo insert) copyright Jonathan Waterman.

For information about permission to reproduce selections from this book, write to Permissions, W. W. Norton & Company, Inc., 500 Fifth Avenue, New York, NY 10110

Manufacturing by R.R. Donnelley, Harrisonburg
Book design by Rhea Braunstein
Map by John McAusland
Production manager: Julia Druskin

Library of Congress Cataloging-in-Publication Data

Waterman, Jonathan.
Where mountains are nameless : passion and politics in the Arctic National Wildlife Refuge : including the story of Olaus and Mardy Murie / Jonathan Waterman.— 1st ed.
p. cm.
Includes bibliographical references and index.
ISBN 0-393-05219-2
1. Natural history—Alaska—Arctic National Wildlife Refuge. 2. Petroleum—Prospecting—Environmental aspects—Alaska. 3. Endangered ecosystems—Alaska—Arctic National Wildlife Refuge. 4. Murie, Olaus Johan, 1889–1963. 5. Murie, Margaret E. I. Title.
QH105.A4W369 2005
333.95'16'097987—dc22

2005001374

W. W. Norton & Company, Inc., 500 Fifth Avenue, New York, N.Y. 10110
www.wwnorton.com

W. W. Norton & Company Ltd., Castle House, 75/76 Wells Street, London W1T 3QT

1 2 3 4 5 6 7 8 9 0

For my son, Nicholas,
and all those who shall inherit the wilderness.

There's a land where the mountains are nameless,
  And the rivers all run God knows where;
There are lives that are erring and aimless,
  And deaths that just hang by a hair;
There are hardships that nobody reckons;
  There are valleys unpeopled and still;
There's a land — oh, it beckons and beckons,
  And I want to go back — and I will.

—ROBERT SERVICE
"The Spell of the Yukon"

CONTENTS

PART I

PART II

AUTHOR'S NOTES

I first traveled to the Arctic twenty-one years ago as a skeptic. I'd already had the opportunity to explore the subarctic as a climbing bum, a Denali mountaineering ranger, and a wilderness guide. But my first experience north of latitude 66½—detailed in chapter 4—opened my senses to a strange new world. The summer sun arced across the northern horizon, the tundra had been ruptured by underground ice, and if you knew where to look, wildlife sign imprinted puddles, riverbanks, and willow stands. Still, the vast plain of tundra could appear utterly barren.

This lonely place did not foster indifference, you either became entranced or you left. I joined the former category and faithfully returned almost every year for the next two decades. Inadvertently, with no scientific agenda, outraged about the wilderness being considered as an oil field and then driven by curiosity to learn more about the landscape and its controversy, I had been snared by the same spell that captured Olaus and Mardy Murie. Olaus first went north in 1914, then, as a husband and wife team, they tracked the caribou in the 1920s, and three decades later they helped create the refuge. My wanderings in the Arctic drew me into the history of the region, to meet Mardy Murie, and to research her family's life. What I discovered about the Muries is detailed in the prologue and in the conclusion of each chapter.

My beliefs about oil development are not all subjective, or enlightened outdoor experiences, or thoughts gleaned from the insight of the Muries. Nor do I think it's necessary to walk the ground of northeast Alaska to make an informed decision on the controversy. For twenty-one years I have kept an open mind, listened carefully to both developers and conservationists, and read widely. I would like to believe that objective-minded readers—if they peruse the diverse titles in the bibliography that I learned from—can make a wise choice on oil versus wilderness. We cannot have both.

While indulging myself in the Arctic, I noted that the real gauntlet of wilderness travel is about immersing yourself into the natural world. Eventually, if a level of mastery is attained, the bears, mosquitoes, storms, rapids, and loneliness seem minor obstacles.

My journeys, which are detailed in the first part of each chapter, were about exploring with friends, often while paddling folding kayaks. Once I drove three thousand miles to Canada's MacKenzie River, and then paddled west alone, until I reached northeastern Alaska. I also guided backpackers, taught a college course, and found writing or photograph assignments to help underwrite the steep bush pilot fares to the remote refuge.

My journals cover eighteen trips to the far North, from 1983 to 2002. This geography is devoid of normal seasons, blurred by mirages, brightened by twenty-four-hour sunlight, and lacks the visual cues of our southern biosphere. The clock becomes oddly irrelevant here. Even with dated journals, travelers' remembrances grow fogged. To cope with this occluded time orientation, I became a zealous observer; I tried to become intimate with landscape, eventually developing a memory bank of animal meetings, as if I had stood in a receiving line greeting each species. My internal map and compass shifted to simple sensory perception—a powerful yet neglected tool among the modern adventurers' gadgetry. Through touching and smelling and listening and tasting and watching this place, I found a rapport with both wildlife and landscape that I'll take to my grave.

This vivid sense of place is strangely removed from my experiences below the Arctic Circle. Yet the dual narrative that follows—my story balanced by that of the Muries—is all accurate. Occasionally, in the interests of concision, I have taken a novelist's license in reordering several events, reconstructing dialogue from journals, and fictionalizing one place-name. Note that when referring to Denali National Park or Inuit in an historical context, I have substituted the older names, Mt. McKinley National Park or Eskimos.

A crucial footnote: During eight months in 1998 and 1999, I paddled, skied, and sailed across the roof of North America until I reached the Atlantic tides in Canada (this journey is described in my book *Arctic Crossing*). On that trip, the continent revealed some of its finest secrets: limestone arches and white-shell beaches and untouched expanses of river deltas. Sublime wilderness all.

Still, the seventeen hundred miles I traveled east into Canada were mostly flat and untroubled by potential oil development. Due to some quirk of my personality, that edge of continent didn't speak to me like Alaska's refuge. I didn't set out to prove this, so much as it surfaced—like the shining fluke of a bowhead whale in the rearview—as I flailed around the next point or surfed onto a new beach. In comparison to the refuge, all places to the east fell short.

Although the Canadian Arctic coast is more secluded, indented by larger bays, and cut by more rivers than northeastern Alaska, it is akin to comparing the subtle grace of the Midwest to the grandeur of the Rockies. I have also gazed into the Grand Canyon's depths, walked past Yellowstone's wonders, been bucked down several wild rivers, and stumbled up the highest peaks of most states. Yet the refuge remains a Garden, our last natural paradise. Throughout North America, no place has such a diverse concentration of wildlife or such an unlikely combination of pastoral and stormbound beauty. Its snowy mountains come booming up out of the sea, surrounded by sandy spits and lagoons, rimming a polygon-patterned coastal plain. The landscape turns and locks your eyes, continually spilling off into a limitless-looking horizon, regardless of where you stand. The slow-fluxing cataclysms of nature have created a world apart.

This corner of continent's edge is oddly unscarred by the most recent ice age, sequestered in summer lushness, and inhabited by millions of migratory animals—poised to flee at the initial chill of winter or the first tendrils of human industry.

To know this place is to desire its protection.

WHERE MOUNTAINS
ARE NAMELESS

THE GREAT GRANDMOTHER

"Am I dying?" Mardy Murie whispered.

"Yes," the nurse said, "but it's okay to let go."

"Can't," Mardy said.

She coughed, trying to clear her inflamed throat. Her nostrils flared beneath the nasal canula that delivered oxygen, and later, as she began choking on her food, the nurse grew increasingly concerned. Mardy Murie, you see, had turned 101 years old.

The obese hunter, Pooto, a furry cat that Mardy named after her favorite Eskimo, often crawled up into her lap. But when he flexed his claws against Mardy's chest, she no longer had the strength to lift Pooto off and set him down on the floor.

Outside, on the isolated Murie Ranch in Moose, Wyoming, the wildlife began behaving strangely. At night, the owls and coyotes and elk joined in a disturbing chorus of yowls. Never mind the grizzlies and black bear and red-eyed moose in rut.

Even the seasons seemed amplified. After a hard, dry summer of fires, snow came early in the fall of 2003. The twelve-thousand-foot-high Tetons were armored with ice so dazzling that people in the valley donned their winter sunglasses early.

In that river-rocked clearing beneath the Grand Teton, just inside the national park, Mardy's breathing grew labored. When her eyes rolled in pain, the doctor came out to the ranch. The pragmatic doctor, who had socialized at the ranch for decades, didn't understand why she was still alive. Although he had diagnosed both dementia and Parkinson's disease, he, like most of her visitors, believed that her eyes showed bright recognition as he moved for the door.

In a tiny voice the next day, as the nurse propped her upright, Mardy apologized that she couldn't be more helpful. That October 18, the nurse prepared the syringe of morphine, tritated in small doses, that would ease Mardy's throat pain. She didn't flinch as the nurse twisted the band on her arm. By now, most of Mardy's friends had converted their surprise into suspended awe, wondering if she would ever let go. The nurse waited for the vein to pop up, then slid the needle under the skin and gently pushed in the gift of morphine.

Mardy opened her mouth. The nurse expected another "Thank you sweetie pie," but this time Mardy fell silent. Still, she kept fighting for breaths.

Many said, with presentiment verging toward fiction, that she was still standing guard over her Arctic National Wildlife Refuge (ANWR), and she didn't want to let go until she knew it was safe. She had been told that another energy bill to open this refuge to oil leasing had reached the U.S. Senate floor. But the energy bill would be blocked, yet again, by Democratic filibusters.* On the other side, since 1978, the House had proposed the Morris Udall Wilderness Bill, which would prevent oil leasing on the 1.5-million-acre coastal plain, nine times. Although the bill was never passed, it gained new cosponsors with every session.

---

*The Energy Policy Act of 2003 had been influenced by the nation's jitters about that summer's blackout, the Iraq War, and demands to reduce dependence on foreign oil. The bill resurfaced and created contentious Senate discussion in 2004. As directed by the Alaska National Interest Lands Conservation Act (ANILCA), Congress has three choices for ANWR: to pass a wilderness bill preventing oil leasing, to pass a bill allowing oil leasing, or to do nothing.

A change seemed to be in the wind. National polls now showed that a majority of voters object to oil leasing in America's last wilderness. Even the oil companies had conceded that they were wary about the costly lawsuits they would face from the environmental lobby if the refuge was opened to oil leasing. Exxon had recently declared all new Alaska exploration off limits; British Petroleum had recently announced that it would confine exploration to already-open North Slope fields.

One of many Washington, D.C., lobbyists (and a repeat visitor to the Murie Ranch) had watched this issue for a quarter-century and now believed that the refuge had become iconic. Every one of five attempts—ending with a defeated Energy Bill in 2002—to open the coastal plain to oil leasing had been defeated.

Although neither side could concede to final defeat or declare victory, ANWR, like Mardy Murie, had become unassailable. So as Indian summer bloomed in 2003, as Congress deadlocked yet again on the issue of Arctic wilderness versus oil, Mardy figured that her time had come.

She knew that her part in the oil-versus-wilderness battle had ended just as she knew that she couldn't let go in early October. After the first storm and snow, her season of glory would come. It had already illuminated the bushes, and, eventually, it would still the wind.

Mardy may have been waiting for something else too. Those who knew about her marriage—a romance that had inspired people from Moose to Fairbanks—saw an explanation for Mardy's tenacity: She was planning a grand exit on October 21, the day that Olaus had died forty years ago. She claimed that not a moment went by without her thinking about her wildlife biologist husband.

She continued to wait and watch. The no-nonsense doctor knew—after Mardy implored him to clean the wax out of her ears—that his old friend also spent an inordinate amount of time listening for owls.

Outside her windows, the early snow had triggered spectacular colors, and while the summer had been dangerously dry, no one could remember a fall as brilliant. With unusual timing, the aspens had let loose their colors with the cottonwoods and the scrub oak.

Stranger still, the forest in the crook of the Snake River came alive with migrating owls. The Grand Teton National Park naturalists had never seen such a plethora of owls. Murie Center employees—fleece-jacketed naturalists who were accustomed to animal calls—became a bit spooked. By Saturday evening, the wheezing ritual between a male and a female northern saw-whet pair rose to a catlike screech.

Sandhill cranes, on their way to warmer climes, patrolled the marsh west of the ranch, confusing passersby with their bugling mimicry of the migrating elk herd— *"K-r-r-r-o-u-gh! K-r-r-r-o-u-gh! K-r-r-r-o-u-gh!"*

Wind shook the roofs. The aspen leaves rattled on the branches outside Mardy's room, just like the trees that quavered around her girlhood home in Fairbanks.

By dawn on October 19, the leaves had fallen onto the old river bottom surrounding the cabin. The sun flooded through the bare branches and into the windows onto Mardy, sitting in bed and fighting for breath. The wind had stilled.

The summer's heat and the quick freeze had turned other aspen groves a rare scarlet. Seen with the golden-yellow cottonwood and the blood-red hawthorn bushes along the blackened thread of the Snake River, the valley had gone afire.

Deep in the forest, a ruffed grouse beat its wings, over and over and over again. The sound—like a broken lawnmower—was felt rather than heard.

By mid-morning, as the valley warmed, it looked like the last good day for heading outside with a picnic lunch and a pair of binoculars to watch the flocks migrating south. As wood smoke poured out of the stone chimney, a riotous bugling of elk surrounded the ranch, rising to a chorus of high-pitched and silvery notes, then gliding back down to a series of guttural grunts known to the Murie family as "Wapiti music." The coyotes joined the cavalcade with outrageous yips and mournful howls, oblivious to the jets rattling the air above the expanded Jackson Hole airport.

In the brief spells of calm, the cabin in a spruce forest clearing— surrounded by beaver ponds and a cold river—seemed more Alaskan homestead than Wyoming ranch. One couldn't help thinking that the Murie lives too came from a yarn more nineteenth than twenty-first century, as much fairy tale as wilderness drama.

Who could imagine making it alone to the age of 101 in a dark and drafty log cabin?

To understand the spark that lit this woman and her husband's days, you must journey north, to the refuge. Here, above the Arctic Circle, in the northeast corner of Alaska, the summer rivers are sheeted with blue *aufeis* and the air clicks with insects. Petite grizzlies and large white bears prowl either side of the coast. Gauntribbed wolves bay toward the heavens. And the hooves of a vast caribou herd shake the tundra.

Go there. If you dare.

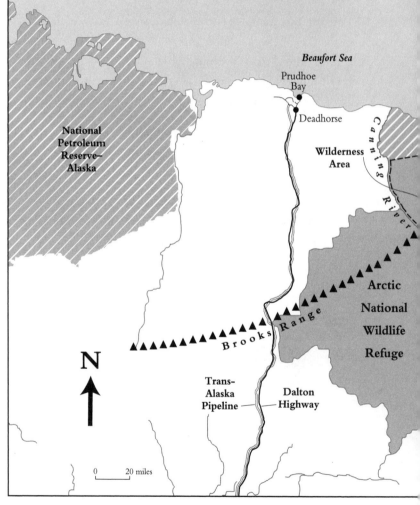

The Arctic
National
Wildlife
Refuge

1 Arctic National Wildlife Refuge
2 Northwest Territory
3 Yukon Territory
4 1002 Coastal Plain

Beaufort Sea

Prudhoe
Bay

Deadhorse

National
Petroleum
Reserve–
Alaska

Wilderness
Area

Canning River

Arctic

National

Wildlife

Refuge

Brooks Range

N

↑

Trans-
Alaska
Pipeline

Dalton
Highway

0   20 miles

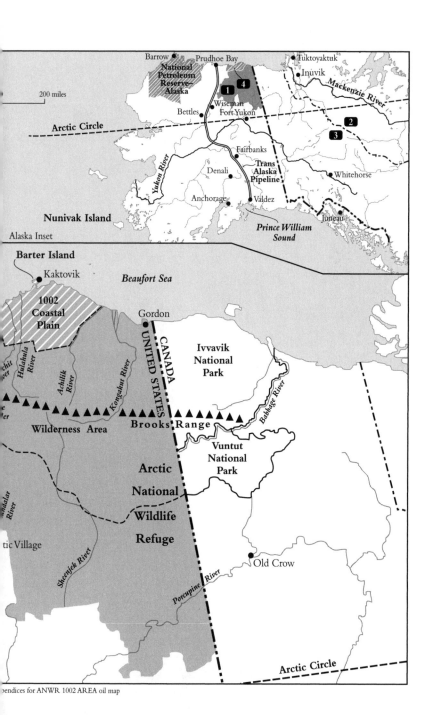

200 miles

Barrow • Prudhoe Bay • Tuktoyaktuk
National
Petroleum
Reserve–
Alaska
1 4
Bettles • Wiseman
Fort Yukon

Arctic Circle

Fairbanks
Denali
Trans
Alaska
Pipeline
Anchorage • Valdez

Whitehorse

Nunivak Island

Alaska Inset

Prince William
Sound

Juneau

Mackenzie River

Inuvik

2
3

Barter Island

• Kaktovik

Beaufort Sea

Gordon

1002
Coastal
Plain

Ivvavik
National
Park

Hulahula River
Achilik River
Kongakut River
Babbage River

Wilderness Area   Brooks Range

Vuntut
National
Park

Arctic

National

Wildlife

Refuge

Sheenjek River

Old Crow

Porcupine River

Arctic Circle

CANADA
UNITED STATES

Sadlerochit River
Chandalar River
tic Village

endices for ANWR 1002 AREA oil map

PART I

Arctic Refuge/Murie Timeline

1889—Olaus Johann Murie is born on March 1; the *Smithsonian Annual Report* decries the bison's extermination.

1901—President Roosevelt creates the first federally protected wildlife refuge: Pelican Island, in Florida.

1902—Margaret (Mardy) Elizabeth Thomas is born on August 18.

1905—The first national conservation group, the Audubon Society, is founded.

1906—Congress passes the American Antiquities Act, which allows presidents to establish protected wild lands.

1916—Congress passes the National Park Service Act to protect scenic wild lands, partly in response to public outcry over the 1913 approval of Hetch Hetchy dam being built in Yosemite National Park.

1914—Olaus Murie spends two years in the Canadian Arctic collecting birds for the Carnegie Museum.

1920—Government biologist Olaus Murie takes part in a six-year caribou study in the Alaska Territory.

1923—Leaded gasoline goes on sale in Ohio. President Harding creates the twenty-three-million acre Petroleum Reserve (eighty miles west of today's Arctic National Wildlife Refuge) to provide emergency oil supplies for the military.

1924—Congress passes a weakened Oil Pollution Act, which prohibits spilling oil within three miles of shore, but does not prohibit spills from refineries.

1935—The Wilderness Society is created by Aldo Leopold and Arthur Carhardt to protect wilderness areas.

1937—The term "greenhouse effect" is coined in Glen Trewartha's *An Introduction to Weather and Climate.*

1938—Bob Marshall proposes that Congress protect all of Alaska north of the Yukon River.

1946—Olaus Murie quits the U.S. Biological Survey and becomes the director of the Wilderness Society; the Survey is renamed Fish and Wildlife Service (USFWS, administrator of national wildlife refuges).

1953—**Park Service planner George Collins reconnoiters Alaska for inclusion in a series of parks or wildlife sanctuaries and recommends that Olaus spearhead the protection of the northeast corner of the territory.**

Chapter 1

ESKIMO LESSONS

uksualungniartik (one who attends to great blubber)
—Inuktitut for *oil company*

I had been alone for weeks when companionship surfaced behind
my paddle and breathlessly gasped, "*Ohhhhh!*" From the corner
of my eye, it bobbed like a polar bear in size and color and swimming ability, but when it spouted a clammy wet breath, I relaxed.
The white beluga whale stretched no longer than my kayak. She
wore a fixed smile as a powerful tail flick sent her back into the
depths.

I took a few deep breaths. The Beaufort Sea glowed impossibly
black and the beach lacked surf, shells, or seaweed. Then, while rolling
my cigarette a stone's throw out from shore, a pink speckled lion's
mane sea jelly, trailing a skirt of toxic reddened tentacles, hovered
past—unexpected as a nighttime explosion of fireworks in the Lower
Forty-eight sky.

I had long stared into and across this frozen water, which didn't
show the blue shimmer of most oceans. It felt more tannin lake
than Arctic Ocean because the ice pack, two dozen miles north,
quelled wave action. I paddled onward, rudely rippling the perfect
black mirror, defying nature's best-laid plans.

I had just crossed the Canadian border into Alaska's Arctic

National Wildlife Refuge. I was headed to Prudhoe Bay. I didn't know what day it was and my wristwatch lay stowed at the bottom of a leaky dry bag. Still, each minute crept by so slowly, and was so filled with nuance, that a sense of wonder began growing over my skepticism.

To chill out, I pulled off the neoprene glove and plunged my hand in for several seconds until the ice water radiated up to my elbow, simulating a pinched nerve. The deck thermometer registered fifty-one degrees. The water lay at its usual thirty-nine degrees, which, in the case of capsize, might allow me several minutes to swim ashore, where I would lock up with hypothermia. So I paddled a stone's throw north of land—allowing a minute to strip wet clothing, and three minutes to torch a life-saving fire with the waterproof matches hanging from a vial around my neck. Firewood would be no problem.

Driftwood had first floated hundreds of miles down Canada's Mackenzie River, then blew west and got plowed by the ice pack up onto thin barrier islands a half-mile offshore. An undulating pile of breastworks stacked as far as I could see. Despite the abundance of wood, walking to the nearest forest would take a week.

In front of the sun-whitened spruce logs, above the high-tide line, the sand had been pocked with animal prints that could be any one of dozens of species wandering the coastal plain. If the caribou herd approached, other hungry species would emerge and give chase. If the herd fled, the bears and wolverines and wolves disappeared. I had learned that you had to key out tracks, smell the air, and pick apart scats in order to understand the local inhabitants. So I lifted the warped binoculars and glassed the tracks for a hundred yards west. The print maker showed unmistakably large, rounded, flipper tracks, striding straight and purposeful into the sea without returning. Just like a polar bear.

I kept paddling west, sweeping eyes back and forth. For seven long days, I hadn't seen people, planes, or boats. Although I woke up many mornings imagining a short obituary about an unarmed kayaker traveling without a radio, this fear went away once the afternoons waddled past and I started interacting with wilderness. In spite of fresh polar bear sign.

For my comfort, a sleeping bag stuffed into a waterproof-duffle-cum-seat insulated my rear end. A gamy black neoprene pullover under a white wool hat lined with nylon blocked the wind and slowed the radiative and convective cooling that dulls the brain. A thermos of hot herbal tea lay stuffed beside my right hip. My feet, encased in neoprene socks inside of rubber boots, felt like blocks of wood. If vigorous toe wiggling didn't bring back some painful circulation, I would soon be pouring the tea directly into my boots.

The ice pack drew closer, whitening the horizon. Clouds cloaked the sun. As the north glowed white, it sent the strange temptation to follow that big white bear out into this Beaufort Sea light, to keep chasing utopia out beyond the roof of the continent.

Pebbles ticked down a bluff, wind spilled around boulders, sea sighed on shore, and birds keened into the big sky. Although I felt delighted not to see border stations, mile markers, outhouses, or ranger stations, I wouldn't have minded some Iñupiat Eskimo, who had a way of putting things into perspective.*

Iñupiat feared getting lost, as in losing track of time and space and allowing oneself to get sucked into capsizing along that bright sucker hole toward the North Pole. They called this hallucinatory state *nangiarneq,* kayak angst. They staved it off by listening to the land.

---

*At the 1979 Inuit Circumpolar Conference in Barrow, the People announced their age-old "Inuit" (Persons) name and specified more regionally correct names such as Iñupiat, Yupik, or Inuvaluit. Canada made the change to "Inuit," but "Eskimo" still persists, while "Iñupiat Eskimo" is often used to refer to those Native Alaskans who have long dwelled north and immediately west of ANWR.

The challenge, at least to my ears and eyes, was that the refuge seemed so difficult to define and so unlike any other place. As the smooth sea folded up against the black skin of land, the earth resembled a green garment: wrinkled by hills, furred with ankle-high plants, and—if I looked closely along those seams chafed by seawater—sheeted with white permafrost ice that lay exposed beneath peaty tundra.

From my cockpit vantage point the refuge did not appear beautiful or particularly inviting. Nor was it warm, easy to walk, flat, colorful, or in any way friendly or familiar. Icy sea air colliding with tepid land air bent the light waves, creating a mirage, blurring the distant ice pack into gleaming skyscrapers and morphing the land into a giant bluish puddle. Up above, the atmosphere swam milky blue and it was no illusion that Alaska's northern skies were free of contrails.

If vision couldn't be trusted, animals here relied on their sense of smell. Unless something just died, or unless I walked over the tundra and sniffed a clutch of perfumed twinflowers or a pile of grassy caribou pellets, I smelled nothing. To my nose the cold sea lacked odors.

I held the shore on my port side and paddled west into a several-mile pan of pack ice held against the shore. Small icebergs caught the hidden sun and phosphoresced like light bulbs under the cloud curtain. I squeezed through the tightening pack—past a crystalline swan and a toothless alligator, carved by wind and water—until the tilting pans clutched my throat with adrenaline. One flip of even a small berg and I'd be squashed and thrown into ice water. I exited north through a long lead.

I scanned for sneaky polar bears. I also scanned for their favorite food—ringed seals—lounging on the ice. But everyone hid today. So I amused myself by paddle sprinting. I clocked out at five miles per hour until my elbows went rubbery; hungry polar bears paddled a lot faster while chasing dinner. Still, to keep in practice, I held the sprint for a mile, rounding the ice pack toward a huge, bizarre-looking iceberg. I needed to confirm it wasn't an ancient bird, thawed from its permafrost moorings.

Every day, for the three weeks since I left the Mackenzie Delta a few hundred miles east, I chased (and was chased by) mysteries: a gargoyle waltzing on the water, unknown sea creatures gently bumping against the kayak, strange humming noises, stones spit up by the permafrost, caribou marching across the tundra in linear formation, or lion's manes dissolving on the shore into spent piles of bloody jelly. Discovery loomed around every corner.* The taxonomic minutia of this ancient land and seascape had its way of keeping one awake.

This confusing monster iceberg was particularly perplexing. The nearest glacial icebergs were supposed to be a continent away, and the winter pan ice here seldom froze higher than I sat. I poked the pterodactyl once with my paddle: rock solid. Did currents carry it all the way from Greenland? Water lapped on its northern rime feathers. Paddling within spitting distance below its southern beak, I imagined the dino-berg taking a quick roll, so I retreated back toward my safety zone, a quick swim away from shore. Alone and tired, it was smart to leave some mysteries be.

With the sky brightening, it must have been midnight. Time to try sleeping. Since the beach lacked large prints, I decided to cook instead of eating granola again. I tested the wind: still blowing east, which would send my food smells in a direction without any bears—or so I hoped. I pumped up the stove, squirted out a thimbleful of white gas, clicked it afire with my lighter, then ran down

---

*In 1954, several miles across the Canadian border, within sight of the ocean, an Inuit elder guided Dr. R. S. MacNeish to a hill above the Firth River. They unearthed nine prehistoric layers, including the oldest in New World history: a four-thousand-year-old, flint-tooled hunting culture that predated the Eskimo.

to the shore and snatched up a pot of seawater. In my titanium pot, it looked like any other ocean, but its low brine made it ideal for boiling spaghetti. The only problem with cooking was that the roar of the stove might block the sound of footsteps, growls, or barks of approaching animals. I unpocketed my canister of bear mace and my air horn and placed them within reach of my right hand.

After a long boil, I twisted the stove valve off. The sudden silence seemed deafening. While I listened and looked for visual clues into a sense of place, it appeared obvious that the so-called nights mimicked the seasons here: midnight rolled right into day as summer got stolen by winter. Evening and dawn were diminished, just like spring and fall.

I ate ravenously with my fingers and, in the raw fastness of that icy day, dinner went cold as I slurped up the last salty strand. I walked downwind, and to keep scent-drawn animals out of camp, I scraped food from my pot, hands, and face with sand. Then I rinsed clean with the black sea and brushed without toothpaste. Time to try sleeping again.

At 2:46 A.M., according to the watch I dug out, it was Wednesday—meaning absolutely nothing. I had no itinerary other than taking my time and getting to know the Arctic National Wildlife Refuge. I was lying somewhere east of the Kongakut River delta that stretched wider than Manhattan, shrunken within a South Carolina–sized refuge. No one knew where I was, and, the way I preferred it, no one cared.

I lay wide awake in a tent that compacted smaller than a toaster oven. Through the bear window, I watched the sun belly crawl across a northern horizon more expansive than any place I knew. I closed my eyes and listened to mosquitoes clicking against the nylon walls like rain.

Then I heard the owl. I hooted back, holding shut my nose and projecting a guttural voice through my cupped hand: "*Brooooo,*

Brooooo, Brooooo." Although the snowy owl never showed its face, the bird replied, if only to let me know that we weren't alone. It was tempting to see this bird as an augury for my journey, and while that kind of thinking might have worked for the Greeks and for the Iñupiat Eskimo—who revered the snowy owl, *opik,* as a being of spiritual powers—I couldn't afford the luxury of getting any more sentimental and scared then I already felt.

"If I die, and it is a possibility out here," I wrote in my sacred journal, "someone is going to think I had planned it." I tapped the pencil against my upper lip, looked out the tent door again for intruders, then continued listing my fears as if they might make some sort of a difference:

Capsizing offshore. Griz mauling me in my sleep. Nanook surfacing hungrily alongside my kayak. Losing my mind (whatever that means) and committing a grievous error in judgment, like trying to practice my faulty Eskimo roll in ice water.

If nothing else, I had learned, the journal was a tool that might allow me a new understanding and perspective of the Arctic. I then turned to jotting map notations about yesterday's wildlife sign and drew latitude and longitude lines to match up the coming day's bearings. Through this obtuse pride in navigation and dead reckoning skills, and through my awareness of the animal beings who shared this corner of the continent, I wanted to believe in a newfound sense of belonging and mastery. I took these skills for granted while traveling with companions. Alone in the Arctic, however, I felt tested every moment. It seemed likely that hungry noses were sniffing after me, but maybe instinct could be subverted by my overactive metabolism—jacked up from the constant daylight.

Finally, so tired and pasta-bloated that I hit sensory overload, I dozed off with the map as a pillow. And I forgot to set the hourly alarm to check for marauding bears.

I woke up at mid-morning with a stiff neck. I pulled down the tent, stuffed it into the dry bag, and ramrodded it up into the bow with the paddle. Two other dry bags followed, quickly. Back before I'd begun stowing the wristwatch for the day's paddling, I had drilled to pack camp within ten minutes—no telling when a bear would demand a rapid retreat. This morning I got it down to nine minutes, forty seconds.

Since I had eaten my way through half the food stowed in the Klepper kayak, I unlashed the book bag from atop the stern and placed it in front of the rudder pedals. I was rereading *Desert Solitaire,* my favorite conservation book, because Ed Abbey advocated going alone into the wilderness to let his sense of self "ebb away." I also carried the last three of Patrick O'Brian's Aubrey/Maturin novels, Herman Melville's *Moby-Dick,* Peter Mathiessen's *Far Tortuga,* two-hundred pages copied from the *Audubon Encyclopedia of Birds,* a Latin-English dictionary, E. C. Pielou's *A Naturalist's Guide to the Arctic,* and Olaus Murie's *Animal Tracks.* My ten-pound dry bag of books gave me more comfort than a shotgun.

I paid close attention to Pielou. She believed that the polar bear lurked just as dangerously as the barren-ground grizzly, and that the two species—related to the same two-hundred-thousand-year-old ancestor—could interbreed in captivity.

Murie had only seen one (wounded) polar bear in the wild, and since it had fled across a field of sphagnum moss, he couldn't cast its tracks, so he settled for a more cooperative bear at the Woodland Park Zoo in Seattle. In his *Animal Tracks,* the rear polar bear foot, nine by twelve inches, was not unlike a wide human foot until you picked out the hair obscuring the pads and how their gait made the rear footprints overlap with the front feet. I often reread Murie's findings about the white bear eating vegetation as well as meat. This offered consolation when you were soloing through the Arctic without a gun because you thought bears could be talked out of camp.

Now that my kayak sat packed and a quick exit seemed assured, I strolled the beach looking for more sign. The Brooks Range— forty miles south and a mile and a half above the sea—had just emerged from a dull-steel-colored cloudbank. Geologists knew this constellation of nameless peaks as the spine of the continent, the lynchpin of the Rocky Mountains. Today it slept blanketed with dazzling snow. Time to pull up the sunglasses.

Plants grew in a tangle up beyond the beach. Dryads, louseworts, lichens, diapensia, dwarf fireweed, horsetails, arnicas—I couldn't begin to identify them all. They formed a vast carpet of muted greens and grays and even a stray daub of purple polka-dotted with white cottongrass. These plants floated on a several-inches-deep sea of plant carcasses, or peat tundra, all blanketing a quarter-mile of permafrost. Looking south across the tundra seemed like looking north over the icebergs: I could only see 5 percent of the plants. The other 95 percent, roots, lay sheltered under this wet tundra. Forests couldn't grow here partly because tree trunks lack insulation against the subzero winters—unlike the plants buried beneath the snow and tundra—and mostly because the shallow peat won't support tree roots.

Early explorers searching for gold or a route to the riches of the Orient called this the barrenlands. Not until scientists such as Murie and Pielou arrived did we come to understand the peat as a biomass, a welter of trapped carbon and roots and larvae and water richer than a forest. But history, combined with ambitious political agendas, has a way of repeating itself: Today's Arctic explorers wildcat for black gold, but they still call this place the barrenlands, a lifeless swamp, even though science shows otherwise.

This wet biomass of coastal plain acts as a kitchen for the Porcupine caribou herd, worn out from a thousand-mile migration that fords ice-choked rivers and rocky mountainsides. As the bands crowd into an aggregation of over a hundred-thousand animals, then birth thousands more calves, the adults chomp a variety of easily digested cottongrass, sedge, lupine, river beauty, leaves, and twigs—an abundance found nowhere else in their range. They go hundreds of yards out of their way for the pink-tipped lousewort, waving its head like a strawberry ice-cream cone. Nursing cows, in particular, depend upon the proteins in this kitchen to nurse their newborn calves.

No landscape in the Arctic—for three-thousand miles from the Bering Sea to the Atlantic Ocean—matches the terrarium accelerator effect here. The continuous summer sunlight cues quadrillions of miniature sun-gathering leaves and plant receptors into a Lilliputian pandemonium of photosynthesis. Then mountain snow melts down onto this Delaware-sized, superfertilized sponge. The glaciated mountains seep, spill, and roar across the tilted plain. From below, the thick lens of weeping permafrost ensures that no plant thirsts. The resulting riot of plants and hatching insects draws millions of birds and mammals.

These were my thoughts while walking east along the windy beach rimming the coastal plain—until I crossed the tracks of another polar bear trailed by two lightweight pawed cubs. The sow's half-inch-deep prints stretched a third bigger than my own size twelves. Since this species doesn't dig like the grizzly, the prints lacked claw marks. And just like the Murie guidebook said, hair obscured the pads. It seemed silly to kneel down then to sniff and finger the prints, trying to snatch some inverse texture from this bear's feet, but it never hurt to pretend that there was still enough wilderness left in North America to permit these small pleasures. I followed the tracks for another mile, sniffing where they sniffed, peeing upon their marked logs, but my friends left no scats—maybe they were starving?

I ran back toward my kayak.

I ran on the balls of my feet, jumping driftwood and creeks and crossing up onto the lumpy tundra, my hands out for balance—a two-legged omnivore could easily trip on this frost-heaved tundra. I held a pace that let me fill my lungs without getting out of breath, stretching the tension out of my legs and bringing a breeze onto my face that thwarted mosquitoes. The land rolled past my distended nostrils with the fennel smell of a ground squirrel home, the licorice hint of ripped-up bear root, and the swampy tundra gassing out its carbons in the warm morning sun. I glanced downward to adjust my foot placements on the spongy mat of earth that was swallowing up rocks and shed antlers and bones, squishy soft then hard then alternately swaying beneath my feet.

It took fifteen minutes to return to the kayak, long enough to feel warmed up. Sweat pooled on my clavicle. With two middle fingers on my carotid, I felt my heart trotting like a wolf. *This is not fear,* I thought. *These are my senses floodgating open to the world.*

Still, the presence of bears and the constant daylight was making me an insomniac. Ten days ago, too jittery to pitch the tent and block my view of approaching bears, I woke up in terror behind a driftwood windbreak as I heard the animal of my dreams rifling through my kayak. I shouted: "Please go away bear!" just as a whiskered fox face popped up out of my cockpit.

Twenty-five hundred polar bears (ten times the number of grizzlies) lived here in the southern Beaufort Sea. The population of polar bears has grown more than 3 percent since 1968, the same year that oil was discovered at nearby Prudhoe Bay. The temptation to conclude that oil development is compatible with polar bears would overlook the Marine Mammal Protection Act of 1972, which prohibited hunting for polar bears in Alaska except by native subsistence hunters, which in turn allowed the bear population to expand. In 1973 an agreement signed between Canada, the United States, Norway, Denmark, and the Soviet Union committed each nation to save the big white bears by protecting their habitat and denning areas.

According to Fish and Wildlife Service (USFWS) biologists, 150 maternal polar bear dens were discovered between Canada's Point Bathhurst and Alaska's northwestern beach during the last two decades. Seventy-three of these dens had been dug along eight hundred miles of shore, while thirty-two of those lay along the eighty-mile-long coast of the refuge. This data—gleaned through satellite tracking of 106 collared female polar bears—showed how the isolated and hilly edges of the refuge offered den sites that polar bears couldn't find elsewhere in Alaska.

Environmentalists and biologists claimed that the proposed oil development would destroy the aesthetics of this wilderness as well as wreak havoc on its animals. In 1995 the USFWS, whose biologists have traditionally opposed oil drilling while its bureaucrats often support it, completed two biology reports suggesting that oil exploration would violate the International Agreement for Conservation of Polar Bears.* Those who supported drilling said that aesthetic values were subjective—one person's wilderness was another's barrenlands. In researched, peer-reviewed reports, USFWS biologists wrote that denning polar bears could adapt to industry. The Department of the Interior report doesn't clarify how this adaptation will happen, but if it fails, euthanasia or tranquilization and helicopter transport were their only options.†

---

*As of this writing, the present Interior Secretary, Gail Norton, allegedly withheld and then rewrote biological information within the two reports before submitting them to Congress, which is in charge of determining the refuge's future. Norton's spokesperson told the *Washington Post* in spring 2001 that the international agreement does not prohibit oil development.

†The seventy-five-page report mentions the population of polar bears surrounding the oil complex at Prudhoe Bay: "Although contact with hydrocarbons can have serious ramifications for polar bears (Amstrup et al. 1989) the polar bears' apparent rapid population growth has spanned the entire story of petroleum in arctic Alaska (Amstrup 2000, Amstrup et al. 2001). This suggests that managed resource development can be compatible with healthy polar bear populations." (See U.S. Department of the Interior, *Arctic Refuge Coastal Plain Terrestial Wildlife Research Summaries,* in the bibliography.)

From my perspective, alone in a sea kayak, the small privileges—chasing an elusive sense of wilderness mastery, flaunting a dream of being an explorer—would be lost amid the industrial infrastructure that the oil companies propose: a series of roads, pipelines, airstrips, drilling pads, and buildings. I was aware, however, that my perspective might not represent that of most Americans. Also, as an oil consumer, it seemed fair to keep an open mind about the controversy—particularly since both environmentalists and oil developers can play fast and loose with facts. Most of what I knew for sure was this: if drilling on the 1.5 million acres got approved by Congress, it would all be built just in front of me on a rectangle of coastal plain twenty-five miles wide by one hundred miles long, surrounded by another eighteen-million acres of wildlife refuge.

My reveries were interrupted by the distant growl of boats. After being immersed in primeval solitude, the whining yowl of approaching two-cycle engines yanks you back into the here and now with astonishing speed. Looking west, I spied steamships with smokestacks that, as they approached through the mirage air, altered into two black skiffs bristling with Iñupiat rifles, crossing over the blurry western horizon and into focus.

My first reaction, after not seeing or talking to anyone for a week, was to hide, but the flat shoreline lacked cover. I braced myself for their arrival.

Now my greatest fear was not the prospect of further solitude, but whether I could hold a coherent conversation. On this neutral-smelling seashore, no nostril would miss the vinegary presence of an unbathed kayaker. Even worse, my shaggy hair and dark beard might offend the clean-shaven Iñupiat. So I reminded myself to smile, to speak in friendly tones, and to resist asking questions—Iñupiat perceive verbal curiosity as rudeness. Suddenly, I wanted to roll over for a quick bath, with the hope that their game-wary eyes might somehow miss the underside of a kayak. Reentering civilization, I had learned, was never easy.

Fortunately, Iñupiat etiquette about withholding questions made them conversational minimalists. And if they thought me crazy, it was partly because I chose to go alone in the wilderness, and partly because I had no engine. Both boats choked out their Evinrudes, and they sat staring curiously at the new species paddling their old kayak.

I smiled. All eight nonswimmers sat in boats with gunnels just inches above the waterline, because the boats were overloaded with an ATV each for chasing caribou. A month earlier, a Canadian coast guard official had told me that the most common cause of death among these people was drowning, but it would be an unthinkable breach of protocol to ask why they weren't wearing life jackets.

The group all looked to the elder so that he could talk first. His missing teeth flattened his pronunciation: "MynameisThomasGordon." Even while speaking English, these noble people annunciated from their throats, as if gargling mosquitoes.

I introduced myself and then we studied one another. His family name marked the map a few miles back as an abandoned trading camp, Gordon. I took a deep breath. Greeting people after solitude seemed challenging, but making conversation without questions was akin to dancing with two left feet.

I wanted to ask what they thought about the proposed oil development. But this was not the time or the place.

"See the polar bear," Thomas said, more statement than question.

"No," I kept smiling.

"He is following you," Thomas looked toward the Canadian border and just to let me know he wasn't kidding about the bear, he spat up from his throat the Iñupiat name, not to be found on any map, of the place he saw "Nanook" digging up and eating my last "poop." This came as no surprise, because hungry wild animals frequently dig up human feces. Then, since he was the elder and I was the unkempt stranger, he broke etiquette and posited a quick question.

"Got a *firearm*?" He put unneeded emphasis on the last word.

I pulled out my little bear banger from the cockpit pocket and proudly held it up. Even if I did feel like talking, I wouldn't mention that the device prompted no more than a glance from grizzlies when I fired it above their heads.

The elder smiled politely. I nodded back respectfully. Inside my head, I wrestled with a newly emerging despair. Before meeting these supremely adapted nomads of the North, I had found an intuition and sense of belonging with my favorite wilderness: sensing grizzlies before seeing them, feeling bearded seals riffling gently below my kayak, keying out plants, smelling animal kills, and concentrating on distant sounds to identify unseen birds. But these Iñupiat thought of me as a foolish loser without a gun.

I couldn't tell if being alone in the refuge had slowed down time or if I was just unaccustomed to the long-suffering and patient manner of Iñupiat, but everything

felt like

slow

motion.

I reached under the spray skirt with the movements of an underwater swimmer to pull out my secondary bear protection—the air horn. The elder suppressed a laugh as we bounced in the blackish swell. Water sloshed in over one of their starboard gunnels, but no one seemed to care. Then a loon brayed from a far-off pond. Someone farted in basso imitation, and the elder immediately grunted his approval of this performance, but everyone else remained deadpan. I smiled again, if only because the kids were staring at me.

Then we all watched reverently as a flock of guillemots undulated across the horizon like a curl of smoke, and it hit me that these people had also come out here in the wilderness to let their senses of self ebb away.

Without shame, I unveiled the final polar bear solution: my spray canister of bear mace. Instead of laughing, everyone in the boats—two aghast children, two taciturn women, and four middle-aged men doing their best to appear nonplussed—looked at the elder for approval. Thomas Gordon cleared his throat as he pointed his crooked finger at my spray canister. The group suddenly began smiling, anticipating his reply.

"*That*," he said, deadpan, annunciating the first and last syllables in high-pitched emphasis: "just piss the polar bear *off*."

BACK IN THE VILLAGE of Kaktovik, Thomas Gordon hung his caribou meat out to dry. Meat and fish hung everywhere, on wooden racks or off rusted snowmobiles, like scarlet clumps of laundry.

Before they realized how many millions of dollars oil development would bring to their unplumbed town, Iñupiat opposed oil development in the refuge. Like the Gwich'in, 150 miles south in Arctic Village, Iñupiat looked forward to hunting the caribou and thought the oil development might chase the herd away. Along with caribou, Iñupiat also harvest fish, seals, and up to three bowhead whales per year.*

As I walked through town, past a putrefying whale carcass dragged up on shore, past faces staring out of windows then darting backward—resembling scenes from a Hitchcock film—it helped to review their past. These friendly yet diffident people had learned to fear white strangers coming to their isolated island.

---

*Over the several thousand years that the greater Inuit nation spread from Alaska to Greenland, the People have not eradicated any species that they hunt and eat. It is the hunters and polluters from below the Arctic Circle who have endangered northern populations of whales, seals, polar bears, and musk oxen.

In 1947, as the U.S. Air Force built its first airstrip and Distant Early Warning (DEW) line of radar sites on the island, several families were forced to move. Nomadic hunters along the coast, who might be mistaken for Russian invaders, were relocated from their coastal homes and camps and moved onto the eastern edge of the five-mile wide, bell-shaped island. As the cold war continued to send forth a chill of northern invasion, the military forced the burgeoning village to move twice more.

Their whole way of life changed. They stopped speaking Inuktitut. They even got jobs, working for *tanik,* the white man.

After oil was discovered nearby, the North Slope Borough was formed by the Iñupiat living in Barrow, roughly 300 miles west of Kaktovik. By 1971, the Alaska Native Claims Settlement Act (ANCSA) gave indigenous Alaskans a huge chunk of Alaskan wilderness and $962 million. The Iñupiat signed, then incorporated as the Arctic Slope Regional Corporation, the richest of thirteen Alaska Native Corporations.*

For Iñupiat shareholders, more than most natives, the deal was lucrative because their lands sat above rich reservoirs of Arctic oil. The Kaktovik Iñupiat suddenly owned surface rights to ninety-six thousand acres of oil seeps immediately south of their village. To the west, where the oil companies had already begun tapping into other oil reservoirs, the Iñupiat owned several times the acreage. The money raised from oil company leases brought in a per capita tax income that out-grossed any white-collar community in the Lower Forty-eight.

While ANCSA gave the Alaskan natives forty-four million acres, a 130-word clause inserted at the last minute instructed the

---

*Senator Ted Stevens sponsored legislation that allowed the indigenous peoples of Alaska to become corporate shareholders. According to a later exposé in the *Los Angeles Times*, Stevens made millions by acting as a silent partner in business deals with the Iñupiat through the Arctic Slope Regional Corporation.

Secretary of the Interior to choose eighty million acres for the people of the United States. These expansions and additions would include national parks, national forests, wilderness areas, wild and scenic rivers, and wildlife refuges. This unprecedented and hotly debated legislation was called the Alaska National Interest Lands Conservation Act (ANILCA),* and it opened up the refuge's oil controversy.

As Iñupiat signed the lucrative ANCSA, the Gwich'in refused "the diseased money" and were given the ancestral land surrounding their village on the southern boundary of the refuge. Historically, these two tribes had been blood enemies. While Iñupiat were wary of the spirit-stealing trees surrounding the Gwich'in villages, the southern natives suspected these tundra-dwelling Eskimos (literally, Eskimo means eater of raw meat) of being barbarians.

However environmentalists might judge Iñupiat Eskimo support of the oil companies, no one can accuse them of being inhospitable. For three days I stayed in the Waldo Arms Hotel, and stocked up on groceries in the Kikitak store, and nobody would let me pay. This generosity seemed linked with the news that had spread through town that some crazy *tanik* was traveling alone across the Arctic in a kayak—their mythical tool.

The mud yards of Kaktovik's plywood modular homes bristled with polar bear hides, sealskins, fish bones, abandoned pieces of plywood, engine parts, toilet bags, tools, hooves, horns, antlers, rusted rifles, and toys. A sled dog howled against its tether on a four-

---

*President Carter evoked his executive privilege from the 1906 Antiquities Act to sign ANILCA in December 1980. As the greatest act of wilderness preservation in the world, ANILCA protected 28 percent of Alaska and doubled the size of ANWR. Yet according to section 1002 of the act, only half of the coastal plain, from the Aichilik River to the Canadian border, would be declared wilderness. The other half, from the Aichilik to the Canning River, would be studied for oil development. Then Congress could declare whether to open the so-called 1002 Area for oil leasing, or close it as protected wilderness.

wheeler. A child walked by dressed in a traditional wolverine-ruffed parka playing a handheld Nintendo game. Fish lay drying next to a rusted harpoon near the gleaming white radar dish of the DEW line station.

In the Inuktitut language, *Qaaktugvik*, or Kaktovik, means seining place, and *qaaktag* means cisco. The fish, some said, were being destroyed by the temperature-changing oil causeways leading out to the man-made islands around Prudhoe Bay to the west.

The people often clarified their main industry, avocation, and passion: hunting. Sixty percent of their food was shot, harpooned, or netted. Each resident ate over four-hundred pounds of wild game a year.

A half-mile outside town, a large pond that froze tight every winter supplied their drinking water. Inside the seventy-odd houses, large closet spaces were equipped with toilet buckets lined with trash bags.* The town population hovered just under three hundred.

I found the mayor and teacher, George, inside the high school, built to fit three-hundred students. It cost $80 million, held a swimming pool, running track, weight room, auto shop, wood shop, and computer lab.

George, a short, stout Iñupiat, who moved from Barrow a dozen years earlier, said that the summer's big election was about banning alcohol in Kaktovik. While he opposed alcohol "in a big way," he shrugged his shoulders as he said, "We're all human."

This remark acted as his segue into the controversial oil development: "We would like Kaktovik to become like a Lower-Forty-eight town, but I'm worried about what the social and economic impact will be if ANWR is opened."

---

*By 2002, more than a decade after putting toilets in Barrow, the North Slope Borough earmarked three hundred thousand dollars per home to install flush toilets in Kaktovik.

He was not opposed to *limited* oil development on the coastal plain, but he was opposed to the Village Corporation shareholders vote for *full* development of the coastal plain. Yet most younger people opposed development because they thought that it would destroy the caribou herd.

The mayor—cheerful through a guarded shyness that is common here—explained that he didn't mind being called an Eskimo, which merely evoked his glorious igloo-building ancestry. He shrugged his shoulders and said, "We just always called ourselves Iñupiat." When I asked what the people thought about the benefits of ANCSA, he laughed.

"ANCSA, ANILCA, ANWR—why such silly abbreviations? What we care about here is the same as *tanik* and people everywhere: having enough jobs and food to eat."

George had quickly come to the heart of the issues, and I admired his concise honesty. Iñupiat, part of the greater race of Inuit spread from Russia to Greenland, were known for their periods of starvation and exploitation at the hands of missionaries, traders, and government men.

⌂ ⌂ ⌂

Olaus Murie and his Eskimo companions tracked the wounded polar bear by following its blood trail across the ice. Several hundred yards up onto the shore, across the sphagnum moss, and beneath a low set of cliffs, they found a white, shivering mass, curled up in a cleft between boulders.

As the Eskimos stood by with harpoons, Murie took off his rabbit-skin mittens and said a quick apology for the Hudson's Bay Company (HBC) traders who had wounded the polar bear that morning with an underpowered muzzle-loader shotgun. Murie then aimed his high-powered carbine at the bear's heart and squeezed the trigger. *Nanook* thrust up its paws, rolled its head, and screamed like a woman in agony. *Nanook* then loosed a final gasp.

Murie cut open its stomach and found only seaweed surrounded by the usual digestive bile. He pared out the heart and lungs and liver, and while pinching the fur above the steaming carcass, he whittled down at the fat to skin the bear cleanly, until he reached the legs. By slitting up the inside, keeping the giant paws intact, he peeled back the entire skin. Then he severed the head by slicing above the last vertebrae.

Murie, a scientist, was oblivious to the stench of exposed organs and the blood crusting his hands. One at a time, he hooked each body part onto his steelyard—adding the bear's weight up to just under a thousand pounds. Then he gave the white-larded meat to the grateful Eskimos. He rolled the skull up into the skin for the Carnegie Museum.

The HBC traders, however, rudely claimed the skin as their own. Since Murie was briefly hitching a ride on their boat, he had no choice but to give up his specimen.

It offended Murie that the traders proudly referred to HBC as Here Before Christ, as if the Eskimos had no place in the Arctic of 1914. Olaus had already seen how HBC had stopped the hungry People from hunting on Sunday—which the Eskimo renamed *naitingujarvik*, time that resembles taboo observance. While the missionaries forbade them from speaking their heathen and throaty language (which Murie had avidly begun learning), the whalers introduced disease, and the traders exchanged alcohol, sugar, and tobacco for furs.

Murie, a twenty-five-year old not yet ready to make waves, couldn't help noticing that the HBC had profoundly changed the lives of Eskimos throughout the Arctic. Steel knives, matches, metal pans, and wooden shacks weaned the People from stone tools, rubbing sticks together for fires, hours of time cooking with stone pots, and living in frigid shelters made from peat or snow. But boredom and debt had set in. Then, in many cases, as the animal parts and furs—walrus, musk oxen, whales, polar bears, foxes, and wolverines—went out of fashion in Europe and the Lower Forty-eight, or were trapped and hunted out by the eager-to-please Eskimos (for traders, or museum and zoo collectors), the People began starving without wild game to eat or furs to trade for "white grub." Previously, the Eskimos had killed the animals that they shared the Arctic with only when hunger dictated. Murie could see that it wouldn't take long before these noble hunters would become wards of the government.

He observed men and women dying, with grim looks of acceptance on their faces, or starved babies stuffed beneath boulders. He gave the People food, and when his own canned goods and flour ran out, he helped them snare rabbits, muskrats, and ground squirrels. In exchange, he gained new knowledge about the ways of the Arctic.

The Eskimos called him *Kopinua angoraka* for the way Little Bird White Man constantly sought out flying creatures. *Kopinua angoraka* gave away the eggs, and after squeezing the bird hearts still, he cradled the remains as he hurried back to his canvas tent. He removed the innards and crop, peeled back the down and feathers, salted the bodies with preservative arsenic, stuffed them with wet cotton, sewed them back together, and pinned them with white identification labels. After they'd dried, he molded their breasts flat, pushed the hollows from their necks, and boxed them up for the museum.

When he wasn't putting up bird specimens or photographing with the awkward glass plates of his Graflex camera, Murie kept careful field notes. For this so-called barrenlands, commonly thought to be devoid of life, he captured an extraordinary collection of specimens, songs, behaviors, and migrations. Whether using his journal or sketchpad, he documented Canada jays, chickadees, sandhill cranes, all kinds of ducks, falcons, hawks, eagles, finches, flycatchers, geese, grosbeaks, grouse, guillemots, gulls, Hudsonian godwits, sparrows, swallows, tattlers, jaegers, kinglets, horned larks, longspurs, loons, magpies, mallards, nighthawks, owls, phalaropes, pipits, plovers, ptarmigan, ravens, redpolls, robins, sandpipers, shrike, snow buntings, Arctic terns, thrushes, warblers, dippers, waxwings, wheatears, snipes, woodpeckers, and yellowlegs.

Murie would eventually ship 1,582 specimens—141 different bird species (mostly ptarmigan)—to the Carnegie Museum in Pittsburgh. He would sell to the museum 280 mammal specimens comprised of 30 different species (mostly small rodents).

He wrote to his brother about how he collected many of his best bird specimens after violent storms, when Pacific fulmars, tufted puffins, Cassin auklets, ancient murrelets, Baird's comorants, and murres drifted in on the tide. "I am painting everything in sight and sketching feet, wings, beaks, eyes, ears," his letter read.

Once he followed a winter wren all day, capturing its voice for his journal:

Rrrrr		*se*	*se*	*serrrrrr*			*sie*
[trill]	*se*		*se*	*se*	[trill]	*rrrr*	*sie*

In the innovative studies he would later undertake as a field biologist, his ear for the sounds of creatures came from time spent with Eskimos. As for the language of these people, he started with only *Shunowna,* What is the name of that? By the end of winter, shivering alongside his companions on dogsleds and in igloos, he had documented scores of animal and plant species along with a working knowledge of Inuktitut.

He had no trouble with nouns, but adjectives, syllables, and complete sentences were tricky. Although saying "hello," "thank you," and "goodbye" had been perceived as presumptuous posturing to a hunting culture that lived off the land, he greeted Eskimos with their new words, foisted on them by the traders: *chimo* (hello, goodbye, and Are you friendly?) and *ko-wanna* (thank you). Mostly, he laughed when he gave his age as "twenty sixes" or tried to refuse water by saying "many water." The Eskimos, too, giggled along with his language lessons.

Murie learned about the Eskimo tongue when its idioms and constructions still had a dynamic involvement with animals and landscape. He had studied Franz Boas's 1886 book, *The Central Eskimo*. This pioneering anthropologist insisted that fieldworkers like Murie collect detailed cultural data, learn as much of the native language as possible, and become a part of the native society in order to interpret native life from within. Beyond his curiosity and compassion, Murie was interested in the Eskimos because their soon-to-be misplaced language provided invaluable information about wildlife that was all but unknown to turn-of-the-century scientists.

To his astonishment, he learned that Inuktitut had no common word for seal or fish. These learned hunters precisely identified each animal as if stating both Latin genus and species. *Natiq* was the ringed seal, *kairulik* the harp seal, *oogrook* the bearded seal, and *qasi-giak* the harbor seal.

On hunts, he observed that the Eskimos used a white screen while crawling toward a seal hole on the white ice. Then they would sit for hours over the breathing hole, waiting for a seal to emerge—the same adaptive techniques that Murie had observed with hawks over gopher holes.

While living with the People, he noted in his journal that much had been said about the filth of Eskimos, but he also observed that they were always cheerful, which he wasn't, since he hadn't bathed in months. If they were starving, they never let on or begged when he came into their camps. He had never seen a people so contented in hungry times, so appreciative for the small favors he gave them.

In spring, as the People gorged on returning wildlife, a hurricane wind blew the ice from the land. Murie observed small birds being pitched about the tundra. As his Eskimo camp struggled to hang onto its tents, *Kopinua angoraka* agonized about how many birds would die in the storm.

Like many northern explorers, Murie used the inevitable tent-bound storm time to catch up on his reading. In addition to Boas, he devoured Fridtjof Nansen's *Farthest North*, Stewart White's *The Silent Places*, Mrs. Bailey's *Handbook of the Birds of the Western U.S.,* and Ernest Seton's *Arctic Prairies*.

As a boy, Murie had been inspired by Seton's canoeing tales, and he thought he had become an expert paddler in a canoe made of barrel ribs and wheat sacks on Minnesota's Red River. But in comparison to the Eskimos, he felt like a city slicker. They taught him things he'd never dreamed about boat travel. He watched laughing men shape frames from driftwood fastened together with sealskin thongs, while the women gnawed on flabby bearded sealskins to make them pliable, then sewed them on as hulls. They placed these remarkable, leak-free kayaks on elevated stakes, away from hungry sled dogs, to dry in the sun.

One day a gust of wind caught his canoe and sent it sailing off their island at "an alarming rate." Without the boat, he and his companions would have starved. Since Murie was the only swimmer in the party, he stripped off his clothes and plunged in—the icy shock of the water left him gasping for breath. Salty waves kept breaking into his mouth. As the canoe drifted further away, Murie's strokes lost their power, and his legs began to cramp. He turned back toward shore, where his companions had started a fire. As he warmed his now-blue body over the flames, his native companions lashed together a driftwood raft and paddled after the canoe. They never said a word about Murie's foolhardy swim. It took two days lying in a fur sleeping bag before he recovered. Murie was now ready to listen to anything.

He learned the Eskimo parable of how lemmings were created from bears that fell from way up in the sky, becoming smaller and smaller as they fell. The substantiation of the story, according to its teller, Pooto, was that the bear and lemming shared the same track pattern. Murie didn't argue; he just wrote down the story and the Eskimo name for lemming, *kilyunmituk*—the one who drops from the sky.

As Murie became entranced with this place and its people, he suspected that the best parts of a trip eluded a journal. Still, as the journey came to an end, he stayed faithful to the daily chronicling:

> It was with feelings of regret that I said goodbye to all and saw [the village of] Moose Factory disappear from view. But soon we were rounding picturesque points, new vistas opening up as we wound about the islands of Moose River. The water is dark brown, the willows and poplars rich yellow and gold, set off with a background of dark spruce.

He would return to the Arctic repeatedly, as if following the impulses of the birds that so obsessed him with "their inherent impulse to go south in fall and come north again to the Arctic in spring." He returned partly to visit its people, partly to commune with wilderness, and eventually to begin his famous study of the caribou. He would never have been capable of such work without his tutelage under the Eskimos and other Native Americans.

Until the end of his life, the time spent in the North gave him clarification he couldn't find elsewhere. He inspired many to follow in his tracks; he fought for the establishment of the Arctic National Wildlife Refuge. And he was convinced that "in the evolution of human spirit, something much worse than hunger can happen to a people."

Chapter 2

CARIBOU

I want to roam over these plains myself,
like the caribou, and feed on lichens,
face the winds, and travel on and on.

—Olaus Murie

Death wet the air as my paddle stroked the ocean boundary of Canada's sister park, Ivvavik, the caribou nursery. Amid my shifting Arctic memories, clearer than the photographs I exposed, my encounters east of the refuge stood out as if they had happened yesterday, before I reached Kaktovik.

The eye-watering smell of flesh and organs exposed to warm air made me beach the kayak. For those who still possess the remnant sensory awareness of our hunting ancestors, this stomach-turning smell came as a warning signal. But I couldn't help myself: the tendon-thrumming monotony of paddling a sea kayak in calm water made me curious, even reckless. I walked up the beach to investigate, warily clutching the mace canister.

Before walking into a thick copse of willow down along a narrow side slough of the Babbage River, I yelled, "Hey bear!" then lobbed in a few river stones to make sure I wasn't interrupting a meal. A flock of ravens jumped skyward, croaking down at me as their wings scritch-scratched through the air. I waited another minute. No branches were breaking, nothing moved, no one growled. Probably just dead bodies.

I walked in, palming branches away from my face, leaning left then right like a linebacker until the brush eased along the river. A wet mat of sphagnum moss sank me ankle deep. I hefted a set of antlers dirty with old blood; it took both arms to lift the rack.

On a patch of nearby mud, wolf prints crowded behind cloven hoof prints. Tawny hollow hairs draped the branches. Thumbnail-sized "boo" pellets, too many it seemed, showed where the fight began: the bull caribou defecating in fear, butting its antlered guard tines at one wolf as another wolf darted in for the hamstrings—or so I imagined. Cows kept their antlers only long enough to defend their wobbly-legged newborns, shedding by midsummer; bulls lost their heavy antlers after the rut in late October. I dropped the bull's antlers (which I had been thrusting out and parrying with), stopped, closed my eyes, and breathed in through my nose: the kill site upstream sent up the smell of leather and grass and methane.

On closer inspection, I could see in their prints how splayed hooves, combined with buoyant fur jackets of hollow hairs, allowed the caribou to swim innumerable lakes, ocean bays, and rivers back to their distant winter feeding grounds. Their hoof-paddles then grew long for traction in the snow. By summer, on the tundra, the hooves would shorten again.

No mammal migrates as far as the caribou. According to fossil records, this herd has migrated here for a million years. According to USFWS satellite collar data, the average Porcupine caribou herd cow runs 2,613 miles each year. Most of the herd stops in Canada's windblown Richardson and Olgiville Mountains; some of the herd splits and winters south of Alaska's Brooks Range.

Their winter bedroom is carpeted with the reindeer lichen that is scattered thinly here along the coast, in dry gravel above the river. Through some inexplicable mystery of evolution, the inch-long, twisted fingers of the lichen, *Cladina rangiferina,* bear a remarkable resemblance to the caribou antlers shed annually onto the tundra, where they mold green. Back in the protection of forests and river valleys, the caribou home in on this antler-shaped lichen. It is no coincidence that in their marching orders for survival, they also chew on shed antlers to recycle the calcium.

As the mercury sinks to the sub-30s, the caribou dig their elongated hooves through the snow to eat vast quantities of this low-calorie, low-protein lichen. Fried up with butter, it isn't bad, but I'd have a hard time making it through the winter on such a diet.

Caribou stomachs have an enzyme, lichenase, that breaks down the difficult-to-digest plant. Since lichen lacks proteins that would demand an additional liquid intake for digestion, the caribou eat snow and forego trying to find drinking water in subzero conditions. The lichen diet of the caribou triggers a mechanism, not shared by any other ungulate, that causes liquid wastes to be reabsorbed back into their rumina to help them stay hydrated.

The litany of caribou adaptations is as varied as the seasons that transform the Arctic. Caribou fat acts like winter-grade motor oil, staying liquid at unusually low temperatures and heating vital organs. The caribou's circulatory system allows outbound arteries to shed warmth to the cold, inbound venous blood; the animal's legs function at fifty degrees, while the main trunk of their body never drops below one hundred degrees.

Here on the wet, silt banks of the Babbage, the front hoofprints of this caribou showed a gap between the hooves and the dewclaws; the rear dewclaws stayed aloft. At a walking pace, the rear hooves overlap the front hooves as the caribou swings its rear leg up to its front track. The front and rear prints were eight inches long and I could match their walking gait with a long stride.

I knew these things because I had ample time to make seemingly inconsequential natural history observations. I also knew these things because I was holding *Field Guide to Animal Tracks*, and because I was trying to get to know its author.

According to Murie, a running adult caribou puts down its dewclaws at right angles to the hooves, as if gathering more traction. Looking a little closer, I spied clods of mud thrown up from the hooves. With my collapsible fishing rod shoved into my pocket, I whiffed the air as I followed the tracks down a river bar. Like the wolves, I too was hungry, partly ogling for fish fins in the river, and partly indulging my curiosity for a more complete kill story in the brown silt. Suddenly, amid a thatch of dwarf poplar greening up the brown willow brake, the air turned so rich that I closed my mouth. A crushed caribou skull, brains and eyes sucked dry, lay in a tangle of knee-high poplar. I kicked a leg bone loose from the chest-high willows. The licked-clean bone was being digested into the biomass of the tundra, its flesh already hoovered up by the clacking teeth of ravenous wolves. The pack had flung a few other bones about, but the main caribou carcass had vanished.

Each year wolves killed 3 to 5 percent of the Porcupine caribou herd (PCH)—up to seventy-six hundred animals. According to Canadian biologists, one wolf eats twenty-nine caribou annually. Human hunters (mostly the Gwich'in) killed and ate up to five thousand of the herd each year as part of a sacred hunt that went on for centuries. Annual herd mortality, combining predation with old age and disease, was 15 percent, up to 26,700 caribou. A balance was maintained, if only because the PCH could birth up to 30,000 caribou each year. But it was a precarious balance at best.

Since 1989, when the population peaked at 178,000, the herd has decreased to 123,000. According to USFWS biologists, the PCH is in some sort of trouble. The decline may have been caused by deep snow, which in some years prevents the herd from reaching the coastal plain. Or, in a late summer, deep snow limits the forage in the caribou's coastal plain kitchen—an area too wet and difficult for short-legged sprinters to prey upon long-legged marathon runners. In those hard summers, calves born outside of the coastal plain in the sort of hilly wolf terrain I was passing through give the short-legged wolves and bears a home-court advantage.* Then the cows' ability to lactate and sustain calves with milk becomes limited by the lack of food. This is only the beginning of the caribou troubles.

Biologists who monitor the PCH—or any of the other dozen great herds migrating back and forth into North America's three-thousand-mile stretch of barrenlands—agree that caribou survival can be severely compromised by weather. Short summers, or conversely, warm winters (which foster a caribou hoof–proof ice layer over their precious lichen) can cause caribou populations to plummet.† The final kicker for caribou, many scientists believe, is that global warming is causing warm winters and thaws in the Arctic. Over the last decade, the ice pack has been reduced by 40 percent.

Over the last four decades, the temperature in northwestern Canada has risen by an average of two degrees Celsius. USFWS biologists were baffled by what they referred to as the PCH's continued "winter mortality," even in those years that the coastal plain seemed to offer plenty of food and favorable calving conditions. After crunching two decades worth of data, they offered five possibilities for the caribou decline: three involved climate warming, one involved the herd exceeding the winter forage, and one involved an increase in human or wolf predation. The latter expla-

---

*The traditional calf survival rate—based on years that the caribou make it to the coastal plain—is 62 percent through June. In 2001, 80 percent of the 70,000 cows calved, with only a 51 percent calf survival rate; in 2000, the calf survival rate was 44 percent.

†In the 1970s, a snowy winter followed by an unseasonable thaw caused a catastrophic die-off among the Peary caribou in the high Arctic. Their population has yet to recover.

nation was refuted by Canadian scientists who believed hunting and wolf pressures did not have a "strong impact" on the herd.

USFWS scientists believe that the proposed oil rigs and roads and pipelines could block the herd's access to their primary kitchen, which the Gwich'in call *Vadzaii Googii Vi Dehk'it Gwanlii,* the Sacred Place Where Life Begins. These USFWS biologists have made four researched arguments to infer that the PCH "may be particularly sensitive to development." Since it's difficult for these scientists to predict exactly how oil development will disrupt the herd, their arguments can be open to interpretation, or even manipulation, depending upon a reader's political point of view.*

The Canadians, who share a vested interest in this international herd, have been following the controversy carefully. From where I stood, east of the U.S. border, along an isolated stretch of wilderness park forever closed to industry, it seemed Canada's chain of command in its Ministry of the Environment is more oriented toward the results of scientific data. Its U.S. counterpart, the Department of the Interior, hosts an ever-changing parade of political appointees. Each new Secretary of the Interior, along with the most senior bureaucrats (but not the scientists), is reappointed with every new administration. Unlike the Canadians, U.S. officials have more ties to industry than to science, forcing new administrations to reinterpret or manipulate the data about polar bears and caribou and oil. Most recently, the scientists, employed by an administration that will not take responsibility for producing greenhouse gases that cause global warming, substitute the less strident "Arctic Oscilla-

---

*The USFWS 1002 Draft Report (1987) suggested that oil development on the coastal plain would cause a "displacement or reduction" of 20 to 40 percent of the herd. For whatever reason, this figure was deleted from the final report, which recommended full-scale gas and oil development. In 2001, Interior Secretary Gail Norton, when reporting to a congressional committee, left out USFWS data that suggested caribou could be affected by drilling and added information stating that caribou calving has taken place *outside*—not *inside*, as her USFWS biologists reported—the proposed drilling area for eleven of the last eighteen years.

tion" to explain how climate change is reducing the PCH population. While NASA and the Goddard Space Center computer models have shown that this "positive" Arctic Oscillation trend is caused
by greenhouse gases, and NOAA scientists say that greenhouse
gases could be the culprit, Department of the Interior scientists
offer no explanation for the causes of Arctic Oscillation.*

While I was trying to interpret the flurry of bear tracks min-
gling with wolves at the Babbage kill site, a magpie floated in and
landed on top of a mound of dirt and gravel five feet from the rushing river. Now I could read the sign.

I rushed backward, burst out through the willows, and pushed
my kayak into the sea. Beneath the mound—cached by a gorged
barren-ground grizzly—lay the rotting caribou carcass. No telling
when the bear would come back to finish its meal, stolen from the
wolves. I aimed west, toward the border, and resumed the labor of
paddling and thinking.

Caribou, of course, do not respond to political boundaries. After
the border was surveyed between Alaska and the Yukon in 1877,
Canada and the United States managed the herd separately. From
the perspective of Native Americans in both countries, the range
of the PCH had been broken in two.

In 1970, petroleum discoveries in the Mackenzie Delta—two
hundred miles east of me—prompted the Canadian government to
conduct a series of hearings among Native communities. These

---

*Arctic Oscillation is the earth's second largest climate cycle—after El Niño—affect-
ing the earth's weather and can be traced back to the beginning of the twentieth century, before greenhouse gases began changing climate. But since the 1990s a shift in
the Arctic Oscillation has caused abnormally cold winters that impede spring caribou migration to ANWR, and warm summers that increase insect harassment of the
herd. The caribou population, clearly correlated to this shift in Arctic Oscillation by
USFWS biologists, has plummeted. Since the science of greenhouse gases and global
warming is not officially accepted by the second Bush administration, in the latest
report, *Arctic Refuge Coastal Plain Terrestrial Wildlife Research Summaries* (see bibliography), Department of Interior scientists refer only to the known Arctic Oscillation
phenomenon.

First Nation peoples universally opposed oil or gas development. In 1978, the Canadian government prohibited industrial activity until a management plan could protect the international caribou herd and assess aboriginal land claims. After this complex business had been sorted out, in 1984, the Canadian government signed the Inuvaluit Final Agreement, creating the 2.5-million-acre Ivvavik National Park. In 1995, Canada added the 1-million-acre Vuntut National Park, south of Ivvavik, also adjoining the U.S. border. Vuntut (literally, marshlands) includes the Old Crow River wetlands, and each spring as the caribou migrate north, an unusual band of moose, logging more miles than any moose in the world, migrates more than one hundred miles from their winter grounds in the refuge, to rip out and feed on aquatic plants beneath the thawing wetlands.

After first reading the U.S. Department of the Interior's endorsement of oil development in the refuge, Canada responded that the 1002 Report (1987) "incorrectly interprets the importance of the area to the PCH, and shows a disregard for the value of the area to other wildlife." Diplomatic lobbying was stepped up in Washington, while the Yukon territorial government began a campaign that showed how the survival of the international Gwich'in people depended upon the survival of the herd.

Lawsuits followed. New bills came to the floors of both House and Senate, yet Congress had not yet legislated the 1.5 million acres for either wilderness or oil leasing. And, as the fate of the coastal plain hangs in the balance, the PCH continues to shrink.

As I PADDLED OUT around the grassy peninsula of Kaye Point, I caught up to a thousand members of the herd. This year, half the migration had stopped in Canada instead of crossing the border to the coastal plain. The band in front of me trotted west on a narrow beach hemmed in beneath a high bluff. Dun-colored calves bleated behind their mothers. Murie nailed their reply spot-on in *Animal Tracks:* "The caribou vocabulary is a short grunting sound, a low pitched '*a-a-w, a-a-w.*'"

I followed the sound of clicking ligaments and hooves hitting the water—*Ka-chunk, ka-chunk, ka-chunk.* The herd put on a burst of speed, cantering up to ten miles per hour as a fertilizer fragrance filled their slipstream. Their antlers swayed and flexed as they ran. A callous on my palm clicked against my paddle, windmilling through air and water as I chased after the herd.

This was not the legendary aggregation of the refuge coastal plain, with caribou overflowing the horizon. Out there, until late July or August, the caribou crowd into a one-hundred-thousand-plus mass until the first breaths of winter or the simultaneous aggregation of insects signals them to break up and run south to their winter bedroom—to begin their rut. Unlike the predator-free terrain of the American coastal plain, the herd can never let down its guard along Ivvavik's coast.

A half-mile in front of me, out on the point, a barren-ground grizzly—frozen like a blonde boulder—suddenly leaped out and charged the herd. The lead bulls turned back east and galloped through the shallows while the cows and calves ran along the mud shores. There were no stragglers. And since the herd was healthy, the grizzly slowed to a nonchalant walk along water's edge. It had been testing the herd, probing for wounded or weak. It would take me fifteen minutes to reach the bear, but it was his prey, vanished into in the green womb of the Canadian caribou nursery, that had consumed biologists for eighty years.

⌒ ⌒ ⌒

To understand the way of the herd, as well as the creation of the refuge, it was helpful to track America's first caribou biologist, Olaus Murie. In 1920, during his first fall studying the caribou,

Murie ran behind the herd like a hungry wolf through the boreal forest. In the wake of the Yukon-Tanana herd he noted how tons of lichens had been cropped away from stunted trees and gurgling streambeds. Mosquitoes filled up on his blood. Wolverines trailed him for scraps, and Canada jays alighted on his shoulders. But "Mr. Caribou," as the local tribes now called him, forgot about birds when he caught up to the herd. On the rim of a narrow, high valley that gave him an unobstructed view, he counted fifteen hundred caribou passing each day—for weeks. Murie eventually counted a half million caribou.

He shot caribou for specimens and filled a wrap of cheesecloth with two handfuls of stomach contents, tagged the bags with dates, and hung it all to dry. When the herd had passed, he pulled out his mouse traps, trying to catch new species. Murie carried his watercolors in a belt pouch and mixed them on a porcelain slide, which allowed him to quickly draw the birds and mice he collected, before their blood drained and faded their colors.

That winter Murie learned how to run his own dogsled without Eskimo support in order to cover vast stretches of roadless, northern wilderness while constantly taking notes and catching birds and mammals, sleeping between his dogs to stay warm and to stop them from tearing one another apart with hunger. In the coldest part of the winter, with sixty-below temperatures freezing his spit before it hit the snow, he lived on only what he could shoot. One week, he subsisted on only a moose heart—the size of a small ham—which threw his dogs into growling fits of frenzy whenever he pulled it out of the gunny sack and carved off a chunk. The dwindling rations of bony and white-fleshed dog salmon kept his companions from starving.

After Murie's exemplary work collecting Arctic specimens for the Carnegie Museum, the U.S. Biological Survey hired him to study caribou in Alaska. Rather than protecting the wild herds, the survey sought to introduce herds of domesticated reindeer. Murie's agency had been created after locusts devastated Midwestern crops at the turn of the nineteenth century. As a utilitarian bureaucracy, it studied animals, then classified them as "good" or "bad" according to what they ate. Then yet another branch of the government, Predator and Animal Control, would set about poisoning, trapping, bombing, drowning, or shooting the "bad" species.*

The survey's scientific findings were often overridden by the outcry of farmers and ranchers whose crops and animals needed protection. Murie's letters home complaining about his boss's disinterest in science showed that he understood the government's blundering science and politically driven agendas. But he felt that by being sent north, he was given a chance to make a difference on a frontier that, while torn asunder by gold miners, was still largely undisturbed by agriculture.

The territory held no shortage of frost-hardened Sourdoughs, tough as bears, who wouldn't think twice about eating their dogs when times got hard. Olaus stood apart not just for his ability to withstand hardship, but for his soft-spoken manners, his nondidactic way of sharing the Latin names for things, and his genuine interest in people. When Olaus Murie mushed into Fairbanks to resupply, his legend—much to his own modest chagrin—preceded him.

He spoke with a "ya, ya" burr—gained from his Norwegian-immigrant parents—mixed with the slow cadences of his Midwestern upbringing. He also avoided confrontation, which wasn't

---

*In 1946, when Murie quit the Department of Agriculture, the U.S. Biological Survey was renamed the U.S. Fish and Wildlife Service (USFWS) and made into a branch of the Interior Department. Predator and Animal Control was renamed Animal Damage Control and prospered until it was disbanded in 1985—long after "the damage had been done, that damage which the Service is now endeavoring to restore perhaps acting as Olaus' conscience" (according to USFWS editors of a 2000 symposium booklet *The Muries*).

easy for a government official with part-time game-warden duties amid a frontier rife with poachers.

This towhead with frost-blackened fingertips said "please" at the Fairbanks Mercantile when he asked for his rifle ammunition. While most men fresh off the trail grew beards, Olaus took great pains, often breaking ice in his razor bowl, to shave each morning. He drank only water, and he abstained from coffee and tea because he believed that force of will supplanted caffeine. Rumors began circulating that his cabin—filled with jars of formaldehyde and animal skulls and hides next to measuring tapes—was also decorated with pen-and-ink drawings. The subjects of these drawings weren't posed animals standing in front of the backdrop of Mt. McKinley, like the bespectacled Lower Forty-eighter suitcoats fancied. Murie's drawings featured the authentic, lean, hungry-looking or placid-faced beasts that miners and trappers met out in the bush. Murie drew and collected his specimens in subzero cold, he often mushed out alone, and he didn't hire guides. Consequently, the local Sourdoughs overlooked the odd fact that "Mr. Caribou" didn't smoke, drink, or whore.

Alaskans in the Arctic villages of Wiseman, Bettles, and Fort Yukon initially feared that Murie, a government worker, came into their villages to enforce prohibition. He had a way of approaching Native Americans slowly, cautiously, the same way he approached wild animals. And he could speak enough words in the Athapaskan, Gwich'in, and Eskimo languages to get the information he needed. To a stranger, Murie looked frightened, even shy, but his gentle manner could be deceptive, because he slowly approached all strangers while he was "waiting to find something to admire." He sought out these people because he believed that the Native American perspective would broaden his knowledge of caribou. Murie started by inquiring about the health of their dog teams. If this didn't work he chatted about politics—since there weren't yet radios, everyone was anxious to hear outside news.

As he gained their confidence, he focused in on the caribou. How many? Where did you last see them? What direction were they traveling? Did you hunt any? Did you see wolves or bears chasing them?

Although the natives, unlike the white hunters, did not waste their caribou meat, that fall, a small tribe near Fairbanks killed twelve hundred caribou to feed their numerous dogs. One village burned down the forest, creating miles of open space through which it was easier to shoot the herd. But in a letter to his boss in Washington, Murie then listed populations of the "Indian" villages, the number of men who hunted, and concluded:

> that there is no "wanton waste" of game. . . . When killing caribou for dog feed [*sic*], all the bones are saved, even the feet, including the hooves. These parts are cooked and are then much relished by the dogs.

Mostly, he complained—in his first offical report, "The Destruction of Game in Parts of Alaska"—about the white hunters. One Fairbanksian, mimicking Buffalo Bill Cody, shot 135 moose and caribou in a day. Many hunters, trappers, and prospectors shot indiscriminately, without regard to bag limits, killing cows and bulls and calves. Families shot twenty caribou each fall to get through the winter. Murie blamed the high price of transportation (bacon cost $1.15 per pound, caribou 15 cents) and the general hardship of life on the frontier.

Over the next couple of years, Murie repeatedly tried to domesticate wild caribou in McKinley National Park. His assignment—herding free-ranging animals into corrals—proved strenuous and time consuming. The few animals he managed to lasso and coerce into confinement were "belligerent" and dangerous. When a bull lowered its hundred-pound antlers toward Olaus and his brother Adolph, who had come north to be Olaus's assistant, they sawed the bull's antlers off. By morning, they found him dead. This experiment signaled the beginning of Olaus's difficulties with the government.

Olaus then had to help bring domesticated reindeer, which are difficult to tell apart from their subspecies cousins, the caribou, into a park that already had a thriving wild caribou herd. In Olaus's mind, this new government boondoggle had all the markings of disaster. The reindeer herders were irresponsible, their herd had cancerous growths and were unable to outrun predators. Even worse, the reindeer needed hay, not caribou lichen, to make it through the winters. Murie worried that they would mingle with their wild cousins and produce "a mongrel race of animals which scientists and sportsmen deplore."

As departmental policy began to favor reindeer over wild caribou, Murie began debating with his coworkers about the logic of introducing reindeer to the North. Finally, he wrote to his boss, Edward Nelson, that it "was premature to exploit the game country before a market has been developed." He also complained about the lack of coordination between the economic and scientific branches of the survey—science again took a backseat to the utilitarian aim of the government, to efficiently develop natural resources. To keep his job, Murie was forced to compromise his ideals about the spiritual and inspirational value of these same resources.

For the next few years, Murie watched the herds and lobbied his superiors not to push ill-conceived policies without first performing careful science. As Nelson tried to grasp Murie's suggestions, it became evident—through incredibly detailed reports about caribou diets, predation, weights, migratory habits, and herd populations—that Murie had learned more about the North than any government field biologist.

In a 1924 letter from Washington, D.C., Olaus wrote about enduring "the ever present supervision and imperial suppression of government work," but the careful and groundbreaking science of his caribou report impressed people. Everyone was treating him with deference and respect, as though he had "really done something."

Murie's report, *Alaska-Yukon Caribou,* is still read today. Along with revelations about how predators actually strengthen the herd, he had shown that the caribou migration patterns made them an international species; the same laws that applied to birds that flew in and out of Canada or South America should be applied to them. After observing thousands of migrating caribou, his report introduced a new grid-counting technique by which zoologists could accurately count staggering herd numbers. Most importantly, Murie stopped the government's plan to domesticate the wild herds with imported reindeer—which could have destroyed the caribou throughout Alaska. He advocated that the herds be left alone with the wolves and bears, and that all species be given large and uninhabited tracts of habitat. He was also the first scientist to show that Native Americans lived in harmony with the northern herds, and to advocate that these people should continue to hunt the herds as a God-given right. Although these conclusions would become more widely accepted a half-century later, in 1926 Murie's science shocked and stunned government bureaucrats, who appreciated wildlife only for its potential economic value.

Chapter 3

OIL

Who laid the foundations of the earth, that it should not be removed for ever.

—Psalms 104:5

A few miles south of the Beaufort Sea, I jogged across huge polygons and into the heart of Alaska caribou calving terrain, looking for the invisible herd. Once in a while I stopped to catch my breath, close my eyes, and put my ear to the ground. Chasing after the spectacular and sometimes overhyped Porcupine caribou herd was an exercise that allowed me to accidentally discover other important nuances of the refuge. Like the weird, polygon-shaped cracks in the earth.

Every fifteen to twenty feet, I skipped across a several-inch-wide crack rimming the tundra's polygon edges. Kneeling, I could see ice water gurgling below. I palmed away the black soil to reveal a gray wedge of icy earth. I stuck my head in deeper, funneled my lips, and drank deeply—happy as a dog—wetting my beard with ice water, contracting silver fillings and numbing teeth.

This polygon, one of millions stretching across the coastal plain, could be fourteen thousand years old. According to Pielou, the permafrost hidden another few feet below is one hundred thousand years old. Like mud in a puddle, this expanse of tundra cracked up as subzero cold buckled and contracted the coastal plain in concert with the permafrost. Water trickled into the cracks and formed ice wedges, which eventually widened the cracks.

From a standing position, polygons appeared to stretch past the horizon. I had never seen anything like it. I could have been on another planet: photographs of a meteorite impact crater's floor on Mars show identical polygon structures.

Alaska's North Slope seems like alien ground compared to topography below the Arctic Circle. In the early 1940s, military airstrips and buildings built on the North Slope all slumped into the frozen ground. Initially, U.S. Geological Survey (USGS) geologists were stumped.

Then they figured out that gravel pads had to be placed beneath airstrips, and piers beneath buildings, to prevent the ground from melting. In 1943 the USGS director, William Wrather, who had made a fortune in petroleum development, hired the brilliant Stanford paleontologist S. W. Muller to help figure out how to extract oil from this permanently frozen ground. The bilingual Muller translated reams of Russian documents to try to teach the U.S. government about its own frozen Siberia. He borrowed many of this landscape's names from the Russians, Norwegians, and Eskimos: *pingos, palsas, nunatuks, tors, talik, felsenmeer.*

With his colleagues' help, Muller then came up with the most important name. One winter day in 1943, he was in a federal office building in Washington, D.C., surrounded by several more adventurous USGS geologists—including Robert Wallace, who had spent years chipping out oil-bearing fossils in the barrenlands. One of the scientists stared at a paper bag that contained the underwear he was bringing home for his wife: a recently introduced brand of underwire bra called *perma-stay.* An anonymous member of the team—none of the male scientists cared to take credit for this historical moment—jumped up on a desk and shouted to Muller as he frantically began pointing at objects around the room: "Perma desk, perma chair, perma walls, perma brain!"

That year, Muller published the definitive 136-page booklet, *Permafrost or Permanently Altered Ground and Related Engineering Problems,* that gave new definition and shape to oil companies and college geology classes throughout America.

These USGS innovators then charted out the zone of *continuous permafrost* north of the Brooks Range, and *discontinuous permafrost* down in central Alaska. They identified the *sporadic permafrost* intermingling with the *discontinuous permafrost* to southern Alaska. From seismic extrapolation and drilling samples, they classified the layers of permafrost soil into an *active layer* of thawing surface tundra six inches to ten feet deep, above a quarter-mile-deep *permafrost table,* above *talik* or unfrozen ground. On the surface, permafrost created frozen *nunatuk* ridges, ancient lakes pushed up into minature volcanoes, *pingoes,* and tiny frost-heaved *palsa* hills. These hungry male scientists, quick to grab handy metaphors, calculated that the permafrost is several degrees warmer near its bottom in the unfrozen *talik* earth, from geothermal heat, like a frozen cake on a warm countertop.

Permafrost blankets 24 percent of the earth's landmass. The common misconception about permafrost is that it's ice rather than frozen soil, but permafrost can also be porous bedrock. Permafrost rarely lies below warming rivers or insulating glaciers. Although permafrost weeps on the top and bottom from surface and subterranean heat, it's impermeable to water.

As I ran, water from the melting permafrost table burbled out of my running shoes. Clouds of mosquitoes bounced off my face and tumbled into the slipstream behind me, where I wished their skinny proteins to hungry yellow jackets. Then, as I jumped an unnamed creek, an iridescent blue sheen whorled the water like tree rings.

I stopped to peek closer. A brown, whining cloud caught up to me within seconds, so I focused quickly toward the ground. No tire tracks or footprints, not even an old animal trail. I dipped in my fingertips and sniffed. The unmistakable rotten-egg smell declared it unpotable. Most places in the Lower Forty-eight this would merely unveil some automobile's oil leak, but here in the Arctic it meant that the original goods were bubbling up through the ground.

They called it black gold. Alaska crude. Petroleum. Fossil fuel. Or ancient algae.

I rooted my fingers down in the underwater mud and dug up a palm full of gooey black putty. If I could have pushed this old, cold algae back into the oil reservoir, a mile below, the earth's geothermal heat would have melted the putty back into liquid oil. I was not the first to stumble across such a seep, which bubble up across the coastal plain in what oilmen call a "string of pearls." According to Alaska's USGS lead research geologist, the low-sulfur content of this "sweet, light crude" makes ANWR oil highly desirable. If mixed into the Trans-Alaska Pipeline with the Prudhoe Bay area "crude" oil—ten times heavier—the commingling would reduce the overall sulfur content of the crude eight hundred miles to the south at the Valdez terminal. Low-sulfur crude is cheaper to refine. And this "lighter, sweeter" fuel fetches a premium price.

But holding it in my hand was a mistake. The aromatic chemicals benzene and toluene, which comprise 10 percent of this "light" putty, stung my sea salt–cracked fingers. It would take days to scrape the goop out from under my nailbeds. At Prudhoe Bay, when the pipeline sprung yet another leak of heavy crude containing up to 30 percent benzene and toluene, the fumes were so dangerous that cleanup workers wore respirators as they mopped up the tundra. Toluene is the same essential ingredient in my repair kit's glue, and if I sniffed the putty again, I would get higher than a kite. If I mistakenly swallowed the putty the toluene might not kill me, but it could affect my ability to conceive healthy children.

Benzene, commonly smelled at gas pumps, is even worse. It is used to make rubber, pesticides, drugs, paints, detergents, lubricants, dyes, and is a natural by-product of the cigarettes that I stupidly smoked for reassurance. Breathing or ingesting benzene can cause leukemia, lymphoma, damage to chromosomes that develop hereditary characteristics, headaches, nausea, tremors, sleepiness, comas, convulsions, and death. In the air, benzene breaks down within a few days. In the water, benzene breaks down much more slowly.

The 360-million-year-old genesis of this chemical mix bubbling out of the tundra occurred when unfathomable tons of algae and plankton sank to the bottom of a warm and shallow sea between the shores of the continents Arctica and Laurentia. Then, 150 million years ago, as Arctica fell under today's Beaufort Sea, the collisions of continents created heat, slowly rendering the single-celled plant creatures into kerogen. Overlain with sediments that began washing off the Brooks Range 20 million years ago, the pressure and heat turned the kerogen into a fine-grained shale known as source rock. After several more millennia of cooking in the earth's subterranean oven, the shale dissolved into liquid or gaseous hydrocarbons and was absorbed by porous and permeable rock formations.

More recently, Iñupiat discovered cooled-down pools of this ancient tar along the coast. Sometimes they found caribou trapped in the tar pits. To the amazement of a culture that deified its marine mammals, the black goop even out-burned seal blubber in their soapstone lamps.

A geologic nanosecond later, the petroleum geologists arrived. With whining snow machines and clattering helicopters, they inventoried the coastal plain's string of pearls, hammering off chunks of oil-soaked shale and red sandstone cliffs.

As THE TUNDRA became even wetter, I slowed to a dogtrot south through tall grass stems waving in the breeze, tipped with cotton-balls and mixed in with pink, scrawny ice-cream-cone–shaped wooly louseworts. In spring, the black seed clusters of the aptly named cottongrass drew heat from the sun, offering a rich source of protein to the hungry caribou herd.

Bipeds, however, were not designed to travel through these tus-socked plant communities, stacked like high-rises ten inches above the water. Hopping them, like jumping rocks across a stream, seemed the only technique. Before I left camp this morning, antic-ipating the swaying terrain, I taped both ankles to prevent an acci-dental sprain. The bugs were now boiling up out of the tussocks and into my nostrils, so I hid my head inside my hood, shoved hands into pockets, and concentrated on my foot placements.

A half dozen miles in from the sea, I jumped a rut—connected to another fourteen hundred miles worth of tire tracks—dug out by seismic oil exploration vehicles inside the refuge boundaries during the winters of 1984 and 1985. Although the tundra was frozen as these Cat trains vibrated the ground and took readings for geologic maps, the tussocks were crushed, exposing the permafrost, which would unnaturally begin melting as the weather turned warm. These water-filled ruts have become permanent troughs across the tundra.

The seismic testing conducted by "thumper" vehicles allowed petroleum geologists to make a subterranean map of the refuge show-ing, based on the time it took sound waves to vibrate through the earth, the thickness and depth of bedrock hidden below the per-mafrost. Geologists drew their maps through a scientific process of elimination, partly relying on what drills hit west of the refuge, and partly relying on fossils and surface rocks along the seismic test lines. Although similar shales and sandstones found west of the refuge have yielded oil, that doesn't guarantee that oil will be found here, but it does give a high statistical probability. Specifically, the USGS estimates a 95 percent probability of recovering 5.7 billion barrels of oil and a 5 percent probability of recovering 16 billion barrels. Sixty miles west of here, at Prudhoe Bay, they've already pumped out 11 billion barrels.

At the southern refineries each 42-gallon barrel of crude—a thick, black stew of hydrocarbons—was thinned through a combination of catalytic reforming, coking, alkylation, and heating into various fuels.* Each barrel yields 50 percent gasoline, 10 percent propane and butane, 10 percent jet fuel, 25 percent diesel/heating fuel, and 5 percent heavy fuel oil.

I finished my rambling run back on the coast in Kaktovik Iñupiat Corporation (KIC) land (see "Native lands" on appendix B), within the refuge's 1.5-million-acre 1002 Area proposed for drilling, at a suspiciously green circle of newly planted sedges less than a mile from the sea. The sedges had been planted on several feet of gravel, used to keep the permafrost below from melting. In 1985, Chevron got permission from the KIC to drill a test well here. The results were never released to the public, and the findings from this Chevron well remain a source of conjecture to both developers and environmentalists. The information obtained from this top-secret well, called a "tight hole," were not shared with any public official.

Even a dry hole could have told Chevron a lot about the strata below. They could have determined the exact depths of the sandstone and shale layers, they could have hit ancient seawater, fossils, or even gas. Since 1985, improvements in directional drilling technology would have allowed their bit to snake sideways for several miles and poke around without moving the drill rig. If the well had

---

*In 1995, a glut of West Coast oil caused the ban on Alaska crude oil exports to be lifted. Up to 7 percent of Alaska crude was shipped directly to Korea, Japan, and China. In 2001, rising oil prices, dwindling supplies, and angry American consumers caused the ban to be reinstated.

been a "producer," with crude oil pushed by natural gas or water pressure through the newly drilled escape hole and gushing up the pipe, Chevron workers—clad in respirators—would have spilled at least a few gallons. But except for the raised surface beneath my feet, there was no smell, no pretty blue oil sheen, nothing to indicate that they tapped into any reservoir.

While the term *reservoir* is part of the lingua franca of petroleum geology, it is also misleading, because hydrocarbon reservoirs are often trapped inside permeable rock formations—from the Greek *petro* (oil) and *leum* (rock)—trapped below an impermeable roof of shale or limestone. The richest oil-soaked strata is speculated to be within the permeable and porous sandstone of the Sadlerochit formation, north of a subterranean feature known as the Barrow Arch, pushing up the ancient sea bottom with all its cooked algae for 375 miles, then plunging miles beneath my feet, under the eastern edge of the refuge.

This science looks impressive on a geologic subsurface map (see appendix C), wrinkled with anticlines and brightly colored with rock stratum, but petroleum geology is never a sure bet. Geologists looking at these maps must constantly remind themselves that they're not just looking at rock formations—Gubik, Sagavanirktok, Canning, Hua Shale, Kingak Shale, Shublik, Sadlerochit, the Lisburne, the Endicott—they're looking at time itself. They're staring back into the formation of the North American continent, beginning with the 65-million-year-old Cenozoic, down through the 144-million-year-old Cretaceous, the 208-million-year-old Jurassic, and into the 400-million-year old bowels of the earth, from the Devonian to the Proterozoic epoch.

Since the coastal plain is closely corralled by the Brooks Range—unlike the productive oil fields to the west—and mountain creation produces intense heat within the earth, it's possible that the oil companies will be thwarted, hitting only worthless gas reservoirs. But if the geothermal heat of the earth deep below my feet has remained at a tea drinker's comfort—90 to 190 degrees—for the last million years, drillers might find oil. Several degrees hotter or colder—enough to burn or cool your lips—and drillers might hit a vein of gas. Let it suffice to say that the tea-drinking temperature, or "petroleum window," is uncommon, which explains the rising price of oil and its declining availability (see appendices D and E).

Nor will it be easy to remove the hypothetical oil just north of the Barrow Arch, slightly south of the sea, a couple of miles below these 1.5 million acres of coastal plain. According to the most recent USGS assessment, "the volumes of oil are expected to occur as several accumulations rather than just a single large accumulation." Meaning that the oil field here cannot be contained within a couple thousand acres; a large infrastructure of connecting pipelines and roads would have to be built. Other difficulties include working in sixty-below temperatures, waking up denning polar bears, and melting the permafrosted ground into a Delaware-sized lake. Such an *extraction* (another suspiciously sanitized piece of lexicon shared by petroleum geologists and dentists) will demand that thousands of workers assemble that infrastructure of heated pipelines, toilets, cafeterias, bunkhouses, warming shacks, distillation plants, and a jet airport—all laid down on millions of tons of insulating gravel, dredged up from the nearest riverbed. Every road or heated structure must be built upon gravel piled several feet high on the tundra, lest the building fall into the permafrost like a hot knife resting on that frozen cake.

The four-foot-thick, fifty-yard-wide pad of gravel crunching beneath my feet was dredged from a river somewhere and then barged into the refuge. To support a new oil field, it would be exorbitantly expensive and incredibly time consuming to barge in gravel through the shifting ice pack of the Beaufort Sea. Contractors would be tempted to dredge the gravel out of the refuge, by driving the bulldozers and dump trucks to the banks of the Aichilik, the Jago, the Okpilak, the Hulahula, and the Sadlerochit. These logistics aren't overwhelming to an ambitious engineer or an oil-company executive in Anchorage or London, but it all changes when you are sifting the gravel through your fingers and marveling at how much work went into the only drill pad within the refuge—alternately shivering, overheating, or being bitten by mosquitoes. Out here on the thawing ground, it was obvious that it would take an impossible feat of engineering for the oil companies to preserve this place.

In lieu of gravel, the oil companies have come up with one solution, at least for winter roads. At the new Alpine oil field west of Prudhoe Bay, British Petroleum (BP) pipes water out of the Colville River and sprays it in ten-foot-wide swathes over the tundra. Once it freezes rock solid, they can freight the myriad of oil vehicles and equipment over it—although the effects of global warming have reduced the cold winter months in which artificial ice roads will stay frozen. By spring, the ice roads begin melting across the tundra and BP is forced to fly helicopters.

One of the biggest contentions against oil development here is an economic and national security argument: that the petroleum below the coastal plain will not wean the United States from Middle Eastern supplies. Comparing Arabian oil reservoirs, conservatively estimated at 699 billion barrels, to the refuge's 6 billion barrels is like comparing dollars to dinars (see appendix E).

Oil leasing here has been repeatedly recommended (although not successfully passed by Congress) as various politicians insist that development on the coastal plain can be conducted without damaging the wilderness.* Naturally, environmentalists don't agree

---

*In 1987, Reagan's Secretary of the Interior Donald Hodel (who replaced the controversial James Watt) had first recommended full-scale oil leasing on the coastal plain. In the controversial *Arctic Refuge Resource Assessment,* Hodel wrote that "Continued dependence on imports for a substantial part of U.S. oil consumption creates many national security concerns." Hodel concluded, "It is my firm belief that an orderly oil and gas leasing program for the entire 1002 Area can be conducted in concert with America's environmental goals."

with this viewpoint. Businessmen do. But there's little doubt that another successful Arctic oil "patch" will boost both the oil companies and the sagging Alaskan economy with a surfeit of jobs and new industry.

Whether the coastal plain's ancient sea yields six or sixteen billion barrels of oil, or none at all, it's not disputed that the United States consumes seven billion barrels of oil a year.

Every forty-two-gallon barrel of crude oil that shoots up from a mile or two beneath the Arctic tundra by the natural pressure of gas or water yields half as many gallons of gasoline. And for every eight-pound gallon burned in a combustion engine, five pounds of carbon dioxide is emitted into the upper atmosphere, furthering the greenhouse effect that's flooding tundra polygons and native villages.

On the northern edge of the coastal plain, around the Iñupiat village of Kaktovik, permafrosted earth has recently begun collapsing into the sea at an alarming rate. Two hundred and fifty miles east, the village of Tuktoyaktuk, Canada, is slumping onto the melting permafrost, as the ocean washes closer to sandbagged Inuvialuit homes.

Several dozen miles south of the coastal plain's shoreline, the Jago Glacier appears as a pale and anorexic whale, its blue crevasses like a mouthful of baleen. But this is no mirage. The Jago—one of two dozen "marker" glaciers measured by scientists during the last decade to show the specific effects of global warming—is shrinking so fast that by 2020 Americans will no longer have any active Arctic glaciers.

As I jumped and hopped back to my kayak through the tussocks, wind lifted up river-borne glacial silt—ancient ground-up rock—into a brown dust storm. I closed my eyes. The airborne till ground against my teeth. The howl increased. A plover cried "*wyeep wyeep yeep yip yipiyyiyiyiyi*" from its nest. The wind whistled against its own reverse cyclonic, shrieking, and karate chopping out into the Beaufort Sea. I stopped and crouched on the balls of my heels for balance. If this kept up, my kayak would get blown off the beach.

At my feet were waxy miniature leaves of yet another plant I couldn't identify. The leaves curled over their furred underbellies, holding precious moisture away from the greedy wind. These tundra plants emit carbon dioxide and methane each year as they wither and die, but the resulting carbons are mostly absorbed by the underlying peat. When I closed my eyes and kneeled down—wetting my knees—against another gust, the tundra seemed like a big sponge, sucking in the silt, the hydrogen molecules, and even my own exhalations of carbon dioxide.

According to Pielou's trusty *Guide to the Arctic*, decomposition—fungi and bacteria eating the dead plants—is slow in the cold north. According to other scientists, 14 percent of the world's carbon is safely locked up in Arctic permafrost. But as the tundra abnormally warms from the positive Arctic Oscillation trend (aka greenhouse effect) the permafrost below the plants melts. The tundra is turning into a warm soup, speeding up decomposition by encouraging the growth of bacteria.

The net result is that the tundra is now releasing abnormal amounts of stored carbon dioxide and methane. Pielou concludes that if this trend continues, it "will enhance the greenhouse effect, and an unwelcome positive feedback will come into play."

Pielou is warning, like many other scientists, that glaciers will keep melting. Oceans will rise. And more acid rain will fall from the sky.

Although I like to see myself as a recycling, conservation-minded citizen, every time I went to look for the caribou herd, my trips north—riding jets, chartering small planes, or driving a car—demanded the distillation of many barrels of crude oil. On this trip, I burned 144 gallons of gasoline in my car, which emitted 720 pounds of carbon dioxide into the upper atmosphere.* Much of my essential adventure gear—rubber-hulled kayak, synthetic clothing, insect repellent, tent, and even my camera film—was made from those ancient subterranean algae and their component chemicals. So, as I lingered in the wilderness and speculated about tundra melt, I had to share responsibility for using fossil fuel that was warming the earth—because it was also powering my journeys.

Until I realized the true cost of fossil fuel, and how badly it could damage the environment, I took oil for granted. In 1989, the spill in Alaska's Prince William Sound made people like me sit up and begin calculating the cost of oil consumption more carefully.

IN 1977, THE SHORES of the Pacific got hooked up to the coastal plain of the Arctic by an eight-hundred-mile-long, four-foot-wide pipeline. It took another twelve years for Prudhoe Bay to reach its record production capacity, pumping eighty-four million gallons per day. Each gallon spends five days traveling seven miles per hour to reach Prince William Sound's port of Valdez.

For a millennium before the pipeline, thousands of glaciers and streams spilled a diversity of nutrients—algae and plankton (that will someday cook into petroleum), freshwater seeds, and fish fingerlings—into these protected waters. With twenty-three-foot tides acting as a blender, Prince William Sound fed a staggering abundance and diversity of life. Vast beds of clams and scallops carpeted the tide pools and seafloor, along with king and Dungeness crabs. Higher up the food chain, orcas and humpback whales, Steller sea lions, Dall and harbor porpoises, more than ten thousand sea otters, and a host of other animals all depended on the rich mix of fresh

---

*Carbon dioxide comprises 61 percent of the greenhouse gases in the upper atmosphere, along with methane, chlorofluorocarbons, and nitrous oxide. Since the Industrial Revolution, these gases have increased to nine times their previous levels, magnifying the harmful rays of the sun, trapping heat energy and warming the earth.

and salt water. Over six thousand bald eagles roosted here, along with countless seabirds. Thousands of tons of small fish, cod, rockfish, sablefish, halibut, squid, and five species of salmon used to splash here.

Past tense.

It all changed on March 23, 1989, when the single-hulled tanker *Exxon Valdez* radioed for permission to change channels. Columbia Glacier, the mother of all iceberg makers in Prince William Sound, had been explosively active during an unseasonably warm winter, and had disgorged tons of ice into the shipping lanes. Scientists had already shown that the unusual glacial melting—measured in each of Alaska's fourteen mountain ranges, from the Brooks to the Aleutians—may have been caused by the greenhouse effect.

The *Valdez*'s skipper knew about the iceberg-filled waters and he wanted to avoid "doing a Titanic." His crew could hear growling noises as the hull plowed through small ice "growlers" and kayak-sized "bergy bits." As the coast guard authorized the course change, the captain put the ship on automatic pilot to get it around a bigger field of bergs that could dent the hull. Then he left the bridge.

At 12:09, while relaxing in his cabin, the captain felt a slight roll followed by a half-dozen shuddering, heartrending jolts as his ship ran up onto Bligh Reef. Eight of the ship's eleven tanks were ripped open in a six-hundred-foot-long gouge.

The captain ran out and looked over the side with a floodlight: oil boiled up out of the sea. The tanker had been loaded with fifty-three million gallons of crude oil, drilled 825 miles away from under two miles of Arctic tundra and permafrost.

The chief mate quickly ran calculations that showed the ship would sink if taken off the reef. But the captain would not listen. He spent the next hour and a half trying to power the ship off the reef. If he had succeeded, the *Valdez* would have capsized, possibly killing the crew, and certainly spilling its entire payload.

Several hours later, the coast guard boarded the *Valdez*. The oil fumes—benzene and toluene are highly flammable—teared their eyes, but they discovered the captain out on deck drinking coffee and smoking. They ordered him to put the cigarette out. No one detected alcohol on his breath, but the caustic chemical fumes deadened their sense of smell. One coast guard officer noticed that the captain's eyes appeared watery, but it took time to round up a Breathalyzer.*

As eleven million gallons leaked out of his ship into the sea, the captain fueled himself with coffee to try to counteract his afternoon intake at Valdez's Pipeline Club. Over the next twenty-four hours, Exxon ships pumped forty-two million gallons out of the *Valdez* and into three tankers, holding just off Bligh Reef with set anchors and engine thrusts. After two days, the main spill spread to a dozen square miles, as smaller oil slicks spread over one hundred square miles. Pilots flying a thousand feet overhead reported their nausea from the benzene fumes.

Then seventy-mile-per-hour winds hit. The red oil-containment booms ripped apart, while the tanker listed dangerously to port. Three days after the spill, Exxon declared it impossible to contain. Meanwhile, the U.S. Energy Department ordered the port of Valdez be reopened to supertankers. Alaskan officials and fishermen took over by surrounding islands near the spill with booms, desperately hoping to save salmon hatcheries.†

---

*Captain Hazelwood had his blood tested ten hours after the accident. His blood-alcohol level registered 0.61 percent; the coast guard allows no more than 0.40 percent while operating a commercial vessel.

†On March 28, President George H. W. Bush sent federal officials north. While the world reacted in shock to Exxon's lack of response, the president, when asked if the spill changed his position in support of oil drilling in the refuge, replied that he saw: "No connection. They've been shipping oil out of here for a long, long time and never had anything of this magnitude or this concern. So the big thing is to correct it."

The slick grew into a forty-mile-long patch, reaching its oily fingers into the most biologically productive parts of the sound. By March 29 the slick extended forty-five miles, soiling islands and threatening the sound's $100-million-a-year fishing industry. Although no roads penetrate this rugged part of the sound, the spill devastated coastal communities such as Cordova—closing its vital herring fishery—and the native village of New Chenega—poisoning the Chenegans' clam beds.

Oil tarred thirteen hundred miles of coastline and killed billions of juvenile salmon and herring. Mature fish died by the millions as oil rotted their fins and tails and supported trichodinid ciliate parasites that attached to their gills and suffocated them. Half a million birds, including 250 bald eagles, died as oil weighted down their feathers and prevented them from flying. Then, as they tried to preen off the sticky crude, they ate benzene, toluene, and octane, causing kidney failure and intestinal damage.

Half of the area's ten thousand sea otters died. Autopsies showed changes in the sea otters' lungs (caused by pulmonary emphysema), livers, and kidneys, along with pathological skin lesions and oil in their blood.

At least three hundred seals died; the oil limited their mobility and they drowned. Twenty-two orcas from both resident and transient populations died, often after eating slower, oiled seals and salmon. Ironically, as oil was ingested by its progenitor species, algae and plankton, the single-celled aquatic organisms were unharmed. But for years, these toxic sponges of algae and plankton would continue to be eaten by other marine species.

Of the eleven million gallons of crude oil spilled, only a quarter-million gallons were skimmed off the sea. Tides, winds, and a disorganized army of cleanup workers repeatedly undermined containment. In the end, evaporation did more work than the $2.5 billion that Exxon spent cleaning up the spill. Many workers became desperately ill with respiratory diseases, caused by benzene or by the toxic solvents used to clean up the oil. The workers' claims for their health issues have not been settled by any court.

As for the oil spill, Exxon settled for a $125-million penalty and another $1 billion, spread over a decade, for Prince William Sound's rehabilitation. Most Alaskans were angry with the judge, figuring that Exxon got off lightly because studies conducted by state and federally funded scientists estimated the damage at $15 billion. Alaska's governor during the 1991 settlement wanted to take less so that attempts to open ANWR for oil exploration would not be deterred in any way by the staggering costs of another potential oil spill.

Immediately after the spill, Exxon fired the *Valdez* skipper. His on-duty drinking cost him a nine-month's suspension of his pilot's license. He was convicted of a misdemeanor for "negligent discharge of oil" but his $59,000 fine eventually got overturned. Because the captain originally reported the spill, an obscure federal statute provided him with immunity from prosecution.

Congress banned the repaired ship from ever returning to Prince William Sound and mandated that all tankers would have to be constructed with double hulls, which would have minimized the *Valdez* spill by 60 percent. Then the powerful oil lobbyists convinced lawmakers to give the oil companies until 2015 to rebuild their ships.

Some pundits painted the disaster as a boon to the environmentalists. The big-gun environmental groups—the Wilderness Society, the Natural Resource Defense Council, the National Audubon Society, the National Wildlife Federation, the Sierra Club, and the Defenders of Wildlife—collectively raised $2.6 million immediately after the spill to increase awareness in Alaska about the dangers of oil development.

That year in Washington, D.C., oil lobbyists announced a $50 million annual budget for their interests.

Still, the public outcry effected change. The Secretary of the Interior's recommendations for drilling, along with the entire two-hundred-page *Arctic Refuge Resource Assessment*, which took seven years to research and write, were scrapped. And Senate bill S 406, which would have opened ANWR to oil development, was shelved in May 1989.

TWO MONTHS LATER, I glided to within a respectful distance of the mile-wide Blackstone Glacier, cocked and overhanging Prince William Sound like a wall of artillery. That June had been one of the hottest on record in Alaska and my friends and I had paddled an unusual seven days without a drop of rain. We had already seen blackened seaweed tangled with dead cormorants and loons. Our eyes watered from the benzene fumes. Red-buoyed, oil-absorbent booms lined many of the outer shores, and except for the throaty breathing of ocean against graveled beaches, punctuated by the splash of our paddles, an eerie silence prevailed throughout the sound. We fled into more protected waters, into Blackstone Bay, hoping to find some remnants of paradise unspoiled.

Below the glacier, we waited expectantly with our paddles poised over battened-down cockpits. We had come to the sound to witness the power of calving glaciers and search for a bit of paradise unspoiled. Bergy bits and growlers bobbed all around us.

As we sat in our sea kayaks waiting for a small natural disaster, the Blackstone Glacier finally shifted. First, a cannon roar, followed by an underground rumble, and then a jagged, Parthenon-sized pillar of jade-blue ice began to sink as the glacier behind it exploded, throwing frozen shards thirty yards out as the pillar splashed into the sea and a river of ice roared down behind in a two-minute-long waterfall filled with more bergy bits and growlers. We put our cameras away and braced our paddles in the displacement swells.

I closed my eyes to swaying water as my senses spilled open among the bouncing peaks and troughs of the ocean. I smelled the briny cordite of rocks sliding and sparking beneath the ice as a glacial breeze fanned my face. I opened my eyes and slapped my paddle down opposite the wake to prevent capsizing—my feet simultaneously cramping as I stiffened my legs against the knee braces. When the moment and its requisite fear passed, the bay surrounding us seemed utterly huge, and we all felt like shrunken bugs.

One of my friends whistled with an intake of breath while jabbing his paddle away from the glacier, toward the mouth of the bay. I cocked my head back, careful not to lose my balance.

A six-foot high, triangular fin knifed through the water. Someone whispered "Ohmygod" as a black upwelling of seawater ran toward our kayaks from the opposite side of the glacier. Then the bull orca rose out of the sea, ogling us with a dinner-plate–sized eye. It slid back down with a quiet splash—all performed fifty yards away, with the same respect for our safety that we had shown to the glacier.

A tiny fin trailed a three-foot-high fin as we paddled into shallow waters to ride the tide back to camp. Although orcas didn't attack kayakers, wilderness etiquette dictated that mothers and calves deserved plenty of room.

Since the oil spill the resident orca population among this, the most highly studied group of whales on earth, had dropped from twenty-two to nine—prompting biologists to call Prince William Sound's resident whale pod endangered. These whales were seen swimming around in oil-slicked waters eating contaminated seals, not their usual diet of fish, because the oil-poisoned seals weakened into slow-moving prey. Subsequently, the birthrate among this pod has dropped to zero.

Back at camp, under a knoll, a clear brook whispered past a gauzy hemlock copse. Mosquitoes were strangely absent, but mayflies hung in hazy brown clouds under a clear blue sky. As midnight approached, I crawled into my tent, pitched beyond the tents of my clients. The sea lapped gently against moss-covered boulders exposed to the falling tide. Clams spat, fish jumped, and barnacles popped. After a long day of paddling, these digestive noises mixed with the gurgling of the brook lulled me to sleep within minutes.

But several hours later, I sat upright and awake after hearing a muffled sonorous moaning unlike any snore. It wasn't a bear; it could have been an owl. I unzipped the tent, peered around, and listened. Two minutes later, a plaintive canto of pain—that, in my somnolent state, spoke to the recent environmental disaster—rose across Blackstone Bay: *"Ooooooooooooooooooooooooooooooooooooooo."*

I couldn't see anything out in the moonlit waters. No splashes, no animal movement, just a silver sheen of tide whooshing in like a river. The moonlight painted a golden fur on the outstretched arms of the hemlocks. Nothing to do but relax and lay my head back down and listen to the whales.

"Ooooooooooooooooooooooooooooooooooooooo."

THAT YEAR I VISITED MOOSE, Wyoming, and a sagging, spruce-logged homestead inside Grand Teton National Park. In my confusion and outrage about how Exxon had damaged Alaska, and how the oil companies might continue to devastate my favorite wilderness by drilling in the refuge, I had gone to seek counsel from the legendary conservationist Mardy Murie. She spoke with a slight lisp about the senseless tragedy of the oil spill. She encouraged me to be curious, to hear all the facts before I came to any conclusions about oil development in the refuge, her "place of enchantment."

She, of course, had already made up her mind, but as she passed me a platter of caloric cookies dolloped with frosting and filled my tea cup, I wondered why she remained so calm. She hadn't pounded the table or expressed her emotions when talking about the oil companies, and even stranger, she seemed blithely unaware that the latest Senate bill to open the refuge had been temporarily shelved. *Who was this woman?* I wondered, looking around the cabin.

On the spruce-log mantel above the fireplace built from Snake River stones was a varnished wooden board painted with black and yellow lettering by her husband, Olaus, now thirty-six years dead. The words came from a Cumberland graveyard, but like many Murie messages, things were not as they appeared on the initial read. This was not their epitaph. This was merely what they wanted people like me to see:

> *The wonder of the world,*
> *The beauty and the power,*
> *The shape of things,*
> *Their colours, lights, and shades;*
> *These I saw.*
> *Look ye also while life lasts.*

Mardy was showing an intense interest in my repeated journeys to the North. She was eighty-seven years old, of Irish lineage, but her eyes were clear and she stepped lightly, quickly, as if she had been dancing all her life. She repeatedly twirled a simple gold nugget on a band, worn on her wedding finger. Her long nose, brown eyes, and broad pale face were revealed by the turquoise clasp holding back her silver hair. She annunciated her words crisply, like an old-fashioned English teacher.

The only suggestion that came close to environmental rhetoric arose after I referred to the refuge by its acronym, which is pronounced An-wahr. She set down her tea cup. "I've always called it *the refuge*," she said, pointing her finger in the air, "rather than *An-wahr*. That abbreviation sounds like something a government bureaucrat might say. And my husband knew a lot about those government bureaucrats."

I excused myself for a bathroom break and to indulge my lifelong habit of exploration. Drafts blew through the log chinks, which Mardy had stuffed with aluminum foil. A placard that read "Those who dare to teach, Must never cease to learn" hung near her bedroom door. Mardy did not use a computer, a television, a dishwasher, or an answering machine. Her telephone was rotary dial.

On my way back to the table, following an inveterate love of books, I stopped to browse amid a thousand titles shelved in the living room. The more obscure books—*Birds of California, Lectures of Stoddard,* and *Natural History of a Sea Otter*—may have been kept as tribute to Olaus. But Mardy's neat, curlicued pen marked the endpapers, denoting page numbers with relevant conservation information or poetic passages. A Library of Mardy & Olaus Murie sticker featured a snowy owl guarding an Arctic river.

Mardy claimed to be a devotee of Henry James, but the only fiction on these shelves was Tolstoy's *Anna Karenina,* Austen's *Sense and Sensibility,* Cather's *My Ántonia,* and Forsythe's *Dogs of War.* No social change, feminist, or self-help titles freighted her library.

Although she and her husband published six books, these volumes were placed haphazardly and unsigned on the shelves. Her classic *Two in the Far North* wore a leather slipcase embossed MARDY MURIE. Inside, the old card pocket showed that the book had been borrowed, permanently, from a public library.

Mardy came over to show me more. "Do you know about Sally Carrighar?" she asked, sliding out the book from the local naturalist's section. "One of our favorites." *A Day in the Life of Teton Marsh* was autographed to the Muries, like all of Carrighar's books. But the author was thanking *them,* as if the Muries wrote the books.

Mardy then excused herself while I browsed. Famous authors—including a dozen preeminent anthropologists, biologists, and politicians—had given their books to the Muries. Surprisingly, many of them were autographed, like Carrighar's, with a reverse appreciation that embarrassed Mardy:

Silent Spring was autographed with neat penmanship:

To Dr. Olaus Murie,
with sincere appreciation
Rachel Carson,
August 19, 1962

Coming into the Country, although already dedicated "For Martha," the New Jersey author's wife, was autographed:

For Margaret Murie
after Martha's, this is
surely my most prized copy
of this book
All best—
John McPhee
Moose 8/24/79

The bard of the North wrote in *Arctic Dreams*

To Mardy—
in the great arc of your life you have
been illumination in the perennial darkness
and we are most grateful.
Barry [Lopez] at Moose

How could this be, I wondered, *a crusading grandmother?* She evoked the Baroness Karen Blixen, who wrote under the pen name Isak Dinesen and whose memoir of Africa I had just read, in the way she quietly mourned the loss of her husband and the wilderness. You couldn't help wanting to learn more.

Mardy's graciousness made me rethink my time in the North. I hadn't even left and already I was planning to come back to the western rim of Jackson Hole, where the Rockies erupt through a fault block in the earth's crust, chained to their Brooks Range beginnings.

This polite meeting would compel me to make more inquiries about her and her family's lives. I would reread their books. In the way that we become propelled by unlikely mentors, the gentler Murie journeys seemed to eclipse my physically challenging Arctic adventures.

She seemed to invite a big hug, but I politely shook her hand goodbye instead. Looking back at the musty cabin, now under the shadow of the Grand Teton, it became apparent that studying this woman's life would offer a key to understanding the refuge.

⌂   ⌂   ⌂

As a teenager, Mardy watched an orca jump onto a humpback whale and redden the Prince William Sound waters with blood. Feeling the whales' wake, hearing them breathe, and making eye contact from a small boat awed her. Although she did not write about Alaska's richest seascape in her buoyant memoir *Two in the Far North*, the first sentence of the book reads: "A nine-year-old girl can see and hear a lot."

Her Fairbanks girlhood, beside a Chena River slough, had exposed her to the last horse-drawn sleighs and the building of Alaska's railroad. She had learned how to stoke woodstoves and live with clouds of mosquitoes. She grew accustomed to whiskey-soused miners and prostitutes and lawyers, all trying to bring form to a wilderness frontier shut into fifty-below for a month each side of Christmas. Her mother forbade her from setting foot on Front

Street, near the fenced-in yards where the prostitutes plied their wares to the drunks. Fairbanks had twenty-three saloons.

The town began as a row of shacks after miners grew rich panning the creeks in 1902. Named after Teddy Roosevelt's vice president (in hopes that the Alaska Territory would command enough attention from Washington to be given statehood), Fairbanks grew almost overnight when the saloon keepers and prostitutes migrated from the Yukon Territories, where the Klondike gold rush had shown the most ambitious entrepreneurs how to mine the miners. Over the next decade, $63 million of gold would be blasted, hosed, dug, chipped, washed, axed, piped, and panned out of Fairbanks' creeks.

Mardy's stepfather, Louis Gillette, an assistant U.S. attorney, had come to bring law and order to this brawling town. The region's new gold discoveries stopped in 1914, and the Alaska Territory stumbled into a stop-and-go, break-it-or-make-it economy that would define the place and its residents. Fairbanks had grown to over five thousand people. Mardy learned the disciplines of chopping wood, canning berries, and smoking fish for the long winters. She learned to accept the grizzled miners and trappers for who they were, rather than judging them by their gruff manners and exteriors.

Fairbanks, along with the previous gold rushes in Nome and Juneau, closed an era on America's mining frontier. It was the end of the hard-bitten Sourdough prospectors, and the beginning of the large corporations that would later grow Alaska. As most of the gold went bust and hundreds of mines panned out, copper mines were built and canneries sprang up all along Alaska's southern shores— splashing with herring and salmon. As out-of-work miners began pounding in Alaska Railroad ties from Anchorage to Fairbanks, Mardy bounced south in one of the last horse carriages to her father's cannery.

Alaska had changed radically by 1918. As Mardy turned sixteen, during her first summer in Prince William Sound, she too would be transformed by the wilderness.

She couldn't tie a bowline, read a compass, row a tender, or tell the difference between a dog and a humpy salmon, but she had come to learn at her father's—Ashton Thomas's—Port Ashton salmon cannery. By midsummer she figured out how to cook in rollicking fo'c'sles, how to camp out, and how not to crowd the avalanching glaciers. She held the tiller calmly as the clinker-built boat's prop rose from the water atop big swells and clicked against air while she waited for the boat to smack down into the wave trough. By the end of summer, she learned to row without spinning in circles and how to withstand the stench of the main cannery floor—by leaving as quickly as possible.

Her lifelong gaiety derived from these days of dancing and foot races and baseball games with her father, stepmother, uncles, siblings, stepsiblings, and cousins. Mardy was photographed at one of the many costume parties with her thick brown hair braided down to a full and corseted chest. Her Native American headdress and buckskin jacket set off her aquiline nose. Even into midlife, these stout and tanned features—her hair tied up with the signature red bandana—show one at home in the wilderness.

That fall she enrolled at Reed College in Oregon. She returned to Prince William Sound in 1920 as a woman courting refined ideas not normally associated with the frontier. Her father gave her the sought-after job of cannery shopkeeper and her second summer in the sound opened the gate for a life around wilderness.

Although Mardy's stories were punctuated with chasteness, the possibility of love—for the perfect man, for untrammeled wilderness—lingers in her reminiscences. She told of women in minor support roles in the 1920s and watched men more closely, craving their rugged lives or demanding careers. She swooned over a World

War I veteran who played bagpipes and the rough-hewn yet well-mannered Norwegian fishermen who came in to purchase Copenhagen snuff and Kavring. Eventually, she learned to crave this crispy Norwegian toast, which came in barrels topped with white muslin to keep the cracker from going moist.*

She continued exploring this horn of plenty, wondering—as the seas fizzed like soda with fish—how so many herring could possibly exist. She tramped in rubber boots up prickly fields of chest-high devils club and through vales filled with wild violets and into marshes of bog hyacinth. She grew comfortable with her callused hands, climbed slimy ladders, and got acquainted with cormorants and murres and all manner of ungainly-legged, keen swimmers. Although these experiences weren't so wild and wooly in a territory full of would-be Jack Londons cracking whips, an educated girl's perceptions in the middle of the wilderness had little precedent.

Mardy noticed that her father did not dump cannery waste into the sea. She remembered the exploitation—hunters shooting whole herds with impunity, gold miners burning down the birch forests, and canneries gutting fisheries—as the end of a way of life. She called it an Alaskan era "tinctured by greed and ambition."

She spent another year at Reed College as an English major, and then a year at Simmons College in Boston, where her snooty classmates denigrated her as "that Alaskan gal." When she returned home, Fairbanks seemed different. She would never use such words as "quaint" to describe it or its women, who were amused by her passion for Emerson, Dickens, and Yeats. She would never malign the ordinary hardworking and garrulous folks who lived within a

---

*Thirty-six years later, en route to the refuge, Mardy searched for Kavring on the Seattle waterfront with her Norwegian-descended husband, Olaus. In *Two in the Far North* she recalled her girlhood prophecy to her mother that she would marry a Norwegian.

great wilderness. She cared about the kindly Fairbanksians, who at their crudest moments merely made her laugh.

Most turn-of-the-century women attended liberal arts colleges merely to become good mothers and conversationalists for their husbands. But Mardy wanted an education that she could utilize. So she finished her college education in Fairbanks with a business degree, becoming the University of Alaska's first woman graduate in 1924. Although she hoped her financial acumen would eventually help raise a family, she mostly saw the world through lilting turns of phrase and a reverence for literature. And for Romance. She spelled it with a capital R; she meant the kind of Romance that she felt for the land. For Alaska.

Long under its spell, Mardy remembered Prince William Sound six decades later. "The beautiful bays and inlets and channels, the forests and the green slopes dotted with flowers, the whales and the puffins and auklets," she wrote in the decade after North America's largest oil field had been discovered in the Arctic and the new state continued to grow on the largess of its natural resources. "All these I think are still there."

Several years after the oil spill, Mardy added yet another book to her library. Art Davidson, the author of *In the Wake of the* Exxon Valdez; *The Devastating Impact of the Alaska Oil Spill*, penned a note to Mardy above his signature: "Let's make certain that a sinking like this never happens again."

Chapter 4

WOLVES

I felt that if I could see one all my luck would change. Maybe
I would track it until it stopped and greeted me and we would
embrace and I would become a wolf.

—Jim Harrison
Wolf

I bolted up from deep sleep and reached to open the tent zipper as
my partner pumped a round into the chamber of the shotgun.
Since our tent lacked windows, we couldn't see the heavy-footed
beast drumming across the tundra and breaking stout willow
branches—*snap, snap, snap*—across the far riverbank. I unzipped the
door and bent back to make room for the gun barrel as the animal
jumped into the river splashing, snorting, and huffing. It all happened too quickly to be scared.

To our relief, it was only a caribou, shrugging off a quick shower
of river water on the shore below as her hooves threw first mud
then clods of tundra, and she breezed past with the smell of wet
sweaters, ogling us with her harvest-moon wide, yellow-brown eyes.
I rubbed my own, trying to resurface from my sleep, while hooves
shook the wet ground below us as if we were sitting on a water-
bed. We knew she was female by her lack of antlers—my friend
reminded me that cows shed during spring calving, while bulls keep
their antlers through the late autumn rut. Her quivering leg mus-

cles showed that she had grown old enough to fear predators.

What was chasing her?

We heard another faint splashing as a large, sandy-colored canine jumped into the river and loped out of the water below us. Soaking wet, her muscular legs and neck were no less magnificent for lacking fur. Although I had never seen a wild wolf, I knew dogs, and this long-muzzled female—her milk teats swaying—had to weigh a hundred pounds dry. But this wolf bore no interest in human beings; she looked right through us as she ran past our tent door. My friend lowered the gun and we stepped outside barefoot to watch the chase fade into the dawn.

Hoarfrost sifted, gathered, and rained through the space between light and darkness. The light hung against the mountaintops like clover honey in a clear jar, while the sun surfaced like a breathless whale over the northeastern sea. A wheatear whistled huskily.

If there had been a pack of wolves, they would have circled the caribou and ripped at its hamstrings to bring it down. If there had been a herd of caribou, they would have "swamped" the wolves by speeding up and slowing down, galloping back and forth and trading places, until their predators became blurry-eyed and confused.

This was what I wrote in my journal during my first trip to the Arctic in August 1983. And as I would learn in repeated trips to the Far North, when I got the urge to finally go alone, regular sleep didn't come easy. The landscape promotes insomnia.

We could smell the minty bloom of Labrador tea. Frosty air rasped our throats, so we zipped the door shut and sat back down on grimy foam pads. The autumn light blushed against the top of our dome tent, while a Bohemian waxwing squeaked in the dwarf poplar, some nuthatches chipped in to the growing chorus, and the Aichilik River swished against the bank below.*

---

*I have changed the name of the river to give these wild wolves the anonymity and protection that they deserve.

Amid the birdsong, I hunkered cross-legged on my half-inch-thick foam, draped the sleeping bag around my waist, blew on my fingers, and tried to find words that sang to the North within unlined seven-by-five-inch notebooks. The entry began with a few sensory observations, then listed the arcana of camp life: how the Labrador tea boiled after dinner tasted like chamomile, and, in the mornings, constipated me. Why grizzlies in close quarters got me going again. How migrating birds allowed me to connect with a pulse I had never palpated.

I worked with a pocketknife-sharpened pencil and wrote in a shrunken script, an attempt to fit the vast Arctic into my small notebooks:

> Enjoying the reddening bearberry on the valley floor, the aqua blue of the stream, the scats and moose-chewed willows and river bends and ocher cliffs and untouched world that spreads before us in the last splendor of a dying summer.

I wrote in my journal that the wolf mattered to me because she offered a key to my own life. I craved the wolf's three-staged mastery of the world: her independence, her effortless manner of surviving in the wilderness, even her ability, as one author claimed, to nuture a family.[*]

Several hours later, we pushed our tandem kayak into an eddy next to the wolf tracks. For a few seconds, I aligned my palms to her triangular pads and tried to feel the power of her strides, but this exercise in wishful thinking only gained me a half-deserved, curious stare from my companion. My cerebral friend tolerated my

---

[*]Walt Disney released a blockbuster Hollywood version of Farley Mowat's *Never Cry Wolf* in 1983, the same summer that I first visited the Arctic. Mowat created a larger-than-life saga about his observations as a biologist for the Canadian Fish and Wildlife Service, which had sent him into the Arctic wilderness to show how the bloodthirsty wolves were eliminating the wild caribou.

compulsiveness and risk-taking while rock climbing in the early seventies and when we attempted Denali in 1976. He put up with my stubborn need to be an autodidact. He also looked after me like an older brother, securing me hard-to-find outdoor jobs, advising me, and most important, introducing me to the Arctic.

He slid into the bow like a gymnast; I plopped in and nudged us off the rooted bank. Mostly we just steered and let the current pull us downstream so we could listen to the croaking of a raven, the patter of suspended river silt tickling the rubber hull, and the fulsome glide of a river sluicing through banks underlain with dirty gray permafrost.

As on the day before, hundreds of caribou ran into the river current that carried our tandem kayak. They swam grunting and snorting, regally lofting their antlered heads and emerging from the far side with showered shrugs of river water. The tundra had gone red with frost, and the caribou-redolent air smelled of sour hay.

This day I realized that, lacking trees as visual cues, this Arctic valley stretched wider than I could accurately discern. Several hundred yards east of the river, a bear sat on a caribou carcass and gorged with bloody jaws. If you weren't paying attention to the distance in these abnormally wide valleys, the distant bear could be mistaken for a ground squirrel sitting on a pile of rabbit fur. Musk oxen stood still with fur draping to the ground, hiding their legs, and appearing as hairy boulders. Migrating sandhill cranes wavered across the horizon as silver arrows piercing the sky, seen long before their rolling bugles reached our ears.

A couple of miles downstream, on the western shore, a black wolf sat on its haunches and stared at us, rather than past us, as the blonde wolf had done. We paddled slowly for the shore; the wolf waited. On the bank, I grabbed a camera as the wolf backed off and we cautiously followed. Along a stand of willows, I raised my camera and the wolf jumped out of sight. Then he reappeared, looking down at us from a conical-shaped *panga*, a hill shoved up from the forces of permafrost contracting then expanding against the skin of tundra above.

No fear showed in this old cur. Comparing him to even a grey-hound would have been unfair, for despite his sleekness and obvi-ous power he seemed to move from within another dimension. Mincing sideways, waving his tail about like a fifth arm, he sprang above the tundra with every step. He never showed his teeth or barked or growled. He refused to run off. He appeared just as curious about us as we were about him. Unlike the magnificent specimen of the morning, this wolf's ribs poked through his brittle-looking fur. Through the binoculars, we could see that he was missing teeth.

We placed our feet carefully among the tangle of ankle-high dwarf birch, then began padding through crispy reindeer lichen as we chased the idea that the wolf could lead us somewhere impor-tant. On the other side of the panga, we heard a mewing and looked north toward the river and a high sand bank. As soon as our attention had turned, the coyote-sized wolf bolted south, dragging its lame rear leg across the tundra. Before I could further consider what wisdom this old black wolf might have imparted, the mew-ing drew us north. While we thrashed through the low willows, the sandy-colored wolf of the morning unexpectedly jumped down from a den site and sprinted for the river. My partner and I looked at one another, aghast. Being in the presence of a large predator is always electrifying.

We climbed out of the river flats slowly, carefully. Then, as we peeked over the final bluff, we saw five pups lying in the sand.

We crawled closer. Their fur riffled in the wind. One looked up at us from the leg bone of a caribou while its siblings lay half asleep and gorged. My partner whispered not to touch anything around the den hole: "If we foul it with our scent they might abandon their den."

As he spoke, the bone chewer tilted his head in curiosity. Then he stood up and walked down to the river after his mother. One by one, the other pups yawned, stretched, licked their paws, then reluctantly stood up also and stumbled—cinnamon-colored furballs atop uncertain legs—toward their howling mother. We stole one last photograph of the eight-foot-deep, empty den hole, then left. Talking aloud would have been akin to interrupting Sunday mass, so we whispered and gestured.

We beelined back to the kayak. Crowberry, diapensia, and heather wafted past our noses in an acerbic riot of fermentation. The blood-red earth crunched beneath our feet, giving its own last desiccated yelp before the snows. Caribou splashed in the river below. Above, the nameless peaks—which I had no intention of climbing—were cloaked in white-hot glaciers, reflecting more heat than the meek and distant sun. But it was the howling that got to us. The three-noted dirge and instructional lament was sung over and over again, saying (we imagined), "*come away, come away, come away.*" Although the usual reaction to hearing a wolf howl had always sounded trite to me, I learned that it was true: The hair does rise up on the back of your neck.

Our minds were spinning. Neither of us had seen a wolf before this morning. And after encountering a den of pups that had never seen people, we began to rethink what it might be like in an Alaska bereft of real wilderness.

We lifted the kayak into the river, and, one at a time, slid into our cockpits and braced our wooden paddles into water clear as dream-time air. My normally nervous friend had a carefree smile and looked as if he had suddenly loosed the world's weight. I cupped a hand to drink from the river, and my fingers went numb and my teeth ached as we scoffed one another about using water filters. "It doesn't get any purer than this," I said. But I meant it.

At the next bend, the pups all reappeared, swimming the river, their muzzles held high and anxiously above the water as their tails worked the current like rudders. We put our shoulders into back-paddling strokes to stop the kayak and watch. As the last pup clambered out onto the silt bank, he sank deep into a quagmire and cried aloud. He was trapped.

The mother sat as a poised statue of muscle and sinew in the reddening tussocks above, refusing to look at us. We floated closer. As the trapped runt of the litter began whining, lolling its tongue in submission, we prepared to rescue it, even though we hated the idea of tainting a wild animal with a human touch and making it more trusting of people than wolves should be. But before we could J-stroke over to the bank and gently lift out the pup, two other pups ran down, grabbed their brother by the scruff of the neck, and yanked him out of the river silt—growling and play-biting all the way.

IT TOOK YEARS to sift the grains of this beach into a lesson that could hold my weight. At first, I felt hugely privileged: I had witnessed wolves up close within the last great wilderness. I was indirectly inspired by *Never Cry Wolf*, which showed the animals as compassionate and family-oriented hunters, as well as describing the author-biologist's transformation while observing the wolves. But as time went by, I realized that my enlightenment also came from seeing a family of wild animals stick together during adversity—witnessed, as it were, by a young man who had seen his own siblings and parents splinter apart after divorce.

I was careful not to let these feelings of abandonment place needless blame on anyone. After all, the trauma of divorce is not an uncommon story, and besides, the split helped compel my independence. It would have been a waste of time to think that my small despair weighed any more than the problems that most people lug around. Instead, while far removed from those who share my DNA, I was searching for a cure to this loneliness. My family's numbing lack of communication and forfeiture of love ate inside me like a worm, and partially explained why I had fled from the suburbs of Massachusetts to the wilderness of Alaska, looking for polar bears and caribou migrations and wolves.

But at the time, on this wilderness river north of the Arctic Circle, I was more worried about having scared the wolves away from their den. We later learned from a wildlife biologist that the family had all returned. Although we may have been the first humans to see those pups, in the intervening years the refuge has grown more popular, and surely we will not be the last people to visit their den.

I located paradise on that trip. I learned that the Arctic demands something different from its visitors because the broad landscape does not hold the classic and spectacular beauty that is commonly found in the more celebrated national parks where I worked as a rescue ranger. The baffling topography of the refuge—even stranger than the rest of the Arctic—makes it necessary to perform a careful study. Summers are chilly without darkness. Large mammals routinely hunt, kill, and eat other large mammals. It's mountainous, it's flat, it's half forest and half tundra, and it's incredibly wet underfoot—yet the region is technically a desert.

In this peculiar place, to become the so-called wolf that I craved, I wanted to learn how to go out into the remotest wilderness and reduce life to its basic necessities. I also wanted to go alone, to practice total self-sufficiency. I had already spent years honing my route-finding, camping, river-running, and general survival skills. More important, I slept better on tundra than in a bed; I was prone to claustrophobia while indoors and among crowds; I preferred squatting outside to sitting on toilets. I felt drawn to wild animals, and cold air vitalized me.

I wasn't going into the wilderness to court death or even take any risks; I was through with the adrenaline-seeking phase of my life. I merely craved physical mastery. I wanted to interact with the landscape, as wolves do, to try to integrate myself into this

Byzantine wilderness by letting my body become the universe in which it walked. And the refuge happened to be the wildest and weirdest place in which I might possibly attain this unfettered state of being.

Then I learned that the Muries too had an obsession with wolves.

⌂ ⌂ ⌂

Olaus Murie and his half-brother Adolph ran out onto squeaking snow to break up a bloody fight between their two sled-dog teams. Tom and Jerry were ripping fur off one another's backs and baring their fangs, Jerry had already laid Brownie out of commission by opening up his side, and Jack was trying to rip Dawson's nose off. Snook danced about excitedly howling, but couldn't reach the other dogs with tooth or claw. Only Irish and Jake and Jumbo weren't fighting—the other dogs gave these beasts wide leeway. Irish weighed 150 pounds; Jake and Jumbo were bred from wolves.

Since Olaus had always gone light with the whip, he and Adolph dove in bare-handed and jumped on the dogs, pried them apart with their boots, and retied them out of one another's reach. "The dogs seem happy over it all so I guess I shouldn't kick," Olaus wrote to his girlfriend, Mardy, in Fairbanks, in January 1921 as the lamp burned dry and the thermometer hit thirty below. "A day's rest certainly puts them in fighting trim."

He loved his dogs' "primeval truculence," their eagerness to travel, to go, to do something—just the way he felt. Every time he and Adolph mushed into a village, the natives would cajole them to show off their legendary wolf dogs. Jake and Jumbo lay awake while the other dogs slept; they howled, inexplicably, across the tundra; they pulled the other dogs out of line whenever they picked up faint sign of moose or caribou.

Adolph, meanwhile, was having the time of his life. He kept Jake and Jumbo in his team, if only because he felt a spiritual connection with the animals. It brokered the definition of coincidence—there beneath the shimmer of magnetic particles lighting up the night skies, while the two men sought to understand the inexplicable urgings that made caribou migrate—that Olaus's time training Adolph in the rigors of field biology would ultimately save thousands of wolves.

Unlike Olaus, Adolph did not suffer fools gladly, although good manners and respect were impressed firmly upon the both of them while growing up. In each other's company they spoke in Norwegian. While Adolph was a loner, Olaus lived for others. They were closer than most brothers, let alone half-brothers. Since Olaus had helped raise him, Adolph constantly sought out his brother's advice.

Adolph—narrow-jawed, dark and curly haired—could be grim-faced and taciturn. Light-complexioned Olaus—the smile lines etched like glacial striations into his face—gave even his enemies the benefit of doubt. Adolph was a born introvert, a skeptic, a sports fan, and a shrewd punster. Olaus was garrulous to a fault, an optimist, didn't understand batting averages, and rarely pulled anyone's leg. Both promoted epic rambling hikes, or "tramps," and fancied plaid shirts and green, forest-colored wool pants.

Olaus often expressed his frustrations to Adolph about the Washington, D.C., bureaucrats in the Biological Survey who chided him for his friendly style of interviewing the natives and who classified Alaskan animals into "good" and "bad" categories based on economic value. Still, he was thankful he wasn't a game biologist "down stateside," where his colleagues were all practicing "suppressive warfare" against predators.*

That winter, Olaus wrote to his boss about his theory that predation of caribou by wolves could be beneficial because the

---

*The 1915 law to exterminate wolves from federal lands and national parks—based on the government's successful slaughter of 366,981 coyotes over the previous thirteen years—resulted in the killing of 24,132 wolves by 1942.

strongest animals survived and preserved the vigor of the herd. "Man's killing does not work in this natural way, as the best animals are shot and inferior animals left to breed." Murie added that wolves were fast disappearing in the country north of Fairbanks. He discovered that the locals' image of the wolf changed according to the availability of caribou meat. If the herd grew abundant, the wolf was forgotten; in times of caribou scarcity, the wolf was blamed. His writing began to reflect a new visionary stance toward the wolf, one based on empirical evidence and free of sentiment— at least in his official reports.

He concluded that the caribou's greatest enemy was "not the wolf, nor the hunter, but man's economic developments." Murie began pushing to preserve large tracts of land years before the celebrated wilderness visionary, Aldo Leopold, who had shown that deer could coexist with wolves in northern Mexico.

Olaus received a petition from the University of Michigan decrying his agency's poisoning of predators. He told the petitioners about his fondness and passion for animals as a scientist, a naturalist, and an artist. He added, "I dislike no animal because he eats. If an animal eats to the extent of harming me unduly, I will retaliate, but only to the extent of relieving the situation and without hatred." He signed the petition, but since the group had omitted wolves because they were "killers," he urged that they too should not be exterminated, writing, "The wolf is a noble animal with admirable cunning and strength."

By today's standards of wilderness appreciation, his support seems what one might expect of a conservation-oriented wildlife biologist. But in the context of a scientist who was striving to avoid emotion in the 1930s, there was no stronger advocate for the wild wolf.

Consumed by other battles that would lead him to the refuge, Olaus passed the torch for saving predators on to his brother. Adolph was so fond of tracking wolves that he couldn't stop himself from measuring the gait of visiting friends and comparing humans to animals. Then he literally followed in his admired older brother's footsteps.

Adolph Murie had performed his graduate zoology work in Michigan, advising game officers to introduce wolves on Isle Royale in order to keep the unhealthy moose population in check. But the state dismissed his advice. A decade later, during a rare Lake Superior freeze, the wolves naturally migrated out to the island and they and the moose have lived in a healthy balance ever since.

After studying coyotes in Yellowstone, Dr. Adolph Murie moved to Alaska to perform wolf research. This hated "killer" was thought to be depleting the beloved Dall sheep and caribou in Mt. McKinley National Park. Here in the frontier, as a National Park Service wildlife biologist, Adolph was pushed to the limit in a cauldron of backwater politics, where people accused him of being a "posy sniffer." Meanwhile, in the Lower Forty-eight, wolves had been systematically exterminated.

In six months, Adolph shadowed the caribou by trekking seventeen hundred miles. But rather than fleeing, he was following the wolves. He sometimes carried his young daughter, Gail, on his back so that she too could hear the wolf song.

The work that Adolph accomplished, without radio telemetry collars or aircraft, was groundbreaking. He learned that wolves cared for one another in a way that had never been documented with other animals. Even as a stoic scientist, he couldn't help naming the animals he followed, or noting their similarities to humans as they played. He spent as long as thirty-three hours at a time hunkered beside dens. He wrote, "Just as a laboring husband comes home to the family each evening after working all day, so does the wolf come home each morning after working all night." When Adolph told the park rangers that the wolves existed in a delicate balance with the caribou and bighorn sheep—eating only the sick and the weak—he was stirring up trouble. Most rangers, most Alaskans, believed that wolves were ruthless assassins (an intolerance and misunderstanding of the biologic order that still persists in the forty-ninth state).

The Government Printing Office released a thousand copies of Adolph's monograph, *The Wolves of Mt. McKinley*. Its controversial conclusion: "Wolf predation probably has a salutary effect on the sheep as a species." While loudly derided by Alaskans, it was acclaimed by scientists and lay city dwellers alike. (The University of Washington Press would reprint the classic work decades later.) The report was subtly interwoven with Adolph's introverted biases against visitor developments, fire control, and predator control; he supported primeval wilderness.

Olaus had profoundly influenced Adolph's writing and philosophies. In a letter to Adolph, Olaus wrote, "I have a feeling that even yet we do not know the animals among whom we have lived for many centuries—and we may not have many chances with one like the wolf. More power to you." Olaus spoke of Adolph's wolf research with unreserved pride.

Adolph became the first scientist to discover that wolves ate mice. He used years of field time to show that wolves propagated herd animals by preying on the sick and the weak. On these points, the story of the Muries' predator research gained momentum through the best-selling Canadian author Farley Mowat, who sought advice from Adolph for *Never Cry Wolf*. Although Mowat abandoned government wolf research after less than a month, he was writing a book about his experiences. In his letter to Adolph, Farley asked for recommendations about how to observe wolves and wrote, "For the hundredth time [I had] glanced through *The Wolves of Mt. McKinley* to see how your observations coincide with my own."

Atlantic Monthly Press sent Adolph a galley of Mowat's book and asked for a publicity blurb for the upcoming U.S. publication. The editor's letter continued, "If there is an outcry, we can say the foremost wolf experts have read the book and pronounce it reliable." While counseled by Olaus, Adolph politely declined by citing the demands of his field research, but suggested that the editor fact-check by reading *The Wolves of Mt. McKinley*.

After *Never Cry Wolf* came out and people asked Adolph for his thoughts on Mowat's veracity, Adolph again declined. He did write back to Atlantic Monthly Press, telling them that Mowat had relied on *The Wolves of Mt. McKinley* while writing about Canadian wolves:

> I think [*Never Cry Wolf*] should be helpful in many quarters. . . . but as I read it it seemed that the book must have been greatly fictionalized. How could he write about the mouse mystery and much else in the book in the way he does if he was reading about McKinley wolves? In the long run, books such as his may do more harm than good.

The correspondence was forwarded to Mowat, who fired back a letter to Murie. Mowat conceded to taking "considerable liberties with time and place," but didn't want to let the truth get obscured by "too much data [while] attempting to do my best for the wolves."

This episode also shows how the Muries, mid-twentieth-century preservationists, and compassionate writers like Mowat were forced to refine their work. During these boom years of heightened industrialization many people were swept up in a wave of patriotic American materialism and comfort. It took a skillful communicator to show that primitive wilderness and predators were desirable public commodities. To reach the mainstream and effect change, as Farley Mowat had done, Adolph wrote, you had to go beyond science and "bring in esthetics, feelings—our stock in trade."

Many of these realizations came from Olaus, and can be read in the reams of letters that flew between the two brothers over seven decades. "Always a note about the weather in your field journals," he counseled Adolph in a tightly woven penmanship filled with self-effacing friendliness. The letters discussed the government's wrong-headed philosophy toward wilderness as an exploitable resource, clothing that would keep men warm at sixty below, skinning techniques, and the sheen of a wolf's fur.

Eventually, Olaus quit working for the government, who had censored his papers and speeches about predators. In a 1957 *Audubon* article, "Wolf," he found the liberty to describe a wildlife encounter, listening to a wolf howl on the banks of the Old Crow River. He called this Arctic experience a high point of his life. "Congratulations," Lois Crisler—famed for writing the first sympathetic mainstream book about wolves, *Arctic Wild*, in 1959— wrote Olaus after reading this story. "You've dared to handle a hedgehog with bare hands."

In the article, Olaus compared the wolf to the endangered whooping crane and black-footed ferret, decried the lack of science put forth by modern administrators, and blamed careless planning. He told—in the first paragraph—of people who dedicated their careers to eliminating these evil creatures.

"From now on," Crisler wrote, " 'professional wolf haters' is part of my vocabulary!"

Murie's early experiences interacting with wildlife popularized him, however briefly, as the first well-known field biologist. Saving predators led to his convictions about first setting aside habitat. After surviving several long illnesses, he rallied to save northeastern Alaska in a protracted battle that may have been the ultimate achievement of his career.

The year before Olaus died, he told an interviewer that meeting Mardy Thomas was the best thing that ever happened to him or his career. Their romance became a fable. Their romance, some said, created the last great refuge.

Chapter 5

MOSQUITOES AND WARBLES

Fair insect!
that, with threadlike legs spread out,
And blood-extracting bill and filmy wing,
Dost murmur,
as thou slowly sail'st about,
In pitiless ears full many a plaintive thing,
And tell how little our large veins would bleed,
Would we but yield them to thy bitter need.
　　　　　　　　　—William Cullen Bryant
　　　　　　　　　　"To a Mosquito"

The grape-seed–sized mosquito, weighing perhaps a microgram, probed my skin with her proboscis. For taxonomy purposes, I named her *Musca*. This Latin root was also used for the Italian *moshetta*—bolt for a catapult—which perfectly described her drinking apparatus.

I could make out the two pairs of surgical stylet tubes—seen like a bundle of twigs through my hand lens—around the two tubes of her proboscis. It looked as if she was poking me. On the fifth try, she finally found a venule by sliding the stylets through my skin and pushing in the entire fascicle apparatus, withdrawing her labium sheath, and nicking open the venule itself. I felt this infinitesimal cut less than the faint pinprick sensations of her stylet through my epidermis. Then, she began drinking my blood.

I felt an almost unbearable urge to paste *Musca*, so I clenched my jaw and continued to observe with equal parts fascination and exhaustion from my long day of tussock hopping across the tundra.

My experiment took place during the height of mosquito season, in mid-July, during my eighth trip to the Arctic. This time, I was guiding six clients across the coastal plain. The mosquitoes had been boiling up out of the tussocks and springing into our faces all day long. These mythical Birds of the Arctic flew in such thick masses, which when seen from the middle distance appeared as brown clouds of smoke, that they destroyed our attempts at photography by throwing the auto-focus mechanisms out of whack or blurring the film. The noise of their wings was scarily reminiscent of being plunged into a field of beehives. Head nets or insect repellant were mandatory. Unfortunately, the only effective repellent ingredient—the pesticide DEET—made the plastic parts on our cameras tacky and melted nylon clothing. Walking at a fast pace kept the swarms out of our faces, but not off our backs. Hundreds routinely settled for a collective probing motion, miraculously revealed through the hand lens as sawing.

Three of the two dozen mosquito species in Alaska can breed autogenously, without drawing blood. Since trying to swat them all would have been an exercise in futility, a calm Buddhist reaction seemed to help. You had to disassociate from the bugs or they would drive you mad.

Ignoring this insect's place in the refuge would be like overlooking the caribou herd, driven to the sea and its breezes in an attempt to escape the biting brown columns of smoke. Compared to bees, the mosquito role in plant pollination is negligible. Even the millions of birds here probably lose more blood to the mosquitoes than they gain protein by eating them.

The most positive effect of mosquitoes, or so I told my clients, was their substantial suppression of tourist visitation. Without the mosquitoes, word would get out about this bizarre and fascinating landscape, drawing crowds to the refuge's fragile coastal plain.

As we squashed a dozen, two dozen, and finally our record fifty-nine mosquitoes with one slap, I told my companions, "It could be worse."

"How could it possibly be worse?" asked one, a level-headed attorney from San Francisco.

"If these mosquitoes carried the diseases of their less prolific cousins," I replied, "we would not be here now."

He replied that he'd never return to the Arctic. As he and my other five companions dove into the tents for shelter, I stayed outside to conduct the experiment. Within ten minutes, as moving humans became hidden under nylon domes from the eyes of mosquitoes, and as our collective output of carbon dioxide and heat no longer registered on the sensors of their antennae, the mosquito cloud—I guessed a quarter-million strong, but the cloud was impossibly thick and blurry for an accurate count—visibly dissipated into the sheltering cracks and crannies of the tundra. A mere thousand remained on the leeward side of each tent, while another half thousand settled in on the shelter of my lower body. Since their cutting stylets were not sharp enough to penetrate my nylon-shell clothing, I exposed a quarter-inch slit of flesh between sleeve and gloved hand.

The so-called *Musca* alighted, sensing the sudden release of heat from my wrist. Although I could nickname her, I could not identify the species, one of two dozen different Alaskan mosquitoes from the family *Culicidae*. What I could do was watch.

Although my companions thought me crazy, I tried to explain that the best way to withstand the onslaught of Arctic mosquitoes was to deliberately encourage several dozen mosquitoes to bite. As

Musca finished sawing through the surface of my wrist and injected saliva with an anticoagulant protein to keep my blood flowing into her fascicle, my body—after the last few days of this deliberate blood-letting—had developed an allergen antibody to the protein, which prevented the mosquito bites from itching. Unfortunately, each time I returned to the refuge, it took several days of exposure to mosquito protein before my system could redevelop the antibody.

Musca held incredibly still. I timed her feeding: seventy-nine seconds. The mosquito pumping action, pounds per square millimeter, is so powerful that my capillaries were being held like a toilet plunger against her labium sheath. In no small disgust, I watched her ingest nearly three times her own weight in blood. At one millionth of a gallon per mosquito, it would take one and a half million mosquitoes to drain me.

Her stomach distended. *Musca* then stumbled across a few wrist hairs onto the black nylon glove. She scraped her proboscis with a foreleg, and began beating her wings, initially to no avail, until she wobbled into the air, taxing her abilities as she glided downward, freighting a bright red balloon of my blood at a speed no faster than I could walk. She crash-landed against a stem of cotton grass.

I pulled on the claustrophobic head net and settled down to witness a Romanesque orgy of digestion. Meanwhile, a swarm of several hundred mosquitoes had settled onto my shoulders, but since their proboscises couldn't penetrate my nylon windshirt, I made myself comfortable and slid my hands deep into my pockets to protect my wrists.

After twenty-five minutes, *Musca's* swollen, blood-filled belly went from bright to dark red. Across the ice pack along the northern horizon, the sun continued crawling east, while an Arctic fox ambled west across the tundra, sending a rock ptarmigan caterwauling into the distance.

As *Musca's* digestive tools sucked the water out of my blood, she defecated four pinprick-sized pink drops onto the cotton grass stem. My patience now evaporated, and the bloated mosquito made ready to fly off and spend a couple of weeks digesting.

My blood would enable her to lay a clutch of a hundred eggs in a nearby pond or tundra puddle. *Musca* would fertilize these eggs with sperm stored from her one sexual encounter with a nonbiting male mosquito, and as soon as a few hard frosts hit the North Slope, *Musca* would saw no more, having served her life's purpose. Thanks to me, another hundred *moshettas* would emerge next spring. I waved my hand in repugnance as the wind dropped and a brown cloud sprang up out of the ground.

Fifty yards west, a lone caribou wandered by. Through the binoculars, the bull had a soft velveteen-covered rack and black splotches erupting on its back. The bull symptomatically kicked up its rear legs and snorted in pain. It was also coughing. I was not the only one being tormented by insects.

Olaus Murie had observed that mosquitoes "should not be ignored" in a list of causes of the caribou migration. But the postmodernist biologist thinking, mostly proposed by Norwegian biologists, points to another species entirely: the oestrid, or warble fly.*

What this bumblebee-sized insect lacks in mouth parts is made up for by its ability to fly great distances without being held down by the wind, as mosquitoes are. Since the adult oestrid's life cyle is only six days, its survival strategy in the cold Arctic, unlike the mos-

---

*The *Journal of Animal Ecology* article "Reindeer Summer Activity Pattern in Relation to Weather and Insect Harassment," published in 2002, and several other Norwegian studies have discussed how the mosquito may be a mere annoyance compared to the oestrid. Rolf Hagemoen and Eigil Reimers wrote: "Oestrids are the primary tormentors of reindeer and caribou" and that "mosquitoes and tabanids cause only a minor annoyance.... However, there exists a widespread but poorly documented belief that mosquitoes are responsible for all, or much of the insect harassment of reindeer and caribou. Many reports of insect harassment are based only on mosquitoes attacking humans. Although repeatedly cited, few manage to document a clear impact on reindeer behavior by mosquitoes alone."

quito, is to parasitize the caribou. The Norwegian studies have shown that the oestrid causes whole herds to begin migrating as the insect buzzes in and glues up the hair of its hosts' forelegs—causing the animals to jump and buck then run away, futilely as it turns out—as the oestrid deposits several hundred eggs.

During the caribou migration, the eggs hatch, and the larvae burrow under the hide. Warmed and fed by its host's fatty tissues, the maggots slowly begin crawling under the hide, tripping off mammalian pain receptors as they follow nerve pathways toward the caribou's back.

After several months, the caribou skin and circulatory system form protective black or brown cysts around each of the warbles. These maggots grow to the size of marbles and cut breathing holes out through the caribou's back, forming infected abscesses. If the host caribou was glued by several oestrids during the summer, with thousands of hungry maggots resulting, it will rub against tree trunks or writhe on the snow, consumed from within. Eventually, unable to eat enough lichen or plant matter to offset the appetites of the voracious parasites, the caribou will drop to the ground in an internal itching agony and perish from exhaustion, dehydration, and starvation. If a badly parasitized caribou is mistakenly shot by hunters, the meat—literally translated and despised as "bacon" to the Inuit, who also avoid pork—is so putrid and soft that the reeking carcasses are immediately abandoned.

Most infected caribou, if they're young and healthy, will survive a couple dozen piggy-backing oestrids. Nine months after entering their hosts' legs, the fattened oestrids burrow out through the breathing holes and drop to the tundra. The pupae, of course, will break out of their shells, spread their powerful wings, and renew the cycle of hunting for the herd.

Then there are the warble's oestrid cousins, the bot flies, clogging caribou nostrils and throats until they're coughed up and out onto the ground—like a wriggling piece of mucus—to renew their life cycle. Which probably explains why the passing caribou had coughed.

Once, and only once, I had an oestrid experience. To this day I remain thankful that warble flies rarely prey upon humans (although oestrids have sometimes chosen young children as hosts, burrowing behind their eyeballs and causing excruciating pain and blindness). While sea kayaking a mile offshore from the refuge, an oestrid landed on the canvas foredeck of my kayak. I put down my paddle. The roundish yellow-and-black bug, big as my thumbnail, stared back up at me with unnerving predatory intent, but then quickly warbled up into the air before I could squash it. With a foreboding worse than my fear of sharks, I began splashing toward shore to set up my bug-proof tent.

WHEN I VAULTED BACK into the tent with my client companions, they quickly zipped the door shut behind me. As usual, it took us twenty minutes to squash all the hungry mosquitoes that followed me in. Then I tried to recapture the wonder of the mosquito in my journal—splotched with rusty bloodstains.

Like my companions, I was too wired by the late sun flooding into the tent to sleep. So after the obligatory journal session I read until long after midnight. I periodically put down Mardy Murie's *Two in the Far North* to listen to the disconcerting drone outside the thin nylon.

The racket—I figured out later—came from their uniquely short, vein-filled, and stiffened wings. The intense fanlike movement of air came from thousands of tiny wings outside our tent beating up to five hundred times per second. Genetically speaking, these shortened wings were a de-evolution, grounding mosquito air traffic in any wind. While the insects have sped up their wing beats and become a noisier species than their ancestors, modern-day mosquitoes have learned to crawl to their breeding ponds faster than any fly.

"It could be worse," I said again to my attorney friend, as he put down *Arctic Dreams* and I picked up *Two in the Far North*. But I hadn't yet told my tentmates about the warble flies. If those wings ripping air outside the tent had belonged to a thousand wind-impervious, parasitic oestrids, we would have all been in serious trouble.

△ △ △

On a chaperoned picnic to Moose Creek, Mardy Thomas and Olaus Murie lit a smoky smudge fire on the riverbank to help quell the thick mosquito haze. The pair joked about how the bugs were light, and while pulling their collars higher up their necks, they moved closer to the smoke and made small talk. This was their first date.

Suddenly, a great horned owl hooted from within the depths of the boreal forest surrounding Fairbanks. The chitchat ended. Olaus answered the owl by holding his nose and cupping his hand over his mouth, and after several rounds of rhythmic hooting, the owl "floated into a treetop right above us on the riverbank and sat silhouetted against the sky," Mardy later wrote. "What kind of magic did this man have?"

She was half-lying on spruce boughs next to a campfire on the high riverbank. Olaus sat next to her and opened up his notebook. He licked his pencil, began drawing, and in several minutes ripped out the page and handed her an anatomically precise drawing of the great horned owl—capturing its softness and its fury, its wide eyes, and every detail down to the aspen bark, the distant scraggly spruce. Mardy thought, "So he's an artist too?"

She would revere owls for the rest of her life.

Later, he helped her with college math, and she taught him how to dance to the Hesitation Waltz. Their letters were carried back and forth by dogsled between Fairbanks and each village where Olaus might stop.

While the amendment for women's suffrage had been passed in all of the states and corsets had recently gone out of fashion, the Alaska Territory remained a male clubhouse, even though Mardy had been exposed to more progressive points of view. She wrote to the man whom she wanted to marry that his letters had "a charming, graphic style," and boldly asked if she could travel with him "over the rolling country, the silent land," wondering if he thought her able and fit enough to share his rugged life and if he thought women "folks" were up to such a task.

He replied enthusiastically, "yes," losing any of the Norwegian American stodginess he might have had left in him.

In a statement more dreamy-headed girl than anything from *Out of Africa*, Mardy told her fiancé that she never expected to find a man willing or capable of sharing the Arctic wonderland with her. Since Olaus had already made a fairy-tale life beyond her own routines in Fairbanks, she asked to be "taken in."

"Yes sweetheart!" came the reply, again by dog team.

MARDY AND OLAUS were married before dawn on August 19, 1924, in a log church filled with wild Arctic poppies and a single, precious rose from a Fairbanks hothouse. As the sun rose above the village of Anvik an hour later, they jumped back across the mud onto the plank of the *General J. W. Jacobs* and watched the dawn splash a fiery, molten gold across the willows. Mardy pressed a poppy in her journal and wrote with an apprentice biologist's eye for detail about the people who stood on the lighted deck: her friend Elizabeth, in cream lace and flowery cloche; the captain, light glinting on his buttons; and the engineer, who became "startlingly handsome, having scrubbed away the engine room grease."

This was the beginning of a prolonged wilderness honeymoon

that coincided with Olaus's work. Mardy assumed a new role as his biologist confidant. Every species they captured had to be labeled with the date and location of the capture, the Latin name, sex, and length of body and tail and hind foot. She wrote in Olaus's cloth bound book, already filled with 1,940 animal entries. At night in the steamship, they tapped their feet and sang to impromptu orchestras: banjo and fiddle, and monkey wrenches beating time on empty oilcans. The newlyweds danced their altered form of the Hesitation Waltz, hands held above their ears like antlers, smiling and closing their eyes against the coruscating sun swinging low across the southern horizon. They danced all winter.

In frost-hung Bettles, and then in Wiseman, Olaus taught Mardy how to "dance" with sled dogs. Like most Alaskan mushers, she quickly learned that the dogs didn't do all the work and wrote in her journal that twelve below zero produced ideal trail conditions:

> We were both running and I was soon too warm. I threw back the parka hood. The crisp air felt good on my bare head. How light my moccasined feet felt, padding along on the snow sprinkled ice at a dog trot every muscle responding to the joy of motion; running, running without getting out of breath.

Despite these exciting interludes, Mardy also happily assumed a conventional woman's role. She would raise the children, then type and edit Olaus's work when they moved to Washington, D.C.

But when it came time for Olaus to leave Washington for the Arctic in the spring of 1926, Mardy told him if she didn't go, she'd just be another one of the many wives that they saw left behind in the city. So they took their nine-month-old, Martin, into the hoards of mosquitoes above the remote village of Old Crow in the Yukon—mixing his powdered milk with silted river water—during a geese-banding study. They kept Martin in an eiderdown sleeping bag and in a wooden packing crate labeled "Mishawaka Ball Band Rubber Goods." Their best daytime escape from mosquitoes was either standing in the smoke of campfires or keeping their boat out in midriver breezes.

They had to pole the boat upriver for weeks after the engine broke. Worse, the "hundreds of thousands" of geese they had been sent to find appeared to be a myth. They had come at the wrong time of year to band waterfowl. The bureaucracy had literally sent Olaus on a wild-goose chase. Most of the time, they were covered with mud and mosquitoes. Even the Athapaskan villagers were appalled to see the biologist with wife and baby, traveling through a section of mosquito country so God-awful that native hunters only braved it in freezing conditions.

Their seasoned Alaskan boatman, Jesse Rust, had introduced Mardy to Olaus. Rust wrote in his journal that "it was the most miserable trip I've ever been on." His bloodstained journal pages all but buzzed with mosquitoes: "fierce, thicker every day... good and hungry... they even eat the hair off my head.... The biggest I seen anywhere.... No end to them...."

Jesse also complained about how devoted Mardy was to the baby, how she wouldn't leave him alone for a minute. Her husband remained unfazed about her or the mosquitoes. Mardy gave him grief when he absentmindedly dropped Martin's diaper into the fire to chase after a goose—a bird that was becoming harder to find each day.

Despite mosquitoes supplanting geese, Olaus's sense of purpose inspired his companions. After the crankshaft broke, forcing them to manhandle the boat upriver, Jesse wrote in his journal, "Olaus wanted to row most of the time but I wouldn't let him. I want to do my share. He is a dandy to be out with."

To Jesse's horror, he often witnessed Olaus shooing off, rather than swat killing, the scores of mosquitoes on his body. Jesse felt ashamed that while he was keeping score of his own death count, slapping up into the hundreds each day, Olaus had only killed a few, by mistake, and his hands were perversely swelling up in a rare allergic reaction to all of the mosquito saliva. His companions even watched him shooing off blood-engorged mosquitoes from his scalp rather than taking the satisfaction of a liquid swat.

As an older boy, Martin Murie learned that these stories were not apocryphal because his father despised killing. It wasn't that he ever expressed belief in Buddhism or a particular fondness for the mosquitoes as a species. Olaus simply believed that gentleness demanded extreme discipline. A young acquaintance—who also braved fierce irruptions of the Alaska State Bird with Olaus—later wrote that no one had changed as many of his ideas as Olaus had, and that people all over the country had come under his spell and his passion for wilderness as evoked by such crazy examples as his preservation of the mosquitoes.

Through Olaus, Mardy and Jesse learned to laugh at each new near disaster. Mardy insisted that they sing, night after night, balancing Jessie's graveled tenor with her trained soprano as the tone-deaf Olaus waltzed with baby Martin. If they didn't make their own music, the wilderness made it for them.

Chapter 6

KONGAKUT RIVER

To my surprise, it was a wolverine—bounding along at an easy gallop on the snow-covered creek, coming steadily and purposefully as though to meet some appointment. The gentle slope of the creek bed made travel easier, and he was making good speed, though his gait seemed effortless. . . . He glanced toward us but continued on his way through the low bushes without stopping. The incident was so unexpected it seemed like a dream and left us exclaiming in hushed voices.

—Adolph Murie
A Naturalist in Alaska

In flood, the Kongakut River canyons demanded that we stay focused on every paddle stroke. Draw quickly right to miss a boulder, then pull hard for a smooth tongue of water through more boulders, and lean left to catch the main current. Gusts of wind blew us sideways.

We shot through the biggest canyon one at a time, exchanging whoops, yet watching each other closely. By now, our third day out in the eastern edge of the refuge, my partner and I had become acquainted with the rhythm of the river. The paddling, by experts' standards, involved more boulder avoidance than any well-honed technical skills. My fingers felt wooden against the paddle, under my wool cap my hair was soaked with icy rain, and the snowmelt water made my skin crawl with goosebumps. But I could still think clearly, stay a step ahead of hypothermia, and read every twist and turn and flux of current.

In this teeth-chattering weather, my partner turned strangely tentative, responding like a beginner, over-leaning, or neglecting his draw strokes. He quickly got off course, clipped a rock, spun sideways to the current, and promptly capsized.

I caught his boat and waited for him to swim ashore, assuring him that it could've happened to anyone. After he changed into spare clothes, we walked his boat through the meanest-looking boulder fields. At the cliff that forced the river into a forty-five-degree bend, I deliberately paddled into its corner. This reverse current eddy gurgled against rock and my boat sat perfectly motionless as the river slipped a paddle's width away at three miles an hour.

The previous summer, in flood stages, the eddy here had been a raging whirlpool that sucked in a companion and nearly drowned her. It took us a half an hour to pull her out with a safety line, but her kayak had been crushed. Since I despised out-of-control epics, I had returned this summer with a more capable companion to try to enjoy the river without any untoward adventures.

Emerald-hued grayling darted down in the dark hole below. The limestone wall—cold as a glacier against my fingertips—stretched up an unlikely red-stained yellow, revealing a swallow's nest mudded into a hand crack, thirty feet higher. Somewhere in the sheltering sky above, a golden eagle whistled shrilly.

I pushed the bow of the kayak out of the eddy water as the invigorating rush of river pulled me back into its center. That night, as my reconstructed left shoulder began tingling hotly, I checked the altimeter and watched it drop a thousand feet. The high-pressure system that heated up Alaska every summer was sweeping north over the Brooks Range and pushing out the Arctic low—shaking our tent with a warm wind.

At dawn, I walked past basil-scented willow to the last canyon. I clutched a fishing rod and sang aloud to warn any sleeping bears. Beneath a granite ledge, the tight-flowing skin of river repeatedly dimpled with a school of Arctic char, snapping at midges. I cast slightly upstream of the fish, let the current take my fly, and felt a char hit, swallow, then sound; my line tightened with the ukulele strum note of a strike. The fish rushed downstream and repeatedly bucked up out of the river like a caribou sporting warble flies.

I ran with it, lofting the rod tip skyward. On its fifth jump near the shore, I flipped my wrists and ungracefully yanked the fish directly from the air onto the sand. Red dots ran sixteen inches down its silvery flanks, which were tipped with white-rimmed fins. I quickly severed the head, cut open the belly, fingernailed out a clutch of orange eggs, lobbed them into the river, and then scraped my hands clean with cold river and sand, resisting the urge to wipe my hands dry on my pants. No sense smelling like fish for the grizzlies.

Salvelinus alpinus is highly prized by both gourmands and anglers. Early Arctic explorers mistook the fish for salmon because of its distinctive-tasting orange flesh. Although the char is considered part of the salmon family, which die after three to five years and a single spawning, both female and male char return to sea after depositing eggs and milting in the gravel of rivers. These cold-water survivors repeatedly spawn, living up to thirty-five years longer than salmon. If you had to be any fish in the world, you could do a lot worse than the rarely fished Arctic char.

My partner torched up the MSR stove on the riverbank, while I parted the char's bones from flesh with my fillet knife. With the help of a small wedge of lemon, a pat of butter, and a lightweight skillet, it took less time than the short drive from my home to the nearest restaurant to catch, clean, fillet, and fry the char. The meat was firm and even fruity. The crisp skin of the fish, the ambience of the refuge, the lack of cloying waiters—I couldn't remember finer seafood. I passed the skillet. My partner deemed the char tastier than any of the five Pacific salmon species.

Before my last bite, I mumbled a quick and silent thanks. Killing for gastronomic reward can never be taken for granted, especially within a wilderness where humans don't necessarily sit atop the food chain.

I SHOWED MY PARTNER how to ride the eddies and we swooped and played, sometimes sideways, even backward, as a larkspur warbled, mysterious (or at least unseen) animals swished through the willows, and the tundra spun past like an unending roll of music on a player piano. Every bird—the nervous yellow warbler, a begging herring gull, an aloof long-tailed jaeger—flew into my waterproof, five-by-seven-inch journal, carried in a Velcroed chest pocket of my paddle jacket.

I wrote in my journal that if I had gone alone this year, the psychological burden of risk-taking might have suppressed my interest in the sensory delights: smelling the sweet alpine azaleas, listening for birdcalls, or trying to will my eyesight over the horizon to scope out the caribou migration. If rapids or storms threatened, as a team of two we could react instinctively and efficiently, striving for that balance of passivity and physicality; a balance that equaled interaction. Only through interaction could I become intimate with the refuge. I knew that Olaus Murie initially experienced it through hunting, and then later in life through photography or long walks in which he would engage the landscape through sketching and by using his senses—feeling animal tracks in the sand, counting caribou, keying out a falcon nest, and tasting cloudberries.

The philosopher Edward Casey called this eccentric pursuit "using the body as a vehicle for implacement and letting the wilderness redefine your sense of space." Since I too believed that

Olaus on a dogsled during caribou study; Fairbanks, Alaska, 1921.

Mardy Murie sawing wood in camp during 1924 research
and honeymoon expedititon.

Mardy and Olaus after returning from their
honeymoon in January 1925.

Olaus Murie painting on the deck of the *Brown Bear*
while traveling in the Aleutian Islands.

Olaus and Mardy at home in Moose, Wyoming, in 1953.

Bob Krear, Brina Kessel, Mardy, Olaus, and Don Macleod
in the Sheenjek River Valley in 1956.

Mardy with Alice Zahniser and Secretary of the Interior
Stewart Udall (far right) during President Johnson's
signing of the Wilderness Act, 1964.

Mardy beneath Denali, 1978.

Mardy Murie at home
in Moose, Wyoming,
July 8, 1990.

wilderness demanded our physical selves—a letting go of linear thinking in exchange for opening up our senses—I had left behind paperback novels, so that for the first time in my life I could attempt to locate myself amid a landscape by *listening* through my body.

While my partner grooved to his Walkman, I swam in cold river pools and stayed up all night as the sun rolled along the northern horizon. We drank straight out of the clean river, and when the urge came to pee, we aimed back onto the filtering tundra. Grizzlies cavorted on the ridges above camp, while small bands of caribou moved in herky-jerky bowleggedness, splashing through the sloughs. On the fourth day out, a caribou cow and calf stopped to look at me in the river, cocking their heads, grunting, and stomping the ground with curiosity. I kept my head sideways, maintaining the peripheral eye contact that most wild animals prefer over direct stares. As soon as I sensed their growing discomfort, I bowed deeply, kept the paddle down, and let the river carry me off without startling them. Although this wasn't the entire herd that I was seeking, the connection felt real. For a furtive instant, I had made eye contact with two souls not unlike my own.

By August 1, we were wearing shorts and contemplating yet another swim in the icy water to cool off. At seventy degrees even the mosquitoes stayed in the shade.

My partner taught grade school and lived a mile down the road from the cabin that I had wintered in, an hour north of Anchorage. Like most competent Alaskans, he came "loaded for bear," as the Robert Service verse goes, equipped with a nickel-plated, sawed-off shotgun. Since we were paddling all the way out the Kongakut River Delta, and then another sixty miles along the Beaufort Sea to Barter Island, a coast frequented by polar bears, he felt it prudent to be well armed. I couldn't argue.

Our paddling expedition had been timed to catch the south-easterly migration of the Porcupine caribou herd as it fled the coastal plain for Canada. We wanted to see if the rumors were true: that the hillsides turned gray with caribou backs and that the herd strolled through your campsite by the thousands, taking days to pass. According to our bush pilot, over one hundred thousand caribou had massed up to the west of us.

We slid the bows into the shushing river, twisted together the long, two-piece, double-bladed paddles, and wedged ourselves into the cockpits—like pulling on an old familiar pair of baggy jeans. Waves splashed our faces, rounded rocks clicked on the river bottom, and bird melodies filled the copses of dwarf birch and willow.

The Kongakut is the only river, from headwaters to delta, entirely within the protected wilderness section of the refuge. Paralleling our course, the other refuge rivers—the Jago, the Aichilik, the Hulahula, the Sadlerochit, and the Canning—all flow through the unprotected section of coastal plain proposed for oil development. The Kongakut first trickles northeast from its four-thousand-foot-high, sidewalk-sized beginnings in the mountains near the Canadian border. Two dozen miles below, it widens into a country road, rolling billions of small rocks across ancient spines of limestone, until the clear river goes miasmic with silt and spreads out over a skein of shifting gravel bars. Most of the year it remains a burbling country road. In spring runoff or rain, the lower Kongakut rumbles straight north, across the coastal plain to the black sea like a muck-filled superhighway.

We steered our kayaks at several miles per hour past colonies of chattering ground squirrels with midge hatches tickling our faces. Eighteen thousand years ago, most of Canada sat under the Pleistocene ice cap, but the V-shaped canyon we were sucked into illustrated the fact that only water carved out the refuge; ice gouges out U-shaped valleys.

Around a corner, we counted sixteen Dall sheep licking the salty riverbanks. *Ovis dalli* and their goat family relatives, musk oxen, are the only horned ungulates in the refuge. Sheep have been in these canyons for a millennia, occasionally chased by wolves, and missed by the Pleistocene ice in the region geologists call Beringia. Four thousand years ago, the first humans began hunting them with flint-tipped spears and arrows.

This band, amid the twenty thousand sheep whitening the slate-covered mountains of the refuge, was almost tame. As we pried ourselves out of the kayaks to walk up and photograph them, they reluctantly trotted off the river flats for the safety of the adjoining cliffs. They leapt gracefully up broken boulders, then hopped onto a narrow ledge bisecting a hundred-foot-high shale outcropping. With cloven, suction-cup-efficient hooves, the sheep confidently grabbed footholds.

On the beach we found a horn. But unlike caribou antlers, horns are never shed. The remnant horn—the size of my hand held back to my armpit—weighed over twenty-five pounds. I lofted the full curl up to the sun and aged it by counting the two-inch-long growth rings. This twelve-year-old ram nearly made it to old age before being eaten by wolves.

Up on the cliffs, through the binoculars, the ewes' shedding wool left clumped and bald patterns on their backs like the unfinished work of a barber. On the sand at my feet, I picked up a wad of this fleece, combed its fine curls between my fingers, held it up to my nose and whiffed lanoline and salt. Thousands of fingernail-sized scats lay on the beach. Deerlike tracks rutted the sand back and forth to the cliffs.

The indispensable *Animal Tracks* describes how Adolph Murie, like a wolf in disguise, herded Dall sheep up a cliff toward Olaus. Adolph shouted, "Baa-a-a-a—they're moving to your right!" as Olaus, out of sight atop the cliff, got in position for his trophy, and Adolph shouted again, "Baa-a-a-a—now they're coming straight up."

"Thus guided," Olaus wrote, "I found myself in camera range when they came out on top."

I repocketed the Murie guide and scrambled up the cliffs with my camera over my shoulder. The ewes and lambs, little nubbin-brown horns poking straight out of their heads like second sets of ears, lay happily on the rubbled ledge. Ewes chewed their cuds in casual yet eerily synchronized unison as their lambs slept and my camera clicked. Above the cliffs, I gazed with a cursory, circular sweep for grizzlies as an ocean wind waved ankle-high sedges and numbed my face.

Down below, a lone ram with a three-quarter curl impatiently stomped his feet and glared up at me. He stood in a steep black shale corner, his winter coat already on, polarizing him pure as an alabaster beluga in the Beaufort Sea. I exposed a few quick frames, bowed from the waist, said "thank you," and then turned back down to the river. I climbed carefully down through portable handholds of shale, circling around the napping nursery.

We slithered into our kayaks and glided downriver. A dozen miles more and we were forced to set up tents as an unbearable polar wind rocked the willows. A rainbow on the river highlighted ruby storm clouds, which floated over with the distant, limb-crackling explosions of a rare Arctic thunderstorm.

The next day, the terrain flattened out downriver. We searched for the caribou migration and found only fresh crescent-shaped tracks, slightly bigger and heavier than the Dall sheep prints, all with the right-angled dewclaw marks pointed east. We scuffed the sand to unveil tracks of bear and wolves, following the herd. Every mile or so along the bank, I stopped and put my ear to the ground like a wannabe caribou witcher, but the plain lay quiet.

Near Caribou Pass, we climbed up into the last hills to study the Beaufort Sea, undulating above the tundra in a big blue zeppelin mirage. A snowy owl glided past, silent and ghostly, inches above fields of Arctic poppies and mountain heather. Down below, the river ripped across gravel bars in a brown torrent of mud. There were no buildings or roads or boats or people to be seen anywhere. No caribou either. But it wouldn't be the last time that I would miss the migration.

At our camp that night, on a low bank at a slow meander, I lay prostrate with the clear river and breathed deep until my pulse dropped to 45 beats per minute. In the eddy below, a grayling hung still as a jewel. I sliced my hand down into the water alongside the eight-inch fish and reached slowly down the bank, extending my fingertips past the pectoral fins and tickling a scaled belly until the fish froze and I could pinch the gills, wrap my fingers around the body, and slip it out of the river long enough to hold it wriggling up in the air. The fish gasped at a world sculpted through geologic catastrophe, through the flooding of ancient seas and colliding continents and centuries of slow-dumped sedimentation.

Thymallus arcticus is much smaller than the char but no less brilliant, with a purplish-green body and a red-spotted dorsal fin, held up like a sail during the spawn, or in the moments before its death when you tickle it out of the water. Although technically a member of the salmon family, the grayling never leaves freshwater. The rivers freeze tight for eight months of the year, so it would hold here in this deep Kongakut pool, below thick ice.

Since I wasn't hungry enough to tempt the bears with any more cut-up and cooked fish smells, and since I was trying to connect with—rather than kill—animal souls within the refuge, I gently, slowly slid the grayling back into the river. Under the water, backing away, it folded the big dorsal fin down and skittered off into the current. I stopped holding my breath.

From a buckled hill above camp, the Brooks Range seemed to rise and fall, breathing like a great dragon under its new blanket of snow. To the northwest, the green coastal plain rippled with heat waves.

Here, on the roof of our continent, no trees or mountains

blocked the northern sun. The kaleidoscopic effect of colorful light shaken across the sky lasted many hours, casting the sea afire as the light bent through the atmosphere, and the red orb of sun contin-ued spinning east above the distant spine of sea ice.

I fell asleep under the chorus of sparrows and buntings and atop the permafrost, chilling my hipbones through the tundra blanket. I dreamed we were camped on a glacier.

In the morning, the land gave off a warm glow, showing that we had gained the heart of the refuge. Permafrost calved off from over-hanging banks like gunshots and cannonballed into the river. Beneath the musty cockpit cover, my wet legs turned numb.

We still had at least ten days of paddling left along the coast to the village of Kaktovik. But now, a week out, as I relaxed and let go of the constraints of time and the pressures of the outside world, the refuge began to assume larger proportions. Each day I perceived the land expressing moods. A rainy afternoon—for a place that matches the Mojave Desert for dryness—became a joyous change. Fog brought on the coastal plain's enigmatic character. Sunshine encouraged a floral vibrancy: the earth juddered beneath the light-catching lilac asters, the alpine goldenrods, and the pink-veined spring beauties.

In the cold, clean air, looking at this landscape was like peering through glass at a watercolor. On the final miles of the Kongakut, where the river cut deep into soft tundra and pulled us along the steaming banks of permafrost, I first removed my watch. My abil-ity to isolate different and unidentifiable smells became incredibly distracting. My hearing seemed to improve.

I could now sense the ocean through the brine air and through the river's sluggishness. The main channel swept our kayaks into a long field of *aufeis*—German for overflow ice—leftover from sev-eral long winters. To either side of us, the river branched off on into gurgling, cobalt ice tunnels. Suddenly we were surrounded by ice rising eight feet above our heads. I paddled into a calm corner, climbed out on top of the ice, and scouted out a ten-foot-wide path through the remaining half-mile *aufeis* field.

Although whole miles of river bottom were tracked and scummed furry with the hollow white hairs of caribou, the herd had once again vanished. Closing in on the delta, I found consolation. Coming around a bend, a wolverine swam confidently against a hard current, then clambered up a black-mudded, steep bank using its claws as crampons. The animal moved with slow deliberation, then froze several feet above me without shaking off its glistening wet coat. His regal, aloof posture and direct eye contact implied that human beings had absolutely no business being on his river. He snarled, wriggled his nose, and showed no inclination to retreat. Even more than the wolf, the rarely seen wolverine symbolized a complete wilderness ecosystem with a diversity of carrion—the animal's primary diet.

Since this particular species depends on the caribou for food, if oil development came and reduced the herd, the wolverine too would suffer. In all likelihood, this male was backtracking the herd from the coastal plain, looking for abandoned calves or adult carcasses. The so-called hyena of North America can consume nearly half its body weight, use its viselike jaws to crunch through thick bones to suck out the marrow, and fend off bears or wolves with dagger-sharp claws.

My fingers trembled with excitement; I gripped the paddle tighter and feathered in two backstrokes. The wolverine, although widely distributed, has never been abundant. Adolph Murie once wrote that most Sourdoughs rarely saw wolverines and could readily recount the instance of such a meeting. This wolverine was my first, and the experience matched that of witnessing the wolf hunting for her pups.

As the wolverine strutted off into the willows above, I spun out into a whirling eddy, and fished, once again, for my tattered copy of *Animal Tracks*. Murie's book includes over a thousand of his careful illustrations—spring and fall scats, mud and snow tracks, nipped browse, tooth marks on bark, scratchings, rubbings, and in the final spread, the mysterious tremblings imprinted upon a snowed-over meadow, unveiled as a windblown aspen leaf's tracks. The beauty of his pen-and-ink drawings is in the contrast; his unadorned lines capture each being with the deft, anatomical eye of a scientist.

Every species—from shrew to polar bear—is given several pages of text, which includes Murie's personalized observations on habitat, beds, hair traces, behaviors, animal voices, and range.

At first glance, only seasoned trackers would recognize the depth of the author's knowledge, let alone his descriptive and illustrative talents. After all, while traveling in this lumpy, off-kilter wilderness, most people are too focused on keeping their own balance to study the footsteps of other creatures.

On page sixty-five, Olaus wrote that it was a red-letter day when he discovered even the tracks of this elusive animal. He would spend hours following wolverine sign, because their inquisitive, uncanny nose allowed them to uncover raven wings or hidden caribou bones.

I jumped out of my boat into waist-deep water and strange black mud. I kicked steps up the steep, stinking embankment, wiped tarry hands off on my lower pant legs, and clutching Murie's book I lost all sense of time while trying to track *Gulo luscus*.

◬ ◬ ◬

Olaus Murie took aim, fired, and knocked down two Dall sheep that stood profiled against a high ridgetop. As he climbed up through the snow toward his specimens, he found half-inch-long scats next to half-foot-long footprints. He kneeled down to examine the sign more carefully. The tracks in the snow showed five toes (instead of the wolf's four), and the path wove around, just like a wolverine's would.

In the gloom of the approaching sub-Arctic winter darkness, it would have been impossible to skin and pack both sheep specimens down to camp and out of the wolverine's clutches. Olaus put down his rifle and contemplated the situation. He couldn't see or smell the wolverine, but the animal could surely sense the fresh-killed sheep.

Gulo luscus had a reputation for stealing men's meat, making the wolverine a sinful animal in the eyes of Alaskan Sourdoughs. Olaus deplored this tendency of hating animals that interfered with men, so he decided to make a bargain with the wolverine.

He gutted the first sheep and put the meat, skin, and skull into his packsack. Then, lest the second sheep's skin and skull be destroyed, he carefully pulled the skin up over its skull, exposing the carcass for the wolverine.

In the morning, magpies sat on the carcass, picking out the sheep's eyes. Olaus found that the wolverine had come, filled up on the meat, and left. "He had accepted the bargain," Murie wrote, "he had his meal, the museum would have its specimen, and the dogs and I still had a supply of camp food."

THE *ANIMAL TRACKS* BOOK idea started several winters later. One of many Biological Survey chiefs told Murie that he could write and draw a "very credible monograph on mammal tracks." Murie had bigger plans than simply publishing another obscure government monograph, but it took another quarter-century and his newly gained independence before he could pull *Animal Tracks* together.

When he quit government service in January 1946, he wrote that the biological arms of the government were a "farce." In another letter, he confided:

For years I have tried to get the clue to the snarl of red tape that chokes the government scientist. I can speak from experience, having been one of the latter. There are so many checks and counter-checks in the government's effort to keep the government employee honest; so many categories of information wanted by some mysterious force upstairs, that have nothing to do with the actual work the poor fellow is trying to do.

The winter of 1953–54 had him on a whirlwind schedule unlike his calm days as a government employee. As both president and director of the Washington, D.C., Wilderness Society he traveled throughout the country speaking on conservational causes. He spoke almost everywhere about the International Arctic Wilderness idea, as well as about other preservation battles. Olaus's testimony became particularly sought after in the nation's capital during congressional hearings whose subjects varied from grazing areas to proposed dams in Colorado, Idaho, and Montana.

On the day after his birthday, Olaus wrote from Washington to his brother Adolph in Moose that the New York–based Conservation Foundation would fund the upcoming International Wilderness Area survey in northeastern Alaska, the place that he wanted to transform into a wildlife refuge. Olaus asked Adolph to mail out his formaldehyde jar of skunks' feet, the plaster casts of ruffed grouse tracks (somewhere on a shelf near the wolf hides), and the caribou foot drawings. Olaus and Mardy had just returned from Houghton Mifflin in Boston, and they hoped to go to press with *Animal Tracks* as soon as he could make a few last-minute changes to the manuscript.

Two weeks later, he thanked "Ade" for sending the animal parts and drawings, which allowed him to make progress on the book. He wrote that the plan for taking a team of biologists to the Arctic had been reduced to only Mardy and him.

These letters defined Olaus, as did the preservation of that large corner of northeastern Alaska. He brought letter-writing and speech-making to its highest potential by flooding lawmakers' desks with mail. Olaus was one of the first to convince his followers that congressmen and senators paid attention to their mail, because "some secretary's going to say you have 65 letters today in favor of the Arctic, and only 5 letters against it." He advocated letter-writing as a second way to vote.

Olaus had grown so exhausted from speaking and writing and lobbying that he often lay flat on his back dictating aloud to Mardy. Back in Moose, their son Donald could hear the clacking of the typewriter and the drone of his father's voice. Mardy often finished his letters after he fell asleep. In between letters, they also produced hundreds of magazine articles.

A frequent correspondent and park service planner, George Collins, wrote to Olaus from the northeast corner of Alaska. He described tame sheep, wandering grizzlies, and how, unlike any other river in North America, this Kongakut River flowed *north* to the sea. He wrote rather apocalyptically that, in terms of preserving wilderness, they could "kiss the coast goodbye" because of the military's cold-war camps every few miles, but just a few miles inland it remained "clean and untouched" and the "game absolutely wild" and abundant.

Collins pointed out that this summer reconnaissance idea came from earlier conversations with Olaus, as if to give credit where it was due. He added that there was "a very strong need for setting up some form of international reservation to conserve that country before it is ravaged of its wildlife resources." Then, in an insightful evaluation of his own employer, he wrote, "I do not advocate any designation incorporating the word 'park.' As you probably know I have suggested 'The Arctic International Wilderness.'" Then, in what could only be construed as heretical language for a senior government planner, he said he wanted the best organization possible for saving wilderness, and the park service lacked the qualifications. He baited Murie to scurry north with the last line of this letter:"It is so much later than we realized in the industrialization of the Arctic."

That fall, Collins and his partner, biologist Lowell "Doc" Sumner, zealously overstepped their bounds by publishing "Northeast Alaska: The Last Great Wilderness" in the Sierra Club magazine. "This area offers what is virtually America's last chance to preserve an adequate sample of the pioneer frontier," they wrote, "the stateside counterpart of which has vanished."

They were only calling it as they saw it, and they had clearly fallen in love with the wilderness as so many Brooks Range travelers do. But as government servants, they had improperly committed an act of advocacy by publishing in such a liberal environmental organization's magazine. The director of the park service privately reprimanded Collins and Sumner, ordering them to back off from promoting their International Arctic Wilderness.

Collins must have known that, as a bureaucrat, his role in saving the area was doomed from the start. He wrote to Murie complimenting him on numerous articles. Sumner called him "the acknowledged leader of the conservation effort now being focused on the subject [of the refuge]."

Someone had to do the thankless work of promoting this wilderness idea among the backwoodsmen and visigoths of Alaska—yet no one in government had the peculiar credentials for that task. But Alaskans would listen to Murie, who knew how to hot load a gun, flip a dogsled whip, and hawk a crackling loogie at fifty below. The fact that people addressed him as "doctor," or that he could give respected testimony in congressional hearings meant nothing to the Sourdoughs.

In September, Murie received a letter from Sumner suggesting that anything he could do for the Arctic wilderness idea would have to be in an unofficial and limited capacity. Collins finally cleared the air by writing Murie and formally asking him to take over the Arctic International Wilderness project. Collins wrote, "We well know that there is no one anywhere who has the background of acquaintanceship with Alaska people, knowledge of the country and technique of discussion in such matters to match your own."

Then, in a devastating setback to both *Animal Tracks* and the Arctic plans, Olaus contracted the same tuberculosis that had killed his father, his stepfather (Adolph's father), and millions of other Americans. Until the stress of the previous year, his immune system had simply fought off the TB. But now Mardy, who had handled all their money and created a detailed budget, called off the Arctic wilderness trip. The prognosis for meningeal TB was the equivalent of a death sentence.

Houghton Mifflin began sending the *Animal Tracks* page proofs to Adolph, who wrote in technical revisions while Mardy corrected grammatical errors. Olaus lay in bed, dazed and helpless to lift a finger for the Arctic or his book. His vision improved, and he had his pillow positioned so that he could see out the hospital window, spending whole days watching a downtown Denver construction project, lamenting a postwar world all but humming with development rather than preservation.

The ensuing industrial boom changed the face of America. Dams choked off rivers and steamrollers flattened hot tar across rural America. The Muries believed that the new appliances and electricity were so welcomed that consumers would eventually forget the value of roughing it in wild places.

In a rented apartment a block away, Mardy tried to keep up with the deluge of correspondence and took a part-time job as a secretary for the Izaak Walton League. In between the three visits a day she made to the hospital, she transcribed a letter for Olaus to

George Collins, with the key line "I am feeling better now than for many years." Collins replied that Murie's recovery was wonderful news and that "neither you nor Margaret ever gave up the positive approach to people and work—in other words, to life itself. That is a great lesson for all of us." Mardy replied, in lieu of Olaus sending a handwritten note, that her husband's twice-a-day therapy for a stiffened right arm cramped his writing. In between the lines, she artfully kept the Arctic project alive without canceling or committing Olaus to the trip.

MARTIN MURIE RETURNED to Denver in early January 1955, relieved to see his father sitting up in a wheelchair and joking with the nurses. To Mardy's horror, Olaus wrote a shaky letter to the Conservation Foundation in the New Year about resuming the Arctic trip: "It is so refreshing to <u>feel</u> like thinking about all these things again!" In April he tried to hold his hand steady for another barely legible letter to Adolph, stoically assuring him that he felt good, and in spite of what Mardy told Adolph, "Really all goes well here."

The hospital released him with a battery of prescription drugs that June. Back at the log cabin in Moose, Mardy forbade him from chopping wood, so he resumed his painting and sketching, but his art betrayed a loose-handed style. His handwriting had improved enough for him to compose a wobbly letter to Adolph in Alaska and relay that Mardy and Adolph's wife (who had stayed in Moose) were "riding him hard . . . to take it easy." He confided to Ade that he wanted to write but that the discipline somehow slipped away from him.

On the warmer days that fall, he managed to walk with Mardy down to her favorite swimming hole on the Snake River, which clattered with bugling elk from a huge herd he had saved through his efforts in setting aside protected grazing lands around Jackson Hole. As Olaus sat surrounded by the high gravel riverbanks in warm sun, surrounded by the rescued elk and the ancient glacial terrain, he became the second-happiest conservationist in Wyoming, next to his relieved wife, performing a backstroke against the river current.

By now, thanks to Mardy, the Muries' letter-writing campaign had resumed its former flow. As soon as a doctor pronounced Olaus fit for the Arctic, he convinced both the Conservation Foundation and the New York Zoological Society (who jointly covered Mardy's $6,929 budget) that he was in "top-notch shape" and ready to go.

In this defining hour of American conservation history, the Muries were not alone. David Brower had started the fight against federal dam-building by firing up the Sierra Club membership— partly thanks to a knee-jerk reaction against the controversial Interior Secretary McKay, who opened up oil leasing on government lands. Yet Brower's antihunting philosophy and intolerance for compromise would have torpedoed the Arctic Wilderness idea among the stodgy Alaskans. The other outspoken Alaskan advocates were unknown players outside of the Territory. Conservation-minded bureaucrats such as Collins, Sumner, and others could work behind the scenes but were prohibited from participating because it would have been a conflict of interest to their government positions.

The ailing man at the center of the Arctic Wilderness concept simply had unmatched qualifications. Alaskans would fall in step behind his ideas, and he could give charismatic testimony on the Hill. Most students of the refuge like to believe that Murie had become a perfect front man for studying the place, but the truth is he was the *only* conservationist capable of performing both the science and complex political juggling acts.

PART II

Arctic Refuge/Murie Timeline

1956—Congress defeats Echo Park Dam in Colorado; conservationist movement gains new momentum.

Muries survey the proposed Arctic National Wildlife Range (ANWR).

1957—Oil discovered and exploited in south-central Alaska, in the Kenai Moose Range (a wildlife refuge).

1959—Alaska proclaimed a state by President Eisenhower after decades of failed statehood bills. Olaus Murie receives the Audubon Medal for his conservation achievements.

1960—**Secretary of the Interior Seaton creates nine-million-acre ANWR by Public Land Order. ANWR lacks "wilderness" protection.**

1961—Secretary of the Interior Udall blocks the Alaska delegation's attempts to overturn ANWR.

1963—Olaus Murie dies of cancer on October 21.

1964—President Johnson signs the Wilderness Act, creating nine million new acres of protected lands in the Lower Forty-eight and the mechanism to study other wild lands throughout the United States for potential inclusion.

1968—Oil discovered in Prudhoe Bay, Alaska (sixty miles west of ANWR).

1971—Congress passes Alaska Native Claims Settlement Act (ANCSA); indigenous Alaskans receive forty-four million acres (including ninety-six thousand on ANWR) of Alaskan wilderness. Section 17(d) (2) of ANCSA instructs the Secretary of the Interior to preserve more Alaska wild lands (see ANILCA, below).

1975—Mardy Murie appointed member of Alaskan task force identifying protected wild lands.

1977—First Arctic oil flows down the completed Alaskan Pipeline.

1978—Morris Udall Wilderness Bill is proposed to protect ANWR's coastal plain.

1979—Mardy Murie receives the Audubon Medal for her conservation achievements.

1980—**President Carter signs Alaskan National Interest Lands Conservation Act (ANILCA) through the 1906 Antiquities Act, and Section 17(d) (2) of ANCSA—103 million new refuges and parks are created; ANWR becomes a "refuge," and its size increases to 19.6 million acres, 8 million preserved as "wilderness" under the 1964 Wilderness Act. Section 1002 of ANILCA directs Congress to study oil drilling on ANWR's 1.5-million-acre coastal plain.**

1987—First of many oil-leasing scenarios and bills proposed for ANWR's 1002 coastal plain.

1989—An oil spill devastates Prince William Sound, squelching the latest bill to lease ANWR 1002 lands.

1998—Mardy Murie awarded the Presidential Medal of Freedom (the highest civilian honor).

2003—Mardy Murie dies; she was 101 years old.

Chapter 7

BARREN-GROUND GRIZZLIES

Someday we shall meet in this world of ice.
When that happens, it does not matter
Whether it is I who dies or you.

—Michio Hoshino
Nanook's Gift

I jumped awake to the *twang* of the tent guyline accompanying the distinctive bass of loosened bowels. From the tent vestibule on my hands and knees, I could smell bear breath lingering sourly in the air. I cautiously poked my head outside and spied a pile of steaming scat. The bear was gone. It had to be a grizzly because a polar bear would've come into the tent.

I had begun traveling unarmed in the Arctic, because a shotgun added an awkward ten pounds to my kit, and because proper bear-country etiquette equaled more firepower than any rifle.

Here's why: A defensive bullet would have to penetrate the bear's heart or lungs to slow the animal. If you shoot a charging bear, such an aggressive human response might earn you a mauling before the adrenaline-pumped bear dies—*if* you are steady-handed enough to place your bullet precisely in a vital organ. The slim possibility of stopping a charging bear by shooting it in its narrow-sloped and rock-hard head would earn you the Rifleman of the Year Award.

I had shot several misbehaving Alaskan grizzlies at close range—rubber bullets into their rear ends, under the tutelage of my fellow park service ranger carrying a shotgun with rifled slugs. Fortunately, we never had to kill a bear.

We experimented with a carcass (run over by a speeding tourist in a Chevy) and learned that rubber bullets do not penetrate the body if a shooter places the rounds in the rump, where protective fat is slabbed thickly by midsummer. Amazingly, a rifled slug fired at the head glanced off. But the second close-range shot sprayed brains over the firing range. We also learned that handguns are inadequate except as noisemakers.

While out on the Alaskan tundra, fulfilling my ranger duty of weaning bears from picnic baskets, I learned that many grizzlies perform "bluff charges." If you turn and run from North America's largest predator as you are being tested, it will happily give chase. If you stand your ground, confidently yet respectfully talking to the charging bear, it will slam on the brakes and walk away looking bored. Shoot a bear in the midst of a bluff charge, and along with hurting it, you could trigger a primordial fight response. Nothing is more dangerous in the North than a wounded bear.

Big game hunters roll their eyes when I tell them that grizzlies smell the aggression in a man carrying a gun. My theory is that human beings emit telltale pheromones in times of danger. To an animal with a nose and an intuition fifty times more prescient—on a cellular, nucleotide level—than our own dormant senses, these pheromones are more accurate behavioral indicators than any lie detector test. So if you are carrying a gun because of fear, and you are putting on a false bravado or trying to trick or kill the bear, *Ursus arctos* would know. *Ursus arctos* would then try to exploit you.

I will never forget sitting on a wild stretch of tundra, trying to entice a bad bear into camp to teach him a lesson. I sat in the tent bracing a shotgun with a rubber bullet pumped into the chamber.

Although it seemed that the retreating bear had lost interest, I left the safety off. In front of the tent, a pot of simmering pork ramen soup blew its irresistible vapor molecules toward the nose of the bear. But the bear feigned apathy and continued walking south. He disappeared around a high riverbank, and unbeknownst to me at the time, he made a long end-run north, back toward the tent. If not for a backup ranger standing guard over the tundra with a radio and binoculars, this sneaky grizzly would've attacked us from the rear, or at least grabbed the soup. After an excited call came over the radio that the bear was blindsiding us, my partner jumped outside the tent, fired a warning shot in the air, and called the bear's bluff. He swaggered off north.

I didn't go unarmed in the Arctic just because I'd tricked a few bears and gotten away with it. Barren-ground grizzlies were poker players. They practiced all the stealth of wary cats. Barren-ground grizzlies deserved my respect.

So I bear-proofed my camp every night after brushing my teeth without toothpaste, which is a proven bear lure, along with fish oil, perfume, deodorant, menstruating women, and hair gel. I emptied the kayak, placed my food bags downwind, and topped the bags with a tipsy hat of noisemaker pots to wake me up if a grizzly touched it. Then, if he began eating my food or snuffling at my tent, I would try to keep my cool by politely asking the grizzly to leave. If this didn't work, I would throw rocks: Wild bears are not accustomed to being pelted by their prey. If the bear acted aggressively—popping its teeth, woofing, or stomping its feet on the ground—then I would have no choice but to slowly back into my boat and leave. Although it took patience (and I'd only done it with companions backing me up), some whistle-blowing, and even some shouting, I'd always been able to persuade curious grizzlies to leave my camp.

I also chose campsites where the wind blew cooking odors away from hungry grizzlies out to sea, *if* the presence of polar bears seemed unlikely. Whenever I passed through active white or brown bear territory—delineated by scats, tracks, or abundant prey species—I ate granola instead of cooking. I only cooked or ate in the tent if it was an emergency. And while alone, I shunned fishing. Frying fish would bring bears running.

In my time in the North, I had learned that men who told grizzly tales couldn't resist the ingredients of a classic fish story. If listeners appeared rapt, all the important data—distance, size, and weight—could be liberally overstated. When a bear approached you in the wilderness, like having a fish hit your line, the adrenaline of the encounter had a way of obfuscating the facts. These encounters lent themselves to fictional field stories.

After tranquilizing a few bears and weighing them, I learned to subtract a hundred pounds from my initial field estimates. These thickly furred beasts don't stand still, they're often seen at a distance, and although they appear heavily muscled, they are usually swathed with a layer of lightweight fat.

Bears are unpredictable. I have seen angry, aggressive, bumbling, and playful personalities, but most wild bears are exceedingly shy. Time and time again, unnatural, metallic noises—clicking on a gun's safety, ringing bells, or banging pots—had frightened bears out of my camp. Shouting epithets—"Dead garbanzos!"—gave some bears pause. Studies have also shown that a variety of other loud noises—foghorns, screaming, and gunfire—unnerve grizzlies. Still, all these techniques are doomed if the bear is wounded, beset by a toothache, or traveling with cubs.

In more pacifistic Canadian circles, the grizzly tool of choice among park wardens is a "bear banger." This marker-pen–sized, spring-loaded device flings a firecracker round into the air above a bear's head. So in lieu of a gun, I was packing a bear banger, a foghorn, and a canister of bear mace—all ridiculed, of course, by the Inuit, who travel with high-powered rifles.

According to studies performed by grizzly experts, bear spray halted 15 out of 16 grizzly charges in the wild, even though three bears (two sows with cubs) later mauled (but did not kill) the sprayers. When bears came into camp but did not threaten the campers, 20 out of 20 sprayed grizzlies halted their behavior, and 18 of the 20 left the area. The capsicum spray, made from ground-up chili peppers, has to hit the eyes or nose to be effective. Capsicum is not as effective on black bears. Members of that species have aggressively jumped in after my river raft, chased me up a boulder field, and stalked me from great distances.

I also learned from one temporarily blinding experience that capsicum sprayed into the wind is more debilitating to the sprayer than it is to the bear. And carrying bear spray canisters in a hip holster is imperative—I once suffered a burning crotch for days after a canister accidentally discharged in my pants' pocket.

Those backpackers who loath dangerously loaded spray canisters or guns often wear bear bells. In thick brush, bells will deter the smaller black bear (found in the southern end of the refuge) and wake up napping grizzlies to prevent surprise attacks, but a hungry barren-ground grizzly would not be long deterred by gentle jingling. Many Alaskan big game hunters, who love sharing bear yarns, claim that the only difference between black and grizzly bear shit is that the latter often contains bear bells and backpacker bones.

Those were my thoughts immediately after the grizzly tripped over the guyline at dawn. I crawled out of the tent, puffed out my chest, and stood up on my toes, trying to look bigger and badder than a scared six-foot-two, forty-one-year-old clutching a chili-pepper spray canister. The food bags were untouched. The kayak hadn't moved. In the distance, a jiggling set of brown hindquarters jogged up a hill, then disappeared into the waving sedges. Feeling thankful, I bowed. Then I unfolded my hand lens.

The bluish scat pile measured nine by thirteen inches wide and several inches thick. Using two driftwood sticks as a caliper, I lifted out a stool. My *Animal Tracks* book showed the average grizzly stool to be 2¼ inches wide, which seemed accurate, although the happy faces Olaus Murie drew on some of the animals in that book seemed enlightened. I placed the stool on a ripped-out journal page and pried apart a surprising amount of green grass and leaves. The smell merely recalled unpleasant bushwhacking through wet alder thickets.

Several thin, crunched-up bones showed that the bear may have scrounged up a mouse. Otherwise, the hand lens revealed the tiny brown matted objects to be wasps. Tapeworms wriggled amid ridged leaves. The blue hue showed this bear's fondness for berries. Cellophane, dirt, roots, hair, and an unidentifiable feather added further texture.

Recent scatological analysis of Arctic barren-ground grizzlies have shown that their diets consist of up to 78 percent caribou in midsummer, although this particular bruin—given the lack of bone and blood—seemed more herbivore. In early summer, green horsetails, sedges, roots, and cotton grass become a staple part of their diet. By fall, after the caribou migration, berries and ground squirrels constitute the grizzlies' main courses.

Yet attempting to profile an animal by what passes through its lower intestines can lead to gross generalization. In the case of the barren-ground grizzly, the science of scatology is muddied because of the bear's opportunistic eating habits. The omnivorous garbage truck of the Arctic will blithely eat fish, whales, moose, ptarmigans, wooden signs, porcupines, labrador tea, bark, paint, aspirin, dwarf birch, voles, seals, ducks, grubs, worms, moths, woolly bear caterpillars, spiders, ants, human feces, humans, male bear cubs, dirt, sand, whole boxes of laundry soap, cardboard, twigs, shoes, and bells.

Scatologists would like to believe that the bear's metabolism is predisposed to digesting protein, because vegetable matter is so easily identified inside undigested, hardened horse turds, like the one I was poring through. Meat, blood, and protein-laden plants were indiscernibly excreted in runny or tar-textured cow pies. In late summer, ripened carbohydrates—crow berries, salmon berries, bear berries, blueberries, and bunch berries—allow the grizzlies to triple their body fat, so they can waddle into their dens and sleep for a half year with up to 33 percent of their weight as fat reserves.

The barren-ground grizzly's nondiscriminatory diet explains another concern for mauled victims, who often remark on their attackers' horrifically bad breath. If I should get bitten by a grizzly, and if I should survive the attack, my main concern would be infection. The lack of grizzly hygiene, augmented by their taste for carrion and their frequent gorging on flesh wriggling with an assortment of pathogens, causes septic wounds in humans who have been bitten. This is a valid concern for those traveling alone through the Arctic with no radio or likelihood of immediate medical help.

In an effort to be prepared, I carried hydrogen peroxide (for irrigating wounds), three courses of antibiotics, a syringe of morphine, and a large assortment of gauze bandages in my first-aid kit. I also had emergency medical technician certification, but in all my time helping injured backcountry victims, I'd never treated a bear wound.

I did research the subject carefully. In a recent study of North American brown bear attacks over the last century, a researcher documented 165 attacks on humans; 88 percent of those attacks involved solitary campers. The cause of most human deaths from bear maulings—matching most peoples' paranoia about the blood-thirsty Arctic mosquitoes—were classified as exsanguinations.

In another study of 105 people mauled by brown, black, and polar bears from 1900 to 1985 in Alaska, twenty people were killed (most by brown bears). Up to 80 percent of these attacks involved campers mixing it up with protective mother bears and their cubs. Surprisingly, the statistics showed no data about stumbling onto buried caribou caches or napping grizzlies.*

No one had ever been mauled traveling in a group of four or more, but what the statistics don't reveal is that these large groups seldom encounter wildlife. I was traveling alone because I *wanted* to meet bears. While at home, the idea of talking bears out of my camp and facing them down unarmed had an appeal that might be explained by a misspent youth studying Daniel Boone reruns on television. But while paddling on a sea that routinely refrigerated my lower torso, all my fuzzy, romantic expectations of connecting with a bear seemed a trifle silly.

As the monotony of sea kayaking inspired my mind to wander, I couldn't help obsessing about bears. Inuit elders still believe that animals and humans share the same souls, and that bears are beings of awesome and uncalculated spiritual powers. This made intuitive sense to me, given the way bear encounters always cause a mild panic, an eerie sense of familiarity, a trembling in my fingers, and a disconcerting pucker of my sphincter.

These irrational fears—along with the idea that bears, as prescient beings, could outsmart humans—kept me awake or gave me nightmares while alone in the Arctic. So I tried to rationalize the perceived dangers. For instance, statistics of northern accidents showed that I stood a much better chance of drowning than I did of getting mauled. As a good swimmer, paddling close to shore, the concept of an ordinary drowning didn't keep me awake at night.

According to Stephen Herrero's respected book, *Bear Attacks: Their Causes and Avoidance*, over the next year my chances of get-

---

*The only documented bear attack in the Arctic National Wildlife Refuge involved a hiker quietly stepping into a tight stand of willows and waking up a grizzly. The startled bear swatted the bell-less hiker and merely left him with a few scratches.

ting eaten by *Ursus arctos* were 67 times less probable than being killed by a dog, 150 times less probable than being sucked up into a tornado, 180 times less probable than dying from a bee sting, 374 times less probable than getting struck by lightning, and 90,000 times less probable than being murdered by a *Homo sapiens.*

In the unlikely event I became a statistical anomaly, I had taken one final precaution, since other grizzly lovers' maulings ironically resulted in their attackers being hunted down and killed. Before leaving on this summer's Arctic junket, I left a holographic statement in Colorado with a friend:

> This last will and testament revokes all previous wills and codicils.... Should I be killed by a barren-ground grizzly or polar bear, it shall be my last wish and command that the bear responsible for my death shall not be killed, tranquilized, trifled with, or placed in a zoo.

As I PADDLED WEST, grizzly claw prints predictably raked the tundra of the Arctic National Wildlife Refuge. I repeatedly noted in my journal that the accompanying scats—firm and reminiscent of road apples—were free of caribou parts.*

Most days I could not find scats to pick apart, let alone clearly delineated tracks. Still, grizzlies had marked every acre of the refuge. On hillsides and riverbanks that held denning ground squirrels, backhoe-sized holes showed where grizzly claws plunged in after their chattering prey. On flatter terrain, the tundra had been repeatedly plowed a half-foot deep and a foot wide for bear root.

---

*While studies have shown that the barren-ground grizzlies have a hard time capturing adult caribou, according to the government's *Wildlife Research Summaries* (see "U.S. Department of the Interior" in the bibliography), eight of the twenty-six grizzlies or families within ANWR's coastal plain surveyed in 1997 killed up to six caribou calves a day.

In canyons sheltering rare copses of struggling poplar trees, barren-ground grizzly rubbings and eight-foot-tall clawings—with hair stuck in the scraped-away bark—appeared as a challenge to other bears. Huge boulders were flipped over in a search for insects. Curly cinnamon-colored or blonde hairs waved in back-scratching willow stands.

This constant awareness of their sign made it less surprising when I met bears face to face. Even if I was in no danger, my heart always beat rapidly (along with other malfunctioning body parts) as I encountered them—implacable and proud—strolling a riverbank, gamboling on the tundra, or inspecting the tide line.

One foggy day I paddled around a high-banked corner and came upon two mothers with cubs, one a flighty-looking youngster sporting an unusually dark chocolate coat, with none of the blonde or grizzled appearance of the other three. They were cropping the sedges like a small herd of hungry cows. This juicy-stemmed grass—*Arctagrostis latifolia*—surfaced in the scat of grizzly bears more than any other food. They were so engrossed by their grazing, in fact, that they appeared disinterested in my paddle-splashing arrival offshore. I decided to test the bear banger.

I screwed in a firecracker round, flipped the powerful spring, and rocketed the round into the sky. As it exploded fifty yards above, the bears jerked up their heads. Within two minutes, the chocolate cub retreated to the other side of its mother, then all four bowed their heads back down to the rich green horsetail and bobbing cotton grass as if I didn't exist.

These sows weighed several hundred pounds, while their yearling male cubs might grow to five hundred pounds, maximum fighting size for a barren-grounder. For now, their mission, like all Arctic grizzlies, was to rake up every carbohydrate and protein they crossed paths with. While their southern *Ursus arctos* brethren—the fifteen-hundred-pound Kodiak brown bears—discerningly select the fattest salmon and hibernate for only three months, the barren-ground grizzly scrounges for every molecule of food and spends nearly seven months hibernating. Each winter, as more than a hundred refuge grizzlies amble south and cross the Brooks Range to search for sunny den sites, several dozen of their northern *Ursus maritimus* cousins—the eleven-hundred-pound polar bears*—will scratch out their dens on the coastal plain.

In the Arctic, lacking laggardly salmon and other abundant, fat-laden proteins, the barren-ground grizzly develops slowly. Females don't give birth until they are six to twelve years old. Cubs remain with their mothers for up to five years—unlike southern Alaska's two-year-olds, kicked out by their obese Kodiak mothers. Average litter sizes are also smaller in the Arctic. And of the two male cubs sheltering behind their mothers in the cotton grass, statistics show that one of these cubs would be killed by an aggressive male bear to eliminate mating competition and dial down the gene pool.

Despite the grizzly's fierce reputation, I felt relatively safe in a sea kayak. So on another overcast yet tranquil day near the refuge, I was excited to catch up to a lone barren-ground grizzly. The bear had been masquerading as a boulder in hopes of catching some caribou, but after the caribou herd vanished from sight, the bear padded sullenly along the shoreline. I couldn't help wondering if he felt lonely.

His shoulder hump—distinguishing the dish-faced grizzlies from the muzzle-faced black or white bears—was larger than nor-

---

*During the Pleistocene Ice Age, the first "polar bear," *Ursus maritimus tyrannus*, was a grizzly subspecies, isolated by glaciers. Over the next twenty thousand years, these bears became smaller, their skulls elongated, their fur lightened, and their paws simulated flippers. As late as ten thousand years ago, according to fossil records, these sea bears still had brown-bear-type, herbivore molars. In the last several thousand years, they finally developed sharper polar-bear teeth, more suited to eating seals and fish. The bears flourished and grew large by eating marine mammals that the grizzlies couldn't catch.

mal, so he may have been a digger. I was betting that his scats would unveil ground squirrel bones. From his lumbering and muscular frame, and by the way he sank heavily into the mud, he appeared to be a male. I guessed four hundred pounds.

I snapped off a quick photograph, hoping that I was far enough away that the metallic click wouldn't startle him. Then I paddled in closer to make contact. From forty yards away it seemed that the bear looked angry—maybe about losing the caribou. I knew (having been chased by grizzlies twice in my sea kayak) that they swam as slow as dogs with life preservers. This bear seemed to know that I held the advantage. He registered my presence with only a sidelong glance.

If he had been human, I would've called his curled upper lip a sneer. If I were a teller of bear myths, standing on the ground (rather than paddling a kayak) so close to this beautiful yet unpredictable being would have been an act of recklessness and contempt—or an embellishment. If he had been an amphibious polar bear, forty yards would have been too close.

I tried to keep my movements slow and graceful, I avoided direct eye contact, and I breathed deep to still my heart and to prevent the bear from perceiving me as prey. I pushed the hair out of my eyes, wondering how he would judge me.

I quietly set the paddle across the cockpit. The bear's breath frosted white cartoon balloons into the air as he inspected the tide line with his nose. *Now or never*, I thought, I filled my lungs and licked my lips to speak.

I said, "Hello, Mr. Bear," friendly, yet loud; the grizzly immediately sprang up onto the sixty-degree bank. He covered thirty feet in three leaps, and each stride pushed fetid air from the great bellows of his lungs as mud flew off his claws. Two gulls—trailing the bear in hopes of sharing food—began dive bombing and screeching in the air space around his head, rebuking his cowardice.

Sudden as a fish, the bear then plopped back into the surrounding ocean of tundra.

The Beaufort Sea lay still. My ears rang. I cupped my hands and tried to blow my fingers warm.

The press of rolling lime-tinted hills to the south, with the glare of pancake-flat sea ice to the north, gave my loneliness palpable weight. I twisted my head and shrugged my shoulders, trying to loosen the tension, amazed about how the Arctic continually shattered my expectations. A needy human being from the land of forests, I merely wanted companionship. The barren-ground grizzly only wanted to be left alone.

△ △ △

Olaus Murie put down his journal and reached for his small Kodak as the barren-ground grizzly appeared above him and his companion on a gravel slope of the Brooks Range. The bear was too far away from the two men for a photograph. Even worse, it was above, and grizzlies often approach their prey from an uphill advantage.

To his side, yellow poppies and bluebells sprang from snowbanks. Flaxen-colored lowlands undulated in the distance, while orange lichens brightened black boulders. Lupines, forget-me-nots, Lapland rosebay, sweet pea, milk vetch, dryas, wall flowers, anemones, saxifrage, asters, and bluebells added vividness. Olaus had come to survey the northeastern corner of Alaska for a wildlife refuge, even though bears had a way of stealing his focus.

Through earlier reconnaissance, Olaus had learned that the region held two unique North American ecosystems: the northern boreal forest surrounding their base camp and the coastal plain north of the Brooks Range. The climate and topography fostered an unusually rich mixture of animals and plant life.

As a scientist, Olaus thought that his personal life and emotions about this place had no place in his journals (which are now housed in the National Archives). They were the same five-by-eight-inch, lined field journals he had used since the turn of the century. Under the date, June 2, 1956, he wrote about grizzly and wolf tracks, their droppings, and the white sheen of two other grizzlies down by the river. And about a pile of moose droppings with 227 pellets, another with 208.

The uninitiated might think of capturing such minutia as a trivial pursuit. Yet Olaus had learned long ago that this level of documentation would allow him to see the big picture and start the groundwork for the grinding campaign to follow. In that same journal, struggling with how this new Wildlife Range would be created, Olaus wrote:

> If we human beings could only understand the little events in our daily lives! I wonder; is the long, timeless evolution of the universe based on the little unobtrusive forces among us? After all, the impetus contained within a single microscopic cell is in certain fundamental respects more important than the shouting of national leaders.

Here in the Arctic, however, a change had come over his journals as he loosened his scientific ideals for those of a conservationist. He noted still more scats and previously unseen birds as he wandered across tipsy tussocks with his pack, "now a piece of his anatomy," as Mardy described it. She teased her tousle-haired husband every time he bent over to dissect a new dropping, pull out pieces of bone and hair, and recount exactly which animals—mice, lemmings, ground squirrels, caribou, and moose—the bear or wolf had been eating. Olaus, sixty-eight, carried on with boyish eyes. The wilder the landscape, the more lost in rapture he became.

Below the nameless peak that he called First Mountain, the two men looked up on the grizzly bear, and Olaus flashed over a lifetime of bear encounters. Initially he shot bears for specimens, but beyond the work and the need to make a careful assessment for his wildlife studies, he found no thrill in shooting bears. To the contrary, he was ahead of his time in believing that grizzly bears had to be protected. After all, their populations had already begun shrinking throughout the Lower Forty-eight.

For decades, Olaus had experimented with using a camera instead of a gun. Beneath a smoking volcano in southern Alaska, along a stream wriggling with salmon, he and his companion had hidden in the tall grass as a fat Kodiak bear approached. The grizzly grew larger and larger in Olaus's viewfinder as his fingers trembled on the camera. Suddenly, the big bear turned away from the salmon stream and started digging after a ground squirrel. Olaus watched the great shoulders lift and pull, as the bear's face became splotched with mud, until the bear gave up and returned to the stream.

Olaus's courage came back as he raised the sixteen-inch wide camera and snapped a picture just as the bear wheeled around after another salmon, splashing in the stream. The rushing water drowned out the clicks and then the ratcheting of the camera as Olaus changed film. As the bear stood up with a salmon in its mouth, Olaus held the bulky Graflex up above the grass to snap another picture—the metallic click made the bear charge Olaus. He dropped the Graflex, grabbed his rifle, and stood up and shouted: "Hey, you get out of here!"

Although the bear turned slightly, he kept coming on; Olaus stood his ground. And just then his companion jumped up, and rather than aiming their guns, they both waved their arms, shouting, "Hey there, you get out of *here!*" which caused the bear to toss his head and sprint off across the stream. Once finished crossing, he swaggered across the tundra as if nothing had happened.

IN THE ARCTIC, below First Mountain, the barren-ground grizzly above Olaus had fallen asleep, and it would take time to stalk and approach it cautiously. Olaus and his companion slowly began work-

ing their way up, knowing that the wind would carry their scent to
the bear and identify them as humans rather than prey. Still, there
was the problem of approaching a powerful predator from downhill.

As they took their time climbing, Olaus gazed down over the
Sheenjek River—the southern counterpart to the Kongakut—
flowing through one of a dozen southern valleys that drain the
nine-thousand-foot peaks in the Brooks Range. Like the Chandalar
River roaring to the west, the Sheenjek headwaters are limned
with ten-foot-thick, cantilevered layers of dense, blue *aufeis*. Along
steeper gradients, the river undresses the tundra banks to a corset
of dirty, gray permafrost, which the Muries used to refrigerate their
milk and cheese.

Olaus could see Mardy down in camp, swatting at mosquitoes
still sluggish from the cold. Stands of poplar and birch poked out
of the riverbanks.

While picking up hundreds of animal scats and wandering this
paradise in wide-eyed amazement, the Muries at first wondered if
they could adequately describe the incredible variety of flora and
fauna surrounding them. At night, as the sun rambled above the
horizon and birdcalls continued around the clock, they couldn't
sleep. Olaus had already filled two notebooks trying to quantify it.

Bumblebee-hued oestrids and stick-like mosquitoes billowed in
brown diaphanous clouds of insect desire, beneath the cacophony
of birds, shaking their shadows across the tundra. Solar reflection
from the glaciated Brooks Range a mile above their camp could
cause snow blindness.

Everywhere he looked, silver threads of snowmelt washed over
lichen-jacketed boulders and jumped into frozen riverbeds or lakes
whose animal names—Sheenjek, Kuirzinjik, Ambresvajun—came
from the local Native American or Gwich'in concept of "Distant
Time," when animals and men were one. *Sheenjek*, he learned,
meant "dog salmon" in Gwich'in.

Several other biologists on this survey were amazed to learn that their world-renowned scientist and leader was so interested in the Indian ways. It didn't surprise them that Olaus never missed a grizzly or a birdcall, but jokes often flew past him. He spent a lot more time listening than talking. He never swore. He addressed everyone, particularly younger people, as if they were his superiors. And he never asked for help while doing the dishes or burning the trash, which inspired everyone to contribute to both the science and the camp chores.

Olaus asked one of the younger men if he would shoot a caribou so that the camp would have fresh meat. No one had wanted to bring a gun, but a Fairbanks friend had insisted that the Muries borrow a .270 rifle in case a marauding grizzly came into their camp. Each night they locked all their food into a fifty-five-gallon drum, in order to keep the bears from learning bad habits.

Out of deference to Olaus and the spirit of the refuge that they were trying to create, the biologists then made a pact that they wouldn't shoot an animal unless they were defending themselves.

Olaus had counseled everyone about the impulsiveness of the powerful and dangerous bears that they would encounter. Yet he also believed that if people in the Arctic audibly identified themselves as humans, even if the myopic bears could not see them clearly, they would respect that the biologists were not prey.

He told the group about meeting a black bear that was chasing a cow and calf moose out of a pond. As the bear came closer, Olaus hurried closer, then veered back from the pond to let him pass. The bear approached, and at seven paces away Olaus shifted slightly so that the bear could finally see him.

The bear turned its head back and forth, "desirous of leaving" Olaus said, "but apparently reluctant to exhibit fear. Finally, as he stood swaying uncertainly, he suddenly leaped away in full flight." After fifteen feet, the bear turned and came back, aggressively.

"Well," Olaus said gruffly to the bear, "what are you going to do about it?"

The bear stopped, seven steps away.

"What are you going to do?" Olaus repeated, showing the bear that he was dealing with a human rather than prey. The bear began making hesitant movements away from Olaus until it sniffed his scent fully, and dashed away. "Blackie" peered from around a tree, "woofed" several times, and continued retreating, growling with every step.

Another evening in their Arctic camp, while they sheltered from the mosquitoes in their tents, three muskrats dove into the unnamed lake and a wolf appeared. For a few minutes the wolf stood staring at one of the biologists without fear. Their eyes met; two souls contemplated each other. Then the wilder of the two shifted and let tundra begin flying beneath his feet. All the biologists' binoculars came out as the wolf sidled away, shrinking down to an indiscernible, wavering gray blur, enveloped by the immensity of the landscape.

This event changed the writing in Olaus's journal. He referred to the wolf by the pronoun "him." Mardy, characteristically, needed to name him, so he became Lobo. Then Olaus (who often wrote letters to federal agencies protesting inappropriate names on maps) consented to christening the body of water Lobo Lake.

His journal conclusion: "This simple wolf episode is the most exciting event so far. How many would be happy to see that wolf."

This paradisiacal idyll changed when three Gwich'in wolf hunters arrived. Mardy loaned them her husband's *Animal Tracks*, which the three hungry men pored over in admiration. She was aghast to see a porcupine paw bobbing in their cooking pot. They became fast friends, sharing Mardy's stretched stews and potato pancakes. The wolf hunters in turn shared the Gwich'in names for animals, approved of the biologists' name for the lake, and later shared meat from a moose they shot.

Olaus had long admired the indigenous people of the North, but his journal commented on another trashed Gwich'in camp nearby: "We think of the Indian as belonging in Wilderness," Olaus wrote. "But lately he has adopted the way of living of the white man and he is doing the trapping for money to buy more things—getting away from nature."

The Gwich'in sat transfixed for hours, watching Olaus skin specimens of dead voles, lemmings, and mice. With shaking fingers, he slit the tiny animals from their anuses to their jaws, then he cleaned out the skulls and peeled the skin off the bodies—as if savoring the intact rind of an orange before scraping out the seeds. He labeled numbers on each specimen to correspond with the descriptions and drawings in his field journal. Then he salted each animal with borax to deter insects, filled them with cotton, and sewed each specimen up.

To the curious Gwich'in, this white man appeared to hold the ancient reverence for the bodies of departed animal souls. He took the drying board back to his tent and set it down facing the late afternoon sun, in between his collection of drying wolf and bear scats.

In the warm evenings, *aufeis* boomed loose below camp and splashed into the river, rafting down channels newly gouged through permafrost. The Muries watched the *aufeis* rushing past broken limestone ridges holding the hydrocarbon remains of ancient algae. Far below the permafrosted earth, these transmuted sea creatures percolated into rock, trapped by layers of shale amid underground anticlines. Other preservationists had claimed it was only a matter of time before the oil companies started seismic testing here. All the biologists knew what was coming to the North.

Olaus and these naturalists had begun to see this resource-rich landscape as more than the sum of its parts. While sitting around the campfire during the late and bright evenings, they talked about how they had never experienced such biodiversity. As they knelt down on springy tundra and smelled the flowers and listened to *yawp*ing foxes, the biologists sensed that the region had a singular living and breathing quality. A biomass.

Yet they continually struggled for a vocabulary that would express the feeling of completeness that the land gave them. Mardy said that the wilderness was not spectacular, but that its value lay in its untouched character. The youngest biologist, a graduate student, talked with a German accent about how the silence of the landscape dispelled the unease that accompanied city life. Olaus repeatedly emphasized "precious intangible values," and how it should be a democratic guarantee—as much as the right to vote, the freedom to bear arms, and the privilege of free speech—that every American could experience a place preserved for no economic gain. The biologists knew well enough that they could agree on most anything when it came to protecting this place. The hard part would be finding the right language with which to convince the outside world.

Olaus saw the creation of this wildlife range as essential to the animals he had encountered here. Over that summer in the Arctic he sampled 125 bear scats, which gave a good idea of the barren-ground grizzly's vegetarian diet; he told the group that the grizzly was doomed without protected habitat.

In the Lower Forty-eight, Olaus was appalled that grizzlies remained in only four states because of the loss of habitat. Around the campfire, his voice quavered indignantly as he said that they needed to take stock of themselves and their attitude toward wild things and the wilderness.

"How many people would be surprised," he asked, "to learn that this horrid beast is preponderantly a vegetarian?" He talked about the many bears he had found eating ants, grasshoppers, or stealing the roots cached by gophers. He talked about how the only hope of saving the grizzly or the wolf was in saving the wilderness, because in no other place but the wilderness could these predators survive. He said that someday maybe they could all look upon the future of the grizzly as an indication of the growth of generosity and the worthiness of man.

These campfire chats showed Olaus's thinking as he took out his Kodak below the grizzly on First Mountain—the tiny camera had long ago replaced the heavy Graflex and freed up room in his pack for plaster, scats, and all the assorted arcana of a busy field biologist's kit. Then Olaus noticed another one of the biologists coming down the mountainside toward the bear, downwind. The bear went into a sudden alarm and stood up on its hind feet, trying to get a scent. The descending biologist, Bob, knew what he had to do. Although it was a cardinal sin to run away from a bear, Bob ran sideways and downhill so that the bear would get his scent. The bear dropped down on all fours and began trotting toward Bob. Olaus put down his camera in horror. Bob froze. Everyone focused on the barren-ground grizzly accelerating toward Bob. No one was armed with anything more than the knowledge that unprovoked bears rarely attacked men. At the last instant, twenty yards away, the bear stiffened its front legs to stop, sniff Bob, then wheel back around. It began running, broke into a gallop, and reached a speed in the tussocks that would have broken a horse's leg in such uneven terrain.

In the days and months and years that followed, the story of this dedicated team of biologists studying everything from harmless microbes to predatory megafauna would become well-known to naturalists. Yet their unarmed encounter with the barren-ground grizzly showed a sea change in the world of conservation: If you believed fervently in preserving wilderness still inhabited with large predators, it was worth risking your life over that of a bear.

AFTER TWO MONTHS the team flew out to Fairbanks. Their Arctic survey became their finest wilderness outing ever—or so they promoted it with their writings and lectures.

Surrounded by friends back in Fairbanks, Olaus and Mardy knew that gathering Alaskan support would make or break the Arctic National Wildlife Range. Then, as now, the fiercely outspoken residents of the North were suspicious of outsiders and government employees. The long-disgruntled Alaskans had begun threatening to withdraw from the Union even before statehood had first been proposed in the century's first decade. Until this wildlife range idea, Alaska didn't have any conservation groups. Olaus set out to create that community.

He had a political advantage that allowed him to outmaneuver even the local politicians. These men, like all Alaskans, distrusted outsiders from the government bearing strange proposals. But Alaskans thought of Olaus as one of their own, one who had quit the federal government, who could face down a grizzly, who could run a dogteam (conveniently, most people had forgotten the stir he created as a federal employee several decades earlier, when he busted the Fairbanks postmaster for poaching.)

Olaus tapped into the anger against military withdrawal lands— private bombing ranges closed to the public—surrounding Fairbanks and the northwestern slope of the Brooks Range. The *Fairbanks Daily News Miner* printed a firestorm of angry letters. Artillery practice repeatedly and wantonly gunned down members of the caribou herd, which were considered free meat on the hoof by hungry locals, and left hundreds of carcasses to rot.

Olaus, biologist-cum-preservationist-cum-statesman, wrote a graceful letter that was widely printed by Alaskan organizations and newspapers. He clarified that this Arctic National Wildlife Range would be open to both hunting and mining, but closed to the military. He said that Alaska could not be a wasteland for military dumping. He resorted to his favorite argument: "Even though we have a defense department, we also profess to have a democracy."

In Alaska as well as the Lower Forty-eight, Olaus arranged

meetings with the women's tea and garden societies overlooked by the manly Alaskan politicians. Olaus contacted the chairman of the National Council of State Garden Clubs in New York, taking him up on his offer to "sic 300,000 ladies" on the Arctic Range issue. These garden clubs—despite their tea-sipping, weed-snipping memberships—emerged as huge, powerful voting blocs.

Then George Schaller, the young student and German immigrant who had accompanied the Muries, finished his brilliant master's thesis, "Arctic Valley." Page one opened with a quote from Robert Service's *The Spell of the Yukon*. George's paper acknowledged twenty-seven expert sources—from museums, government agencies, and universities all over North America—for their help in confirming the specimens (including sketches, wolf scats, casted tracks, photographs, insect vials, fish scales, stuffed birds, mice, and lemmings) of eighty-five birds, nineteen mammals, and dozens of fish, mollusks, and arthropods. George alone collected forty species of lichen and one hundred and thirty-eight species of flowers in his plant press. "And my vials," he wrote later, "contain twenty-three spider species, to give just one example of the invertebrates." He also wrote with surprising fluency about the human experience available in the Arctic and the meaning of wilderness.

The report showed the biologist's magnificent passion.* Olaus knew how to pick them. George could have been Olaus reborn, substituting a German for a Scandinavian accent, mountaineering for dog sledding, and cats or gorillas for wolves or elk. Two years before their survey, accompanying the celebrated alpinist Heinrich Harrer, George made the historic first ascent of Alaska's 12,010-foot Mount Drum.

---

*George Schaller dedicated the first of his many books, *The Mountain Gorilla*, to Olaus, and would later become a world-famous biologist. In 1972 he won the National Book Award for *The Serengeti Lion*; in 1978 Peter Matthiessen won the National Book Award for *The Snow Leopard*, which chronicled a Schaller quest.

In the winter of 1957, while returning from Olaus's carefully targeted Alaskan lecture tour to women's garden societies and men's hunting clubs, Mardy discovered a lump on her husband's back that turned out to be cancerous. Olaus underwent two lymph gland operations in an effort to stop the melanoma from spreading.

When Olaus got out of the hospital, he and Mardy wrote a script for a film they'd shot in their wildlife range. They called it *A Letter from the Brooks Range,* made several prints, and arranged for it to be shown all over the country. That summer, despite Mardy's objections, Olaus resumed his grueling lecture tour.

In Washington, D.C., Olaus showed his slides to a committee that included the Secretary of the Interior. "Here," Olaus said, in accompaniment to his photograph of two thousand caribou moving by their river camp, "the scientist, be he professional or amateur, will have the opportunity to study an undisturbed ecosystem. Here also," clicking to an image of a bear, "people sensitive to natural beauty can gain inspiration and enjoy a primitive recreational experience."

Then the Muries hit the road, carrying the film, slide carousels, and projectors. They lectured for garden societies and conservation groups all over the country. Everywhere Olaus spoke, the range gained allies.

In Fairbanks—at the Tanana Valley Sportsmen's Association, two Garden clubs, the Rotary Club, the Chamber of Commerce, and the university campus—people agreed to give their support and drafted resolutions. Although these people were voting for the future of Alaska's wilderness, they could just as easily have been putting Olaus in some higher office. He spoke with great humility. He never argued with his audience, and when they asserted themselves as proud Alaskans—*this is my land and damned if anyone will tell me when and where to hunt*—Murie nodded his head in patient support.

The Muries' campaign took place during Alaska's glacial climb toward statehood. Decades of bills had failed. But everything changed in July 1957 as oil exploded out of the pipes in south-central Alaska's Kenai Moose Range, a USFWS wildlife refuge. In the ensuing oil rush, the Interior Secretary sold cheap leases on 250,000 acres in the protected Moose Range (and another 33 million acres of federal land across the country). Although the oil companies were delighted with the opportunity, scandal erupted. The newly empowered conservationist community complained to Congress that the secretary had provided the oil companies with a yard sale. After two months of hearings, Congress decreed that the Department of the Interior must now ask for approval whenever leases were proposed on federal lands. This mini–oil boom and land giveaway triggered a new suspicion of Washington's ulterior motives and foreshadowed latter-day events. The public's mistrust of politicians mixing with oil companies would never go away.

After the president appointed a new Interior Secretary, oil leasing was closed on all federal ranges and wildlife refuges as directed by Congress, but the secretary began working on an exemption for Alaska. Setting a pattern for future northern development, saying "no" to the generous and powerful oil companies became political suicide.

In 1958, black crude began flowing at 900 barrels (49,500 gallons) a day from Alaska's Kenai Moose Range. The territorial government levied an oil tax, and the soon-to-be state was collecting $84 million a year.

Up in the northeast corner of the territory, the ice pack congealed over black seawater as the coastal plain lay blanketed under a subzero pallor. Dippers used their wings like flippers in the thermal springs, pregnant polar bears sauntered into sandy dens, and Dall sheep curled up on grassy ledges. That winter, millions of hungry birds and thousands of caribou had long since fled over the passes, across the Porcupine, on past Gwich'in hunters to the ancient wintering grounds in southern boreal forests, as the snow geese picked through the cornfields of Alberta and Arctic terns winged their transatlantic flights over the eastern seaboard, where the president sat in the Oval Office and smiled in front of popping camera bulbs.

After the proclamation line, "Done at the City of Washington at one minute past noon on this third day of January in the year of our Lord nineteen hundred and fifty-nine," the president signed his full honorific and officially admitted Alaska into the Union.*

New federal legislation loomed like a storm cloud over reluctant residents, whipped into greed by the *Anchorage Times* not to relinquish any of their precious land to outsiders. There were several new federal parks and refuges proposed in the huge forty-ninth state, but none was as controversial as the Muries' Arctic National Wildlife Range.

---

*Although statehood bills had been previously blocked by Congressmen and Senators who feared the new state would produce more Democrats and change the strong southern Republican majority, potentially overturning civil-rights legislation, Washington lawmakers now had to take notice. The Alaska Territory supported an emerging oil industry and its own revenue.

A recently recruited Fairbanks lawyer, Ted Stevens, known as "Mr. Statehood" at the Interior Department, mounted a subversive yet extremely effective media campaign, baiting President Eisenhower with Alaska questions whenever the press corps assembled. In Stevens' words, they were "violating the law [by] lobbying from the executive branch, and there's been a statute against that for a long time." At first Stevens only provided legal counsel, but over the years he would become the keeper of Alaska oil and wilderness legislation.

Eventually, through Stevens, Eisenhower got what he wanted. The young attorney drafted Section 10 of the Statehood Act that would allow the president to take control of all the Arctic and the Aleutian Islands (occupied by the Japanese during World War II) in the event of a new military emergency.

Chapter 8

FAIRBANKS

I feel strongly today that science today is way low—we are just counting and marking. We are not getting down to live with the animals and plants, to learn principles, how they live and what they need. We do not have understanding.

—Olaus Murie,
in a letter to Adolph Murie

In a creaking, clapboard home like the house that Mardy Murie grew up in, the director for Alaska's Northern Center for the Environment made a gaffe. He called the refuge "America's Serengeti," the environmental community's most popular, yet inaccurate analogy.

One of the brightest and most outspoken students raised his hand and interrupted, "Is it true that there are herds of wildebeests, gazelles, elephants in the Arctic then?"

"Well," the director conceded, "*American Serengeti* is a good comparison for an incredibly rich ecosystem. There's a herd of 170,000 caribou, and their aggregation on the coastal plain is the most awesome wildlife spectacle in North America."

"But are there any other herds in ANWR?" another student asked.

"We never call it ANWR," the director retorted, "that came

from the PR people at the oil companies to sterilize the Arctic National Wildlife Refuge. And there might not be other herds but there *are* bands of musk oxen, wolves, and polar bears."

"So it's not really like the Serengeti then, with millions of herd animals?" the first student countered.

"There are millions of birds." And the director ably expanded upon the role that the refuge plays for several hundred thousand snow geese, using the coastal plain as a refueling stop, and Arctic terns, preparing for the longest migration in the world. The younger male students paid rapt attention to this ropy-armed, shaggy-haired, articulate outdoorsman. He carried himself like a trail runner, quick on his feet, with energy to burn.

"Every bear and wolf are radio collared now and the Interior Department wants the coastal plain totally opened to oil," he continued, as the floor creaked beneath him. "But they [the fish and wildlife service] can't talk publicly because of all the environmentalists. Unfortunately, the environmentalists have limited resources and big oil has unlimited resources.

"It's a black-and-white issue," he said, "not at all gray. There can't be any compromise because it will be like slashing the face of the *Mona Lisa* if the refuge is opened [to oil leasing]. And politicians love to compromise."

A third student asked, "Do you know how much oil is under the refuge?"

"Less than half a year's supply," he replied.

"How many barrels is that?"

"Less than we need to run our techno-military industrial complex."

OUR UNIVERSITY OF ALASKA COURSE, Oil Versus Wilderness, would include a week in Fairbanks, several days in Prudhoe Bay, and three weeks in the refuge. The fifteen students would gather information, make conclusions, and slowly decide what position they should take in the controversy. On our return to Fairbanks, they would shower off the black peat and write their papers supporting oil development or wilderness protection.

I was seeking a new perspective of the refuge by signing on as an instructor for these young students. Working under the philosophy that Mardy had placarded in her bedroom—Those who dare to teach must never cease to learn—I hoped to come away with a new and more objective understanding of the development controversy.

The students, aged sixteen to twenty-two, were mostly high achievers. Since the course was college-accredited, this helped inspire parents to pay significant tuition and travel costs, while the excitable kids masquerading as adults were all drawn by the romance of Alaska's ultimate wilderness.

Students and instructors got to know one another by discussing our expectations on a hill above Fairbanks, watching cumulus stack above the distant and vaporous-looking peaks of the Alaska Range. More than a few students were afraid of being mauled by bears. A sharp yet shy high-school senior had never been away from home, and this college course intimidated her. An overweight Dartmouth undergrad hoped to get in shape but had never camped out.

In the amazingly hot and dry summer afternoon, they aired their nervousness about kayaking, carrying a heavy pack, and how to interview the experts we would be meeting in days to come. After two hours, we drove the van down the hill for pizza, and then took a tour of town.

Considering that Fairbanks lies directly alongside the pipeline, 150 miles south of the Arctic Circle and within a long day's drive of America's richest oil patch, the city of seventy-seven thousand has been oddly unconnected with Alaska's largest and most lucrative industry. Unlike Anchorage, population 225,000, 360 miles to the south, spiked with high-rises and showered with oil money, downtown Fairbanks buildings rarely climb several stories from the unstable permafrost. The local phone book shows only two major oil companies. Anchorage hosts fifteen major oil companies. Outside our van, nameless people walked crookedly down the sidewalks past innumerable fur shops, while heater plug-in cords swayed under passing car bumpers.

On the congested double-lane spokes exiting the hub appeared a melee of low-slung chain stores, a couple of malls, a salmon bake, and innumerable tourist shops. Two miles east of town lay the Fort Wainwright Army Base; twenty miles southeast was the Eielson Air Force Base. The town seemed—like most midsized American towns lacking urban planners—to sprawl upon the premise that automobiles could take you anywhere. Giant supermarkets were grafted onto hardware-department stores where a surfeit of grape-shaped people dressed in tan Carhardt overalls pushed oversized carts. Small planes constantly buzzed overhead. Someone in the van asked why the sun was still shining at ten-thirty. The local movieplex was showing *Empire of the Sun, Back to the Future II,* and *National Lampoon's Summer Vacation.* As we passed McDonald's and Burger King, the students sighed in disappointment: no one imagined the frontier would be this civilized.

A ten-minute drive north, west, or east of town and it came as a shock to most of the students that Alaska has no interstate highway. The long strip of Fairbanks's double lane was replaced by straight, narrow stretches of single-laned, frost-heaved asphalt surrounded by a sea of boggy black spruce. It looked like the earth would suck at your boots every step for weeks on end. As the mosquitoes homed in on our heat signatures, we closed the windows. No one got out.

"A few more days," a student said as the radiator ticked, "and we'll be *out* there, in the bush."

"Where we're going there won't even be any trees," another instructor said reassuringly.

The Dalton Highway to Prudhoe Bay is four hundred miles of gravel lying in momentary stasis with floury silt. The van climbed up out of the boreal forest away from all things familiar and over a low pass through the Brooks Range into a treeless fantasy land, on past a corner of the refuge boundary and down to the braided gravel bar expanse of the Sagavanirktok River. This featureless plain caught the back of your throat with starkness and road dust. If such a wilderness felt too strange, comfort could be found in the four-foot-wide silver ribbon of technology that parallels the so-called Haul Road. More than half of the 800.3-mile-long pipeline is aboveground so that its warmth won't melt the permafrost. Four miles are refrigerated below the ground, and along 376 miles of nonpermafrost areas, the pipe is buried. The pipe crosses above or submerges 834 rivers and streams.

The students curiously watched this pipeline rising and falling across the hills like a roller coaster, then diving underground until enormous brown dust clouds occluded the view. As oncoming oil trucks appeared, our windows were quickly pulled shut and the formerly sky-blue van—plastered over with thick layers of brown flour—entered another dark cloud of road silt temporarily risen from its gravel bed.

When the windows were pushed back open, a porcupine waddled in slow gear across the treeless landscape. In lieu of setting, the sun veered north in its eerie Arctic parabola. Snowshoe hares sprung across the road, forcing the driver to hit the brakes. Despite all expectations, our group had not seen any caribou.*

The students believed that their final meeting in Fairbanks with

---

*In April 1923 along this untrammeled stretch of tundra, Olaus and Adolph Murie counted twenty-five hundred of the Central caribou herd, covering the hills in stick-like formation during their northern migration.

the university's caribou biologist, Dr. David Klein, had been the most informative and objective interview so far. Unlike the conservationists and federal employees we met, Klein, at sixty-two, a lanky and droll scientist, presented facts that appeared unbiased by conservation or development allegiances.

Klein concluded—while chalking out a rough map of the refuge on his blackboard—that oil development in the refuge would irreparably damage the Porcupine caribou herd. While the environmentalists among our students claimed that this scientist alone had put a nail in the coffin of the oil developers' lid, we asked the students not to make conclusions until they finished fact-finding and queried the oil-company spokespeople in Prudhoe Bay. So we reviewed Klein's presentation carefully.

Klein insisted that we understand the caribou. For thousands of years before the last ice age, Alaskan herds of *Rangifer tarandus* have migrated from boreal forests to regions of open tundra. Although some Alaskans could recall "millions" of caribou annually migrating past Fairbanks until the 1940s, today the collective populations of caribou in Alaska are found in thirty-two herds totaling, roughly, a million animals.

When cows are calving, the caribou avoid all buildings, roads, humans, and oil rigs, even in areas that had been used as calving grounds prior to Prudhoe Bay's construction boom. Dr. Klein believed that if oil development comes to the refuge the calving members of the Porcupine herd would be forced off the small coastal plain and up into the foothills, to be preyed upon by wolves and bears that normally avoid the coast.

As the pipeline disappeared and our van approached the warehouses and heavy equipment of Deadhorse, Alaska, south of the oil fields, the course director implored the exhausted students—whose emphatic journal highlighting had been replaced by mere doodling—to retain their neutrality with the oil-company representatives. He reminded everyone that it was too early for anyone to take sides, and to review Dr. Klein's information so questions could be generated during our tours of ARCO and British Petroleum facilities.

△ △ △

The outspoken miner stood up and shouted to the Fairbanks audience that he disagreed with the proposed range's rules about not being able to drive his bulldozer Cat into the region. "I would bet you that any one of them that's ever been in the niggerheads [tussocks] on foot would welcome an old Cat trail." He described how slag piles looked like natural moraine and the beauteous remains of mining added life to an otherwise monotonous landscape and how miners had saved lives of passing tourists.

He then complained that the local newspapers wouldn't print his letters about Olaus Murie because the editor said he had been getting rough with the elderly gentleman, but where Alaska was concerned the miner would get rough with anybody if it infringed upon his rights. By now, even the chairman, Senator Bartlett, had had enough of this gadfly.*

The hearing was being held in the university's Shiable Auditorium in Fairbanks, hometown for both Mardy Murie and the senator, as well as the Alaskan haven for mining and gun-wielding anarchists. This was the last of eight public debates about the range held throughout Alaska in October 1959. A nearsighted librarian stepped forth to declare that the only threat to the wilderness came from the handful of "wilderness extremists and federal officials." Numerous miners opposing the bill complained that national parks

---

*The miner, Joe Vogler, became known in the 1970s for his Alaskan Independent Party campaign for the U.S. presidency and an armed showdown with rangers when he illegally drove a bulldozer into Yukon Charley National Park to access his gold mine. He was murdered in 1993, his body duct-taped into a blue tarp, an unsolved crime that the Alaskan Independent Party still blames on a conspiracy of outside politicians.

and refuges would prevent them from exercising their right to bear arms. Others argued that the need for guns to protect themselves from bears was "grossly exaggerated" and shouldn't be a point of discussion.

In Fairbanks, when yet another garden-club representative testified favorably for the bill, the senator came to understand his real opponent. He asked if the issue had been brought to the garden club's attention through Dr. Olaus Murie. She hedged. He pressed her, asking if Murie and his wife had spent some little time in the proposed range? She answered yes. Bartlett demanded to know if the club's vote had been unanimous. She hedged again. Finally, under pressure, she admitted that the vote had not been unanimous.

Written testimonies were read into the record, including yet another outspoken miner who called it, "that wildlife range withdrawal foolishness. Of all the absurd things for those bird-watchers to come up with, that is tops." The audience erupted with laughter. Then the miner's testimony continued:

> There probably wouldn't be ten people a year visit the place to be chewed on by mosquitoes. As long as there is a chance of finding oil or minerals, why set it aside for a few selfish bird-watchers? Besides, they wouldn't let anyone hunt wolves as most of those crackpots are wolf lovers and in a few years there would be no caribou or moose.

This collective anger toward wolves showed the cards of those who opposed the bill. Olaus had sensed this Alaskan aversion to wolves as soon as he started the campaign, so he had warned those testifying not to mention the controversial animal. But Senator Bartlett couldn't resist baiting several Fairbanks anti-wilderness witnesses with the four-letter W animal as an attempt to supplant the conservationists' erudition with some old-fashioned Alaskan miner–style know-how.

An Alaskan state congressman stood up and told stories about how he had defended sheep and moose from killer wolves along the proposed range's coastal plain, which he referred to as "mostly a big swamp . . . I don't believe that you're conserving anything by making a reserve out of that."

A miner associate of Bartlett's who moonlighted as an Alaskan game commissioner took the floor to respond to the senator's prompt about the decline of caribou by blaming it on a "tremendous increase in wolves." The miner windily warmed up to his story about getting an affidavit from a young hunter out at Eagle Creek, scared by all the wolves. So the miner–game commissioner went out to Eagle Creek to inspect a wolf trail that looked like a highway. It was all true, claimed the miner–game commissioner. He said that a lot of caribou get killed, "when you get two or three hundred head" of wolves running in a pack like that.

The next witness had accompanied the Muries to the Sheenjek. She gave a half-hour's eloquent testimony, telling the audience about three rare Asiatic birds found nesting in the proposed range: "I know these birds don't mean much to you people, probably."

The affable senator told the audience that he had never heard so many witnesses starting with the same facts coming to such different conclusions. He facetiously suggested that Alaska had better pass the range bill if only because a bigger range would be proposed if this one failed. When the laughter died down, he told the ornithologist that, until her speech, he hadn't heard the word "ecology" in several days.

She apologized and sat down.

Several more conservationists testified in favor of the range. Bartlett had to acknowledge them. Another local conservationist recruited by the Muries attached reports that showed the precedent for equally large game preserves throughout North America and a recent economic survey for Alaska's annual revenue, showing mining's contribution at the bottom of the slag heap.

The dogged male audience couldn't help but notice that this lady, Celia Hunter, was a looker. Equally impressive, she flew airplanes. But the miners were ultimately deflated by her speech: "I submit that the mining interests are no longer in a position to dominate the state's thinking," Celia said. "It is becoming a case of the tail wagging the dog." Then she reminded the audience that prospecting and mining were permitted in the present range bill.

It went on like that. The few tough-as-nails miners who found the courage to stand up and speak, pickaxing their grammar with colorful fits and starts, pleading that people too needed living room. Not just the wolves.

Only in Alaska could such testimony then be concluded by an old woman standing up to recite Robert Service:

> *The summer — no sweeter was ever;*
> *The sunshiny woods all athrill;*
> *The grayling aleap in the river,*
> *The bighorn asleep on the hill.*

The woman closed by saying that primeval Arctic wilderness should be preserved for posterity.

When the Alaskan testimonies ended Senator Bartlett counted up seventy-eight Alaskan "witnesses," including an equal number of miners and biologists, four women representing clubs that Olaus Murie had infiltrated, seven Alaskan politicians opposed to the range, eleven guides or outfitters, three conservationists, four businessmen, four state officials, one librarian, one logger, and one trapper. Of these people, forty-five were in favor of the range, thirty-one were opposed, and two suggested that the bill be rewritten. Thanks to the Muries, the tide—albeit a miniscule vote—had turned in Alaska.

In the waning days of the Eisenhower administration, on December 6, 1960, the Secretary of the Interior proclaimed the

Arctic National Wildlife Range by Public Land Order 2214. Although the nine-million-acre range had been closed to mining—making Bartlett and other Alaskan politicians appear to have shot themselves in the feet—the fine print read that the range could be opened for oil and gas exploration.

As early as the mid-twentieth century, forces in Washington, D.C., were maneuvering for Alaskan oil. The dense and shrewdly written Public Land Order 2214 revoked Public Land Order 82, lifting military closures on millions of acres west of the Arctic National Wildlife Range, allowing Alaska to acquire the oil riches of Prudhoe Bay. The Interior Department solicitor cannily acknowledged this as quid pro quo for creating the new Arctic National Wildlife Range.*

Meanwhile, in Fairbanks, Celia started a letter to Olaus and Mardy about cabling the Interior Secretary with congratulations, but "we all know the real credit must go to you whose vision conceived it in the first place." Celia also mentioned all the other work to be done with her newly formed Alaska Conservation Society—tipping her hat to Olaus for the good idea.

The next day out at the Moose post office, Mardy received a telegram announcing the creation of the range. She gasped, slid the telegram into her pack, ran outside, and pulled the scarf over her face. Normally she took her time, listening to the juncos and chickadees, but today she bent at the waist to walk faster, as a thin layer of snow squeaked under her Sorrel boots and each breath hung in her slipstream—the strongest breeze that day in all of Jackson Hole.

---

*Ted Stevens authored the land order and would later become famous for crafting hard-to-read legislation. In a 1994 feature story about the Alaskan senator's advocacy for the forty-ninth state, the *Anchorage Daily News* investigative reporter David Whitney wrote: "Stevens works his way most effectively by tagging add-ons to major bills. The bills are usually so long and complex that Stevens' special Alaska provisions are difficult to spot and harder still to decipher."

She made it through the meadows and back into the dark spruce in record time, stopping only long enough to pull her scarf down and take her hat off. Five minutes later, she scurried through the porch; the storm door slammed behind her. She ran past the fire to Olaus, working at the dining-room table on his book *Journeys to the Far North.*

"Oh darlin'," she said, "there's wonderful news today!"

He read the telegram. Then Olaus—the undemonstrative stoic—took Mardy in his arms, and they both wept.

Chapter 9

PRUDHOE BAY AND THE PIPE

This perfection is much more likely to be realized where the hand of man is only reverently and lightly laid upon it.
—C. Edward Graves
"The Wilderness of Beauty"

The ARCO environmental consultant issued our Oil Versus Wilderness students hard hats and visitors' badges as we boarded a tastefully plaid-upholstered, white bus for a tour of Prudhoe Bay. We drove by signs that read CARIBOU HAVE THE RIGHT OF WAY and KEEP IT CLEAN—questionable enforcement, as it turned out, against the reek of spilled diesel fuel and rusted parts and the profusion of steel against tundra. As the bus sent up dust plumes, we bumped north out of Deadhorse and into Prudhoe Bay.

We stopped for the obligatory photographs of a fox den, a single caribou, and a distant family of tundra swans on a hidden pond; long white necks magically gliding back and forth across the tundra. All the while, ARCO's spokesman talked into a microphone. With a vernacular that lacked the southwestern burr usually heard on "the slope," he mentioned how carefully oil companies had integrated themselves into the wilderness, and how unprecedented oil-company studies were making ground-breaking strides toward a new understanding of Arctic bird life and mammal behavior.

"The caribou herd here has increased five times since development," he said. "And the pipeline offers them shade and insect relief."

A hand flew up: "Insect relief?"

"Yes," he replied, "the pipe is cool to the touch and repels bugs."

Our guide pointed to another lone caribou, grazing fearlessly under the pipeline. The bull loped off as our students stepped out of the bus and walked toward the huge oil-processing facility building. "ARCO is entirely self-contained with its water, energy plant, and employee housing," the spokesman said. "Eighty-eight percent of Alaska's economy comes from oil—mostly here at Prudhoe Bay."

He walked us over to the Rolligon, a Cat vehicle used to haul equipment and conduct seismic surveys. Its seven-foot-high, balloon-shaped tires seemed shrunken next to the mobile crane with its ten-foot tires. As the students mugged and posed for photographs beneath the leviathan vehicles, the spokesman explained how the fat, soft tires prevented the vehicles from damaging fragile tundra during oil explorations.

Although the students had prepped with numerous readings, interviews, and "Oil in the Arctic," an environmental report, for the most part they just took notes as our host escorted us through the oil-processing facility. We could not help marveling at the spotless rows of dials and gauges measuring the temperature of "ancient algae that rises naturally out of the ground," our guide said, "at 490 pounds pressure per square inch at 150 degrees Fahrenheit," then are cooled down to 40 degrees with water, which separates gaseous algae from liquid algae, then shot off into "the forty-eight-inch-wide, eight-hundred-point-three-mile-long pipe." Natural gas liquids mixed in with the oil are pumped south into the pipeline.

Since natural gas shoots up out of most of the productive Arctic oil reservoirs, flares above the stations burn around the clock to prevent an explosion. For two months every winter, the gas flares substitute for the total lack of sunlight, and the skyline becomes an otherworldly mixture of yellow light and brown haze as the thermometer bottoms out as low as sixty-two degrees below Fahrenheit (the previous January 27). Gases—worthless on the North Slope without a natural gas pipeline—were separated out during the cooling process and whatever didn't burn off in the flares was pumped back into the underground reservoir to help maintain the underground pressure.

At the drill station, we learned how mud was pumped down nearly two miles to carry back up drill-pulverized rock and lubricate the drill bit. Mud holds down the pressurized petroleum, preventing the well from blowing or gushing out. After the hole is drilled, a narrower steel pipe casing is inserted and injected with cement, which flows out the bottom and lines the hole around the casing. After the cement dries, the casing is removed and holes are made with guns that shoot charges at periodic depths to access the "pay zone" of oil-bearing rock: pressurized oil, gas, or water then flows up the hole.

With directional drilling, the oil companies can bore down several thousand feet, and then drill out at a forty-five-degree angle, reaching as far as six miles from a single platform. They hit pay dirt in rock formations as deep as nine thousand feet and as old as 120 million years; the algae had originally percolated and permeated through formations 200 million years older.

They claimed that each drill bit lasted only ten hours and cost $3,000. The oil companies paid the Iñupiat-owned North Slope Borough $1,000 for each dumpster of trash they disposed. The consultant impressed upon us a myriad of overriding operating expenses, salaries, and transportation costs. Then our brightest student asked, "How many barrels a day are going down the pipeline?"

"Two million," he replied.

"How much does a barrel of oil sell for?"

"Twenty-nine dollars, so you can do the math: ARCO made a profit last year. But millions go right back into exploration and environmental studies."

The students scribbled. The consultant talked. The students asked more questions.

Our guide had been with ARCO for a dozen years, he had a graduate degree in biology, and he was polite, articulate, and solicitous of our comfort as he led us to the cafeteria and a hot meal. At the spotless table under blaring white fluorescent lights, our group looked as tranquilized as the morning's caribou.

"What about the fish here?" another student asked. "Isn't it true that oil development along the shore will endanger millions of passing fish?"

The consultant replied that it wasn't his field. He answered another question by saying that the gravel roads would be completely rehabilitated when the oil companies left, although there would be some "imprints." When asked what would happen to the toxic drilling muds seeping back up into the permafrost he replied, "ARCO is committed to leaving no footprint."

To answer a question about the effects of toxic substances and air pollution on the tundra he said, "It's still being studied." And when "Oil in the Arctic" was invoked, with its charges of oil-company damage to the tundra, he retorted, "*That* report is filled with errors." A momentary silence came over our group as he continued, "The report's claimed decline in predators at Prudhoe Bay is not based on any study."

As ARCO's hired flak-taker, he was long accustomed to being grilled by politicians and environmentalists. In comparison, our young group might have resembled the easily separated mixture of subterranean oil and gas: We just needed a bit of chilling.

He could see that the students were lethargic from their lunch and the previous day's marathon drive on the 400-mile-long Haul Road. The public face of ARCO, our guide had presented himself as a fair-minded yet intelligent savior of the Arctic. He also knew what our upper-middle-class, well-dressed, and respectful group of young people wanted to hear, so he adroitly shifted gears and maneuvered out of another combative Q-and-A session:

> ARCO is heavily committed to alternative energy sources, and although oil is where you find it, we plan to incorporate location into compromise and make good solid judgments for the best use of the land. For the future, we need to conserve energy, find more oil, yet find alternatives, because conservation is like finding oil.

THAT EVENING, in our sagging Deadhorse hotel, I performed the weekly review of student journals. Most of our group remained respectful of the consultant but unmoved by ARCO's blatant display of technology. The lined pages were filled with more questions than answers. One student facetiously wrote that "the environmentalists really have their work cut out for them to convince consumer America that caribou and flowers are better than a strong, proud country with no dependency on the commie Arabs." Someone noted the black smoke wafting past our hotel. Another student found it "highly doubtful that a three-foot raised gravel highway will ever reseed and revegetate the same way the tundra does."

Lit by the midnight sun, I walked with a small group of the students. It was a surreal evening, and since most locals here moved about in huge trucks, we blocked traffic until we jumped off the road's high shoulders down onto soggy tundra. We were bathed in light that warmed our skin, reddened the tundra, and softened the hard edges of an abandoned I-beam. For a moment, I imagined our intimate little group plunged into a French impressionist landscape portrait—until I lifted my head up for the big picture.

Airplane hangers filled the foreground. In the distance, oil derricks and giant flares candled the sky; six oil-producing fields surrounded us. The icy north wind blew litter past puddles of mud and oil. A fox chewed on an apple core while a snowy owl glided low across the tundra, then swerved to miss an oncoming truck. The swath of tundra and its animals appeared so twisted against the imported tons of steel and raised gravel that a wilderness lover could only feel that everything was broken—but perhaps an industrialist would see this as landscape miraculously transformed. We turned back to the hotel.

Culturally, this itinerant blue-collar town of two thousand men and perhaps twenty women was attuned to newsstands selling pornography and renting videos. Alcohol and weapons were forbidden, yet security guards routinely shot hungry bears—both brown and white—as they broke into buildings or chomped on garbage. Oil-company time comprised a week on, then a week off with a quick 727 flight south, heavily stocked with booze, courtesy of ARCO or BP.

The two hotel restaurants did a brisk trade in steak and potatoes, and after we sat down one of the students inquired about vegetarian entrées. Our waitress put the pen on her lip, stared down at her check pad, and laughed with what seemed like apprehension.

We were surrounded by barely graying plumbers and welders and truck drivers and mechanics advertising state-of-the art heavy machinery on their ball caps and forking up dinner with great gusto. Beards and even waxed moustaches abounded. These hairy faces paid no attention to the longhaired, upper-middle-class students with soft hands and fleshy, innocent visages. The men were coughing, wearing bags under their eyes, and the tension in their necks and backs showed that they worked hard for a living that would allow most of them to retire young.[*]

---

[*]Initially, the lowest-grade, uneducated pipeline laborers were making $10.67 per hour, double the standard construction wages of the mid 1970s. Overtime pay, then and now, allows many North Slope workers (often from out of state) to double their income. According to the 2003 Alaska Department of Labor Economic Trends, today's "average" Prudhoe Bay oil worker earns $96,158.

A clean-shaven Princess Tours bus driver—who had just dropped off three dozen senior citizens to admire the oil facilities—stopped at our table to try to figure out what could possibly attract this group to visit the slope. He asked, "What brings you all to lovely Deadhorse, Alaska?"

He had a receding chin, his gray uniform sleeves were too short for his long arms, and he spoke with an unusual falsetto. Under the circumstances, his friendly curiosity seemed like a breath of fresh air, so we invited him to sit down and join us. He perked up and listened intently as he learned that we were studying oil versus wilderness. The title of our course made immediate sense to him.

"Twenty-five years ago this was all a wasteland," he said. "Now look at it: It's a modern industrial complex!"

▲ ▲ ▲

Olaus Murie's eyes went wide as he stumbled upon the Pan American Oil Company's abandoned gasoline cans, boxes, and oil containers. The tundra was burned and brown where toxic chemicals had spilled. Cigarette butts littered the ground, and a grizzly had strewn cans and garbage in a broad swath. Over two days, Olaus returned to what he called this "debris of civilization devastating the Arctic wilderness," to lug it back to his own camp to burn or bury it.

Although abandoning trash in the wilderness was a routine practice through the 1960s, Olaus and the small crowd of conservationists he kept company with were ahead of their time in burying and eliminating all traces of their passage. If he had lived into the 1970s, he would have begun flying out all of his trash, following the new environmental ethic that promoted the value of untainted wilderness.

That June 1961, as a show of his belief in the restorative powers of the Arctic, he and Mardy had returned to their range. They spent the first two weeks alone, camped at the headwaters of the

Sheenjek shooting motion picture film, studying birds, and reading to each other from the mannered Henry James. Mardy fussed over her husband and his insomnia, and they spent rainy hours in the tent, listening to Wilson's snipe and the whistle of the upland plover with their eyes closed like opera fans.

When the rain stopped, Mardy could not help but envy how her terminally ill husband could still pad smoothly across tussocked tundra, his head cocked for the movement of all creatures from grizzlies to ladybugs. By now the reputations of Olaus and Adolph Murie had been firmly cemented: they strode like cats because in their years studying animal gaits and tracks and sign, the cat family proved cleaner and more efficient—claws retracted, light footed, high leaping, scat buriers—than people, wolves, or bears.

If Olaus tired while springing across the tussocks, he'd drop to the ground (to Mardy's initial consternation) and spend the next hour ruminating. He wrote in his journal: "I watch [the nymph] and see him intently exploring, obviously seeking what he must have, whatever that is, just as important to him as our presidential election to us, probably even more vital, though it be encompassed in a small world of bark and grass and water a few feet in diameter."

While the Sheenjek Valley was a remote and intact wilderness, the Muries worried that ordinary nature lovers might not feel stimulated. Without an interest in Latin taxonomy, or basic botany, the omnipresent mosquitoes and midsummer snowstorms were distracting. Paddlers too might feel bored by the river's meanders, while mountain climbers would find little more than aerobic, uphill plods on ancient, shattered seabeds. And those who sought only material gain—be it black gold or sport hunts—habitually harvested their quarry and left quickly, often dumping their trash (witness the Pan American debris). But for people who took delight in birds or wrote articles titled "Adventuring with Arctic Flowers," or "Why Birds Sing," the region seemed miraculous.

Olaus had expanded his interpretation of birds beyond pure science and into the realm of both art and intuition. Originally, he had shot and enjoyed eating birds and other animals as part of his work as a scientist and as a collector for the Carnegie Museum. Now as a graying conservationist, he had moved onto a different level of appreciation.* He no longer believed in hunting, let alone carrying guns. He had shot enough bears in his life to know that it took more than a rifle to defend oneself properly.

While looking for grizzlies and categorizing hundreds of birdsongs around the Sheenjek River, he began to wonder if their voices involved more than simply establishing territory. He wondered if scientists had become timid about assigning the mental or psychological traits of man to birds, as if to deliberately build a wall between humans and animals. Although he knew full well of the danger of anthropomorphizing, after a half-century of observing animals he knew that nature could never be so simple. He decried Walt Disney's childish cartoon renditions of wild animals. Still, he drew his specimens in *Animal Tracks* and elsewhere with Buddha-calm faces.

On his last trip observing wildlife in the Arctic, Olaus had begun preparing "Why Do Birds Sing" for the *Wilson Bulletin,* an ornithological journal. The editor cautioned Olaus that his ideas about birds might not have wide scientific backing; Olaus merely

---

*In a 1913 letter to his brother, Olaus wrote, "I shot a fine male harlequin duck! . . . . I crept up to the rock cautiously, looked over the top, over across a little hollow, and there, on a point of rock, on a little ledge, with the surf dashing all around sat the little speckled beauty. It seemed a dream, but I raised the gun automatically and fired, and the duck fell into the surf." The year before, Olaus wrote home and carefully detailed a silver pheasant and how he tried to capture it with an oil brush, following the tradition of Audubon, Agassiz, and Seton, who shot many animals before resurrecting them in paintings. Olaus also traded his paintings for a sawed-off shotgun and sent it home. And he reminded his brothers to keep up their subscriptions to the ornithological journals the *Condor* and the *Auk.*

smiled in response, knowing that the editor was really trying to protect his reputation. Olaus didn't care.

His writing remained uncluttered and free of overstatement, if only because of the years of scientific training. Yet he had come to believe that animals shared characteristics of human behavior that old-fashioned scientists were unwilling to acknowledge. And equally important, that humans shared the same instinctual processes as the animals.

In the Arctic, he spent hours listening to great horned owls hooting back and forth, one in a low tone—"*hoo hoodoo hoooo hoo*"—the other in high tone—"*hoo hoodoo hoooo hoo.*" He couldn't help but wonder if the birds were saying something to each other, and what would they care to repeat over such a long period of time? Olaus thought it more scientific to assume that they "liked" hearing one another's voices. No different from two singing humans. After a lifetime of contemplating this animal music, he believed that he had developed an ear for birdsong and he began to enjoy the rhythms and the transitions and the poetry as an end unto itself.

Although the air filled with returning birds of spring, Lobo Lake was still ice covered. Behind his and Mardy's tent, the tundra stretched south in a sea of lumpy, waved tussocks. Looking over the tangled willows and dwarf birch and snow-streaked mountains, Olaus thought that most people might not enjoy the stillness. Sometimes it grew so quiet you could hear ringing in your ears. But he and Mardy reveled in their distance from civilization, their freedom and their closeness with nature. Still, in its remoteness and its strangeness, he couldn't help comparing the Arctic to the moon.

As they first made camp, Mardy shouted, "There are two Bohemian waxwings!" Then a yellow-shafted flicker and some bank swallows flew past. They saw a diminutive-looking short-eared owl, numerous tree and white-crowned sparrows, two ravens croaking, northern phalaropes bobbing for bugs in the open water, a lesser yellowlegs walking stiltlike on shore, and least sandpipers pecking the tundra.

A golden eagle sailed gigantically across the cloudless sky. On the opposite shore of the lake, a common snipe winnowed and cliff swallows flew by, making Olaus and Mardy wonder if the birds would nest up in the cliffs on the mountains behind the Sheenjek.

All throughout the continuous, twenty-four hours of daylight, they took inspiration from the banshee-like, guttural cry of the male ptarmigans. The white-bodied, brown-winged males crowed ubiquitous and loud, perching on treetops and knolls, advertising their sex. Since nesting season had begun, the females had lost their winter-white camouflage, turning silent and brown-speckled as they sat hidden on their nests.

The old squaws cried "*a-ha-we, a-ha-we, a-ha-we*" from nearby lakes. Mardy observed a flock flying upriver, only to ride back down again, then fly back up and repeat their ride, gamboling and splashing noisily in the current. Since she couldn't see them catching food, she felt certain that the ducks were simply expressing that which was normally only ascribed to mammals: a reverence of life found through playfulness.

Their summer passed with exquisite slowness. Ice melted off the lake. Birds splash-landed in flocks. And the sun circled round and round the visible horizon. Olaus, it turned out, was engaged in a radical experiment: trying to heal his cancer by listening to the squawking of American widgeons, green-winged teals, white-winged scoters, scaups, pintails, and shovellers.

They also shared the Sheenjek with Bonaparte's, herring, and mew gulls. But what excited the Muries more than any other bird was the pair of nesting Arctic loons on the lake. Olaus would never commit to such speculation in writing, but Mardy was romantically drawn by the knowledge that the birds mated for life. Her husband spent hours painting the birds—their luminescent black-and-white striping, the gracefully curved necks, and the red fire in their eyes—for an oil work that he would present to Mardy.

As he compiled his notes about these bird encounters, he and Mardy discussed how people were so scared of anthropomorphizing that they were no longer using their imaginations. Then he finished drafting the *Wilson Bulletin* article, with its quintessential paragraph:

> I would urge the validity of drawing upon human experience in the interpretation of bird song. This sentence by itself can be shocking to the scientist and misleading. . . . It appears silly to deny to other animals a sense of well being, of satisfaction, enthusiasm—many of the fundamental reactions that we all share. Of course we must be extremely cautious in imputing to other animals the more specialized reactions of man, especially those resulting from his cultural experience. To say that a bird sings "in praise of his maker" may be logically assailed by the scientist, since it is a concept out of man's formalized organization of thought. But to say that a bird sings because it is happy may not be incorrect, if we consent to use terms out of the vernacular, with their fundamental meanings.

Before leaving, he and Mardy walked over to the river. They couldn't get enough of it, this remote Walden that had come to define their lives as modern-day Thoreaus. "We looked and looked," Mardy wrote, "and then we looked through tears." Olaus uncharacteristically waxed sentimental in his journal, as if he was writing his own epitaph:

> How we feel about this place! The birds, the flowers, the place—yes, even the clouds out there above the landscape,

even though they bring us rain. We looked at each other. It is not sure that one person can read the feelings of another. Yet as we looked at each other, I am sure each of us read [one another] all right—a sad but deep feeling when you say goodbye to what you love. . . . How we will miss it all. . . . How we love it all!

MARDY AND OLAUS spent the winter in dry and restorative Tucson. In February 1963, he managed to finish an article for the *Naturalist*. In the cover letter, he wrote, "There is not much time left."

Another journalist met with them back in Moose. She expected them to be woodsy hermits, but quickly learned that they were well traveled, between various Congressional hearings, and trips to New Zealand, Norway, and Europe. Olaus had turned seventy-three, but came outside thinly clad and bareheaded on a cold day. He gushed with his usual "O gee whiz," and "Shucks" as deep creases lifted his face up into a set of parallel smiles. The journalist wrote that his gray-blue eyes looked young, but the photographs accompanying her story showed a man stooped and whittled by cancer, despite his outlandish smile.

A month later, he convinced Mardy that they should travel to Alaska one more time, for the annual Wilderness Society conference. Adolph's photograph shows the brothers posing atop Cathedral Mountain above wolf country in McKinley Park. They stood a foot apart, hands on hips, with their arms and torsos framing the airy depths of braided rivers several thousand feet below. Olaus wore a tan chamois shirt and squinted into Adolph's camera with a wan smile, waiting for the timer to trip the shutter. His half-brother, sixty-one, sported a stylish crew cut. Adolph's hair had gone white twenty years earlier from pernicious anemia, a chronic autoimmune disease that prevents vitamin absorption. Still, he grinned like a wolf amid the pack, shouldering the rucksack frame that Olaus could no longer carry. Collectively, the brothers fought for and accomplished more on behalf of Alaskan wilderness and wildlife than any pair of biologists gone north. But the Murie men had now shot their bolts.

By the time Mardy helped Olaus limp back to Moose in early August, he croaked, "We made it!"

Within weeks, Mardy began trying to relieve the pain brought on by the cancer, now consuming his lungs and stomach. Olaus did not flinch when she twisted the band on his arm, waited for the vein to pop up, slid the needle under the skin, and then gently pushed in the gift of morphine.

On their August 19 wedding anniversary, she took Olaus to the Jackson Hole hospital. He couldn't walk, let alone stand. Mardy read to him from a new book about the Minnesota boundary waters, finding that she could scarcely control her emotions, even though Olaus loved to be read to. Still, Mardy wrote upbeat letters, and told the author Sig Olson how much *Singing Wilderness* meant to Olaus.

Adolph stayed in Moose. He couldn't watch his brother die in such a compromised state.

Numerous friends visited, and while Mardy stepped out, Olaus insisted to one couple that Mardy had more books to write, and they should make sure that she used her talents after he was gone.

On October 20, his lungs had filled with fluid. Mardy's half-sister Louise thought he was dying, and Mardy begged him not to leave, even though he'd hung around to make it through their wedding anniversary, which they always celebrated two months late, on October 19. So Olaus found the strength to sit up. To persevere. And to cough his lungs clear. He smiled and while he seemed to regain lucidity, the doctor had to repeatedly tell him what he was suffering from.

The next morning, thinking that Olaus had improved, Mardy

ran into town on an errand. Suddenly, Olaus sat up again with a superhuman effort, and speaking more eloquently than in the last few weeks he told Louise, "You know, we have to find out what we're here for. That's what life is all about."

He took a last gasp. His lungs wouldn't clear. His face stilled.

Louise, characteristically a stoic, burst into tears.

MARDY SCATTERED OLAUS'S ASHES about the ranch, reading aloud from the epitaph about autumn that they'd included in a book they had been writing together. Despite the help of friends and family, her best consolation still came from Olaus, through his reams of letters. Although she had steadfastly replied to and then ripped up other letters, she kept everything that Olaus ever touched with a pen. She eventually typed them all, to save them for posterity. He had written to her:

> You are in my heart forever. I will go on and will enjoy these Arctic days, and when I see the growing moon, the shifting tints in these winter skies, the mountains and all, to my mind you will be beside me, doing it all with me.
>
> Best wishes to your family, and to you—all I've got.

The *Washington Post* obituary mentioned his numerous commendations. The next day's edition read, "To the thousands of people who had hiked or camped with Olaus J. Murie or had talked with him on a mountain trail, he was Mr. Wilderness." Although Olaus never professed to be more than a country scientist who tramped the streets of the capital, dismayed by the manner of politicians, puzzled over cracked vases and Japanese art, the editorial concluded that he was "a highly civilized being who had acquired an aura of nobleness from the wilds that he loved so much."

The flood of clippings, letters, and support gave Mardy some small help. But for nine months she couldn't put her life back on track. Since living at the ranch reminded her too much of Olaus, she fled to live near her mother in Seattle.

Mardy's sense of mission returned at the end of her first summer without Olaus. She came back to Moose and installed a telephone. Early one morning a call from the Secretary of the Interior's office woke her up with news that the president would be signing landmark environmental legislation that Olaus had fought for.[*]

She was so overwhelmed that she lay in bed, thinking, " 'Oh, go 'way; leave me alone, I just don't feel like doing anything!' But as I lay there I got to thinking, and remembered the thing that Olaus said so often to me: 'Say yes Mardy, don't say no.' " Next she had to battle her chronic fear of flying. But once the bouncing, twin-engine plane climbed above Jackson Hole, she took consolation in the lurid orange sun lighting the plane's eastern course into the darkness over the nation's capital.

As MARDY SOUGHT IMMORTALITY for her husband by publishing more of his work, Washington politicians helped bring progress to northern Alaska. Mardy began writing letters to these lawmakers, trying to prevent the eight-hundred-mile pipeline from "zippering the state in two."

In 1968, ARCO and the Humble Oil & Refining Company announced a major Arctic oil strike. These companies, along with the other major oil consortiums, believed that there were at least nine billion gallons of oil beneath the coast just west of Mardy's

---

[*]President Johnson, as a powerful senator, had been courted by Senator Bartlett and Solicitor Stevens to end the Alaskan statehood blockade. The Wilderness Act Johnson was about to sign would set aside nine million acres of federally protected land, without roads or logging, and review another fifty million acres (eventually including ANWR) for potential inclusion. His Secretary of the Interior, Stewart Udall, had already foiled Senator Bartlett's repeated attempts to overturn the Public Land Order for the Arctic National Wildlife Range.

sacred range, and in a year's time, Alaska sold off a half-million acres of Prudhoe Bay for $900 million. What developers and politicians had called the quid pro quo—the Arctic National Wildlife Range for oil—had finally paid off. The next trick would be piping all this black gold to waters that weren't blocked by sea ice.

Mardy suspected that it would only be a matter of time before they began seismic explorations all over the North Slope. She wrote to Phillips Petroleum in 1970 that "they were taking over so much of the Arctic for one purpose alone." The manager of public relations replied that "their oil operations would occupy a very small part of this forbidding wilderness area," not realizing that the old maid had run dogs and bivouacked beneath the northern lights in fifty below—in a place that she thought of as anything but forbidding. His sanctimonious reply shocked Mardy, with its platitudes that the oil companies were actually "protecting the environment" and just going to where "nature placed the oil in the ground." She made a note in her journal to send another letter to the Pan American Oil Company, along with Olaus's photographs, showing the mess that they'd made in the Arctic National Wildlife Range.

Even reluctant activist Adolph briefly took up the letter-writing campaign. Without Olaus around to temper his lofty ideals, Adolph's correspondence had grown surly, complaining about diminished book royalties, roads being built through parks, and biologists who stooped to radio collaring wolves instead of taking the time to watch the wolves without tranquilizing them or otherwise interrupting their lives as wild animals.

Several years earlier, Adolph had been diagnosed with epilepsy, which added to the annoyances of chronic malaria and pernicious anemia. He had long since learned to distrust doctors, beginning with his father's and stepfather's deaths from tuberculosis, his brother Martin's death during routine tonsillitis surgery, and the limitations of modern medicine that may have cured Olaus's TB but only seemed to bring on his cancer. Adolph also hated the idea of being medicated in the same way he objected to modern biologists who tranquilized and radio collared wolves. His family noticed him discreetly slipping the prescribed Valium pills into his pocket rather than into his mouth.

In February 1971, he wrote to the president and the Secretary of the Interior to protest the proposed Alaskan pipeline. He suggested a long-term freeze on the project, and reminded them of a tanker collision and oil spill several days earlier in San Francisco Bay that had killed thousands of birds. Even eight years after his brother's death, Adolph repeatedly mentioned Olaus's name in that short letter.

But the pipeline was unstoppable.* Japanese steel mills shipped over one hundred thousand lengths of forty- and sixty-foot steel pipe. Workers in Valdez and Fairbanks then welded forty-two thousand double joints, connecting two sections of pipe together, before the sections were trucked to the field and laid down in a fashion that would allow the pipeline to expand and contract in a zigzag, rather than lengthwise. This engineering novelty allowed the pipe to move according to 200-degree variations in temperature—each forty feet of pipe expands or contracts 0.031 inches with each ten-degree change in temperature. Despite the excess of overpaid laborers speaking in colorful Texas oil patch twang, "the pipe" burgeoned into a working man's fantasy. No one dressed in overalls

---

*In October 1973, Syria and Egypt invaded Israel. To retaliate for American military aid to Israel, Arab members of OPEC stopped exporting oil to the United States. So began the panicked and oft-repeated oil lobbyists' cry: America must wean herself from foreign oil and further develop her own resources. In November 1973, after Alaska senator Mike Gavel wrote a pipeline amendment, after Senator Ted Stevens crafted legislation to quell noisy environmentalists, and after Vice President Spiro Agnew broke the tie vote in the Senate, President Nixon signed the Pipeline Authorization Act. Some twenty-eight thousand workers began plumbing the eight-hundred-mile-long pipe. Soon enough, most Alaskans were touting "the pipe" as the Northern version of the Egyptian pyramids and the Great Wall of China.

cared that the pipeline had been budgeted at $900 million before costs doubled, and then tripled.

Three years prior to the pipeline's completion, Adolph Murie took an evening stroll toward the Snake River. He walked past the garden toward the deep forest on a trail imprinted more by hooves than Vibram. Ever the purist, Adolph ducked under and climbed over the log blowdowns he refused to ax off this route to Mardy's favorite swimming hole, shared with the big ungulates of the forest, a badger, and cavorting common goldeneyes. Alone and without medication, when the seizure hit, it prompted a fall, cushioned by the soft forest litter. Alone in his woods, Adolph choked to death.

He had reached seventy-four, the same age that claimed Olaus. Adolph's friends knew him as a skeptic, the darker and more complex half of his adored brother. In death, Adolph had managed to escape the awkwardness of bedside visitors in a hospital reeking of the solutions that he used to jar insect specimens. Adolph died as he lived his life, avoiding compromise.

Mardy and Louise scattered Adolph's ashes outside his north-facing cabin and Olaus's south-facing studio. They flung Adolph's ashes into the wind, under the ripening serviceberry, and onto the spruce-needled earth. They scattered the ashes with the same care that they had spread Olaus's about the ranch eleven years ago. As an autumn zephyr swept beneath the granite Tetons, shaking the bows of thick spruce, rattling the aspen leaves, the Murie brothers merged into the archetypal nitrogen cycle that they had dedicated their lives to as field biologists and ecologists.

While their ashes released nitrogen into the soil, the roots of *Pinus contorta, Populus tremuloides,* and *Picea pungens* drew the molecules of these two scientists up toward the sky, and with their donated nitrogen, the arboreal Murie Ranch soon converted the sun's energy into food and new leaves, which would eventually fall back to the ground from whence they came—feeding insects, fungi, animals, and other plants. It may have been a small if not uncommon gesture, but there atop the ancient glacial moraine, Murie atoms continued to mingle in their forest amid the everlasting ecological cycle.

The brothers have also managed durability through their public and private acts, their science, and their art. While Mardy proudly turned down several proposals to tack Olaus's name onto northern landscapes, Louise proudly accepted the McKinley National Park officials' offer to rename the Toklat River flats and its wolf dens after Adolph as "the Plains of Murie." Somehow, this titular honor never made it onto the USGS map.

It remained a blessing to the family that neither of these tundra trampers lived to see Prudhoe Bay, alongside the Arctic National Wildlife Range, bereft of wolves and wolverines, who flee the noise and commotion of this industrial site. The oil fields were all hooked up to the forty-eight-inch steel pipe that snaked its glittering course to Valdez. The pipe ended up costing $8 billion, nine times its original budget. Then the conglomerate of newly enriched companies tried to stake the pipe's claim as the Eighth Wonder of the World— along with a railroad built to Key West, Roosevelt's Panama Canal, a bridge in Montreal, and later oil pipelines in Kazakhstan and Libya.

When oil finally ran down the pipe on June 20, 1977, the *Anchorage Times* headline proclaimed "FIRST OIL FLOWS (After 8 Years, 4 Months, 10 Days)." Four minutes after oil gushed into the pipe, a valve leaked and ignited a catastrophic fire and explosion, killing a man. The would-be Eighth Wonder of the World reopened nine days later, until the next of a dozen leaks—a quarter of a million flammable gallons, rich with toxic benzene and toluene, spread over eight hundred miles and two dozen years—shut it down again.

Chapter 10

TEACHING MOMENTS

Yes, the caribou will have to move again.
Yes, another place, but smaller still,
  will have them.
Yes, their habitat diminishes in increments,
  but we will not notice.
Yes, the tundra is a habitat.
Yes, the tundra is black muck, moss, lichen,
  herbs, small flowers, dwarf shrubs.
Yes, the tundra holds a subsoil of permafrost,
  delicate, and beneath that, a long way back, oil again.
Yes, oil again. The past lives there.
            —Laurie Kutchins
            "Hey Mom, What Does Refuge Mean?"

In an unnamed valley high in the refuge, a grizzly pretended he
didn't smell us and worked his nose back and forth over the tundra—sniffing for ants and grubs and roots—like a Geiger counter.
I asked the students to talk aloud so that the boar above wouldn't
mistake us for a passing herd of caribou.

I held my chin high and walked proudly yet stepped lightly,
hoping to show grace and humility to the bear, as if I were a diplo-
mat for the human race, trying to correct all the aggressive souls
who had come here before me with a gun. Proper bear etiquette,

after all, entailed constant awareness and adept acting. So I tried to pretend that I wasn't carrying a 12-gauge shotgun loaded with two rounds of bird shot and three rifled slugs. Grizzlies might be myopic but they could smell cocky, armed men a mile away.

Night and day, I kept that Remington Wingmaster shotgun within arm's reach. The responsibility for guarding eight young students who might mistakenly surprise a sleeping grizzly in the willows couldn't be taken lightly, in spite of statistics showing that bears never attacked a group of four or more campers.

As we walked, the students discussed what their friends might be doing at home. Shed moose antlers littered the stream bottom; a porcupine sashayed east with us.

After seven days of backpacking, a pretty, freckle-faced twenty-year-old tripped and stumbled under her heavy pack. It all happened in slow motion: her scream, the twisting fall, and my immediate fear that I would have to somehow evacuate her; we were fifty miles from the nearest village. She stoically bit back the pain, her right ankle twisted beneath her. We set up camp early, and she sat on a boulder along the snowmelt creek, icing her foot in the water. She also took two anti-inflammatory tablets to help keep the swelling down.

In the morning, I stirruped her ankle with eight foot-long strips of adhesive tape, mimicking the protection of an intact ankle ligament. She limped, but her ankle was safeguarded under the tight tape, and she would be okay if she kept up the icing sessions and held her foot above her heart during rest breaks.

Like most summer visitors to the refuge, we were hoping to see the Porcupine herd migration. That night while we lounged on a spongy carpet of caribou lichen, as if to whet our appetites, a lone, lost-looking bull sprinted through camp, its antlers flexing and swaying, tight and buoyant as a beauty queen's perm.

We skipped rocks, flipped pancakes, told jokes, and woke up

early the next morning to climb a five-thousand-foot peak. We pushed through calf-nicking willows, hopped up boulders into skies blackening with storm clouds, tiptoed across creaking blocks of limestone, then kicked steps up a final snowfield. The Canning River dropped away at our feet. To the south, purple-turreted towers rose into eight-thousand-foot peaks, spiraled with green glacial ice. To the north, an ocean fog swirled toward us. We caught brief, binocular glimpses of the tepid Sadlerochit springs, the tawny sea spits, and the *aufeis* bluing the muddy deltas. The air smelled faintly rusted and stung my nostrils with the moist premonition of an approaching thunderstorm.

At dawn in clearing skies, I woke up to the liquid notes of an American robin's phrases—"*plurri, kliwi; plurri, kliwi; plurri, kliwi*"—with a long pause in between, before repeating the phrasing. Alternately, the robin whistled or called softly or sang in an eerie duet: producing two notes at once. *Turdus migratorius* (migrating thrush) was a species that our group expected to find plucking worms on a suburban lawn, not plucking microbes out of a glaciated stream in the Arctic.

Several hours later, as if to dispel our chagrin at finding such a familiar bird in this unfamiliar latitude, we heard the clatter of wings above camp: several hundred robins flew up toward the Brooks Range, in mimicry of flocking snow geese. They flew on past earth-twisted towers of brown limestone and gray shale bearded with orange lichen. Their brief shade-cloud alarmed a colony of ground squirrels into high-pitched whistling. And as they continued circling to gain elevation—chirping "*piik, piik, piik*"—a peregrine falcon soared past, too shocked to dive into such a multitude. I couldn't have been more surprised if I had seen the herbivorous caribou eating a fish (which my Athapaskan neighbor once witnessed outside Denali Park).

DURING OUR THREE WEEKS in the refuge, we identified the songs and cries of eiders, thrushes, old squaw, gyrfalcons, warblers, ptarmigan, Lapland longspurs, snow buntings, Canada geese, semipalmated and golden plovers, dowitchers, Arctic terns, northern wheatears, tundra swans, dunlins, bluethroats, sandhill cranes, and several sandpiper species. We often discussed the songs, squawks, caws, crows, bleats, burps, barks, and chips of these and other birds' territorial cues, flight calls, predator warnings, and sex lures.

Dead mice were cached in the forked branches of willows. Predatory shrikes would later fly back to retrieve these meals, landing precisely at one willow cache among a stand of hundreds of willows—a task that would defy cats or monkeys.

This wasn't the only event that made birds appear superior. One evening, a migrating flock of Canada geese came honking over our heads like a team of synchronized swimmers. They stroked their orange-lit wings fluidly and glowed with a collective intelligence and intuition greater than a flock of human fans standing up in a football stadium and performing a wave.

We watched gulls and magpies following bears in anticipation of sharing an animal kill. But most interesting of all were those residents who survived the brutal white winters here. Since I too had made my own adaptations to spend time in the Arctic, maybe I was looking for kindred souls.

One afternoon, craving the animal or bird encounters that could only be found in solitude, I left the students and took a long walk. I stopped at a small, green-scummed spring rippling with insects. Two feet below, the Canning River rushed past with gray turbidity. From an overhanging granite slab, an American dipper bobbed on spring-loaded legs. Quick as a falcon, it dove underwater for a bug. Then this oil-winged amphibious bird of the Arctic popped into the air without shaking off the water.

Cinclus mexicanus, according to most bird guides, does not make it as far north as the refuge and is not considered an Arctic resident. Yet this bird—metallically buzzing *"dzeett, dzeett, dzeett"*—would stay all winter, supported year-round by aquatic insects in the tepid spring.

From the dwarf birch several feet above the river, another year-round resident, the rock ptarmigan, made its distinctive call *"Go backa, go backa, go backa."* Suddenly and noisily it burst from its hiding place, raucously wobbling away in flight. Seen through my binoculars, the notch on the trailing edge of its wing revealed how the ptarmigan, like the other phasianids—chukars and grouse—made quick, explosive takeoffs to evade prey.

As the Canning gurgled by at several miles an hour, grayling skittered through turquoise pools whirlpooling holes into shale. An anorexic-looking yellowlegs nesting in the sedges jumped up and sprinted away calling *"tew tew tew!"*

I passed the tracks of lightweight ground squirrels, web-toed sandhill cranes, cloven-hoofed moose, and a running wolf.

At a stream confluence, I kneeled on a muddy bank for one of my favorite investigations. I grabbed a small stick to poke apart a large grizzly scat sweatered in coarse brown fur that the grizzly had licked off during frequent grooming sessions. The pile was glued together with half-digested and dusky-green wet stems, grubs, and leaves, blued with the omnipresent berries, then laced with white fur, jellied fat, and bone shards.

Adjacent wolf prints showed how an envious *Canis lupus* slowed down to a walk. Rather than primitively poking through the grizzly's digested meal, the wolf stopped and aimed its long nose like a radar gun. Using a sense of smell a hundred times more prescient than mine and his uncanny ability to isolate smells—grizzly fur, willow, moth pupae, dwarf alder, blueberries, Dall sheep—the wolf identified the grizzly's diet with a quick sniff.

Alone next to this wondrous scat pile, I sat down to write in my five-by-seven-inch journal. It seemed an irony of wilderness leadership that guides are transformed into social hosts, rather than being physically challenged. I let out a quick, rejuvenating scream. To my relief, nothing screamed back.

What I had long needed, I scribbled in the journal, was more solo time in the Arctic. And a chance to see the caribou migration. Being alone amid this vast and silent horizon, with polar breezes caressing my hair, would present an excellent opportunity to corner all of my demons, chase away obtrusive self-consciousness, and learn how to simply breathe like an animal.

Feeling better, yet slightly guilty about my absence from camp, I slid the journal and pencil into their fanny-pack residence and turned back north. Like most guides, I worried about stoves torching tents, sprained ankles, and the students taking a miscalculated swim in the ice-cold river. Even worse, I worried about curious eyes peering down the muzzle of the Remington that I left in camp with the experienced sixteen-year-old hunter, so that he could defend his fellow students in case of a marauding grizzly.

I was also excited to get back and share my discovery of a sheep-eating grizzly. Predictably, no one would care about my bird encounters. If any of the impressionable young guys asked me whether I got scared being alone, I would happily admit to it.

Then, with the timing that shows how wilderness intuition is free of coincidence, a chesty and inhuman bawling stopped me in my tracks. An electric shiver went up my spine. I closed my eyes, took off my hat, tilted my head, and waited.

"Owww-ooooooooooooooooooooo." The wolf call rolled down the mountainside for another ten seconds. Then all that remained was the river, whooshing like wind and the thundering within my chest. Every being within a mile listened to that call. I had no idea what the howl meant. The wolf must have been watching me; I couldn't see him. I waited another fifteen minutes, crouched over

the river bar, but the wolf was gone. I stood up slowly, pushed the hair from my eyes, and trotted back to camp.

WE SPENT TEN DAYS floating out to the ocean. Distant bands of caribou and musk oxen wavered past like fuzzy puppets, blurred by the mirage air. As we cleared the muddy deluge rinsing the Brooks Range out to sea, the water turned limpid black. I cupped it into my mouth repeatedly, but I couldn't taste brine until the Canning delta faded from sight.

We tied our kayaks together into rafts, raised a giant tarp tied to our paddles, and sailed west toward Prudhoe Bay. Wildlife disappeared, and in its place we identified oil barrels and gravel-drill pads and the detritus of oil exploration.

Although I hid my opinion about whether I supported oil or wilderness, the students interrogated me. At sea, and in camp, they wouldn't let up.

"Jon," asked one long-faced, pony-tailed teenager who would become an internationally renowned alpinist, "you don't really think that we believe there's any chance you would support the oil companies?"

"Why not?" I asked.

"Because oil-company supporters aren't interested in spending time in the wilderness." This student had all of the qualities of a fine adventurer: patience, curiosity, and a willingness to forgo comfort. It came as no surprise that he was adamantly opposed to developing the coastal plain.

I nodded my head, showing that I'd heard him, and instead of voicing disagreement or support, I asked, sincerely, "Why not?"

He looked exasperated.

On the next-to-last-night out, while keying out rock jasmine and glaucous gentian on the tundra, I saw an opportunity for another teaching moment. I surprised the group by pumping a round of bird shot into the chamber of the Remington. To the west, we all heard the familiar cry: *"Go backa, go backa, go backa."*

"Hold your ears," I said. Double-checking that all eight students stood to the south, I aimed into the northern sky. I clicked off the safety with my forefinger, led the white-brown flying dapple, and kept pivoting the muzzle while gradually squeezing the trigger.

My ears rang from the gun blast as the ptarmigan tumbled out of the sky. The students, appalled, gathered around me as I knelt down and spread its wings two feet across. "Beautiful, isn't it?" I said.

"It's dead," said one girl.

"These birds will turn all white in another two months," I said. "This red supercilium above the eyes means it's a male."

I showed them how the polar-bearish feet and legs had a broad range of feathers that insulated the toes and effectively gave them a set of snowshoes for winter travel. Then I started yanking out quills.

"What are you doing Jon?" one of the boys asked with an accusatory tone.

"Preparing dinner," I replied, "so we can talk about whether eating canned chicken is any different from eating this ptarmigan."

The students, vegetarians and meat eaters alike, were confused as I placed our dinner on a driftwood log and split the naked-looking, foot-long bird down the middle with my Swiss Army knife. I scooped out its crop, which stored intact mosquitoes, green grass, and brown willow stems. My bloodied fingers were shaking, but I hadn't drunk coffee in weeks. I had just killed a bird, a being that instilled lightness and wonder in my time in the wilderness. I knew how to use guns, and I liked to fish, but hunting had never appealed to my sense of sportsmanship.

As we brought noodles to boil in a large pot, I sautéed thin gray strips of ptarmigan flesh in the frying pan. "Has anyone ever thought about the morality of killing your own food," I asked, "versus someone doing it for you at a slaughterhouse?"

Several sets of narrowed eyes said that the students were disgusted. I told the group that I admired the vegetarians' resolve, but that I preferred taking direct responsibility for killing an animal if I was going to continue eating meat. I didn't mention that I had never shot a bird in my life. The students, at least before the shooting, had respected me as a wilderness lover, if not an environmentalist. But their leader suddenly transformed into a hunter, and the students' assumptions were challenged all over again.

As the boiling noodles steamed our red pyramid tarp, we lay in a circle on our stomachs facing dinner, with our legs outside, spoking around the tent. From the hub, someone asked, rhetorically, if we should be hunting animals in order to get to the answers about choosing oil versus wilderness. Someone else pondered aloud about whether the two were mutually exclusive.

I said that the Muries had originally created the refuge so that people could express their love of wilderness by backpacking, bird-watching, river running, mountain climbing, performing science, or hunting. "For forty years, the refuge has been open for hunters to shoot birds, caribou, musk oxen, moose, even wolves. And none of these animal populations have declined as a result. But tell the general public that ANWR draws hundreds of hunters each year, and animal lovers everywhere would be appalled."

Since none of the students cared for the stringy ptarmigan meat—which tasted of soured pond scum—I resolutely ate it myself, and made a silent pact to never again carry guns in the refuge. Let alone kill an animal.

Out in the tundra swales to the west, toward the oil flare at Endicott, a loon deepened the space surrounding us, yodeling: *"owiiil-ka, owiiil-ka, owiiil-ka!"*

The future alpinist got everyone back on track: "Well here we are in the Prudhoe Bay oil fields, and since this land belongs to all of us, how are we protecting the wilderness by allowing the oil companies to drill here?"

BACK IN FAIRBANKS, in spite of our best efforts as teachers not to unduly influence the students, only one believed that oil development should be allowed in the refuge. The other fourteen students rode this "developer" mercilessly. The latest Alaskan poll declared that our lone voice of development belonged to a huge majority of the state's population who supported drilling on the coastal plain.

Our student advocate for oil development was also the oldest and funniest member of our tribe, so he defended his position without losing face. He proposed that 15 percent of all federal money from the development of the coastal plain be used to establish a conservation fund to promote natural resources, that we raise automobile fuel standards from 27 to 30 miles per gallon to lower our nation's demands for oil, and that as a remembrance, the development of the coastal plain "will make us think of the heavy price we have paid for the gains, so that perhaps this solution will never be needed again."

In the university dorm, we sat cross-legged on the floors, since we had become unaccustomed to chairs. The other instructors and I smiled as the students argued their positions. I had come to know and respect all fifteen of them. I had learned from their idealism and shared the wilderness with them, but more than anything else, they had given me hope. They *all* really cared about what happened to the wilderness, and *all* of them, pro-wilderness or pro-development, went home pledging to present public lectures about the refuge.

Everyone flew home deeply affected. Even the instructors were struck by the inevitable consciousness of reentering civilization: how not to take hot showers for granted, the perplexity of mindless speeding in city traffic after contemplative paddling in wilderness, and the delicious foods from which we had abstained so long. Many of us had lost weight.*

---

*Some of the students were so moved by this wilderness course that they would describe it to us years later as the most powerful experience of their teens. No one failed.

As a guide, my lessons learned from our Oil Versus Wilderness course were different from the students'. I never thought myself a teacher, because we were all learning together—withholding hasty judgments, listening to all sides of the controversy, and carefully making our final conclusions. Our teacher was the refuge. If we came away with any new insights, it was because we let the wilderness speak for itself. As a facilitator of that experience, my conclusions also came from years spent gauging the strengths and weaknesses of my outdoor companions. Although I had splinted broken legs and performed rescues of people not attached to my groups, it was not just luck that partners, clients, or students hadn't been badly hurt or killed during my trips. I shepherded my charges like that wolf hidden on the mountainside, figuring out what scared them and made them laugh, or how they could keep on walking after they sprained their ankles. And when people were frightened, I could feel it coming, even though being scared didn't deter people from revering the wilderness. To the contrary, primal experiences often became a reawakening.

The inexplicable genetic coding that allows some people to withstand discomforts and appreciate wild places—like that of the birds and mammals of the refuge—has more to do with intuition than intelligence. To revere wilderness one needs a capacity to revere natural beauty or art, an active curiosity tinged with humility, and an ability to accept fear.

⌂ ⌂ ⌂

Several decades before his death, the humble scientist sat with pen in mouth admiring a winter thrush burbling a melody over Wyoming's Wetstone Creek. As the four children in camp began building a fire ring, Olaus jumped up. After all, this was a training trip, and he was the experienced woodsman.

"Martin," he told his son, "there's a big flat one; let's move it over a little so the girls can use it as a kitchen table." As Olaus began pushing the sharp-edged boulder, it slipped and fell, gashing his thumb. Blood gushed out. The children froze. His teaching moment had arrived.

"Well," Olaus asked, "what have you learned in first aid?"

Alma Ruth recovered her poise and directed their elder woodsman to sit on a rock while she wrapped a handkerchief around the bleeding thumb. She then produced a bandage from her pack, while Martin, under Olaus's gaze, started the fire with only two matches. As the boys heated soup for their injured father, the girls fashioned a sling to hold Olaus's arm up and keep the thumb from throbbing.

He then took them down to Wetstone Creek. Since they were now in charge and ready to listen, he introduced them to *Cinclus mexicanus*, bobbing on a rock above the stream, crying "*dzeett, dzeett, dzeett.*" Olaus let them wade in and find the dipper's nest of sticks under a waterfall as he stood back listening to their muted squeals of delight. Later they found a band of elk, passing on the skyline above the waterfall. By trip's end, he felt wiser from his time around these kids, three of whom were his children. He felt that young people with a balanced education and an ability to act on their curiosity would make the world a better place to live in.*

AFTER OLAUS DIED, Mardy kept up their legacy of honoring young people. In 1967 she began mentoring the summer biology courses at the Teton Science School (TSS), across the valley from the Murie Ranch. Eventually, the school developed a year-round environmental-education curriculum. The TSS, and other schools from around the country, began visiting the Murie Ranch. Mardy

---

*Six decades later, Martin wrote an introduction for a book of his father's stories: "One thing to watch for—he's trying to catch you, enlist you in the struggle for wilderness. That became his agenda, sometime in the thirties, if not before."

served the students lemonade as she pulled out her husband's note-books and card files and paints, trying to imbue students with a sense of wonder for how an old-time naturalist worked. Mardy claimed that she never caught a look of boredom on anyone's face.

As she grew more and more impressed with their powers of retention, she began taking trail walks with children on a regular basis. She avoided preaching, at all costs, and eventually the children began teaching *her* about sense of direction, where to find the fish, and the habits of wildlife they encountered.

In May 1974 a Jackson Hole High School teacher—who knew of the power of such role models—challenged his students to find a graduation speaker. So three teenagers wound up drinking tea and eating cry-baby cookies in Mardy's living room. Since they had grown up in a Wyoming ranching community, none of them resem-bled suburban environmentalists, but they were "aware" as one of them put it, "of the outdoors." They had come to ask Mardy to speak in front of their class because of her reputation as an author and a local who had seen some of the world. Since they had no clue that Mardy was an "icon of conservation," they asked what she could speak about.

"Whatever you think you should hear," she replied.

So in mid-June Mardy Murie stood up in front of the Jackson Hole High School graduating class. She deliberately abstained from proselytizing wilderness and used only a minute of her half-hour speech to mention that it was important for young people to dis-cover who they really are, and that this can't be done without learn-ing about the natural world.

Mardy then looked them in the eyes and told them to take part in what was happening in their community, their state, and their nation. She told them to get into politics.

She told them that they were going to be the decision makers—"but don't be afraid to get in there; it will be a big adventure. Bring to it what my sea-going father called 'That divine thing: Enthusiasm, and that other life-giving quality: Curiosity.' "

By now Mardy had become accustomed to standing ovations, and clearly she had inspired the 1974 graduating class of Jackson Hole High. The speech changed at least one eighteen-year-old's life.

Something about Mardy—her interest in kids, her warm empathy, her ability as a teacher—made the boy, Mike, want to get to know her. Over the years, as she became more in demand as a speaker, he graduated from Colorado College and moved back to the valley, even as his parents moved out. Unlike Mardy's many female disciples, the young man was not a bird-watcher, a granola cruncher, or even a Democrat. He was not looking for a surrogate mother either, but since his grandmothers were long gone, she filled this niche perfectly.

He spent several holidays with her. He teased her about hand-feeding wild pine martens within a national park; she encouraged him to marry a good gal who would make him happy. In the falls, and particularly on October 19, after the sandpipers and cranes had migrated through, in yearly celebration of a wedding anniversary celebrated two months late, she read to him from her husband's letters: "How I wish you were with me right now," Olaus wrote, as he and Adolph embarked on the caribou study:

> We are up on a summit, the night is silver clear, with twinkling stars and a pure crescent moon. I was out a moment ago to look at it and think of you at the same time. The spruces stand all around, straight and still. The dogs lie curled in dark blurs on the snow.

Since getting to know Mardy had sparked Mike's interest in conservation, he went to law school at the University of Oregon and became involved in the Jackson Hole Conservation Alliance.

Eventually, he got involved in politics while living in Washington, D.C., and working as the executive assistant for the director of the USFWS.

Call it serendipity or fate, but the director, John Turner, had grown up in the same valley. Since he was a dozen years older than Mike, his boyhood role model had been Olaus. Mimicking Olaus in the late 1940s, John had expanded his scat collection: coyotes, moose, elk, mule deer, bears, and even a few owl pellets. Since this large and uncontained assemblage quickly became inappropriate—his family's Triangle X outfitting ranch in Moose hosted many dude visitors—John turned to casting tracks.

Several years later, during a pack trip along the Yellowstone River, he excitedly found what appeared to be wolf tracks. He mixed his plaster carefully in the bucket. When it reached the consistency of concrete, he poured the plaster into the track and waited several hours for it to dry. He pulled the cast off the shore, dusted away the sand, and brought it back to the Muries.

"Wonderful track!" said Olaus. He took him to the extensive collection in the barn and pulled out a box full of casted wolf prints. Olaus never said that his young disciple's cast wasn't a wolf print, but when the thirteen-year-old held his narrower paw cast next to Olaus's broad-casted wolf paws, he knew he'd only captured a coyote. Olaus let him discover, on his own, that wolves no longer existed in Wyoming, a realization that helped stir his devotion to protecting wildlife.

John Turner was one of many inspired by the Muries who would change the face of modern environmental politics. He went on to earn a graduate degree in wildlife biology at the same University of Michigan where the Murie brothers had studied. As a state senator in the 1970s, Turner backed a Wyoming Wilderness Bill. As the director of the USFWS—under the first Bush administration—he revitalized the refuge system, promoting environmental education for children, completing recovery plans for more than a hundred endangered species, revising plans for more than twenty additional species, and doubling funding to protect endangered species. Turner even endorsed the legislation that would reintroduce wolves to Yellowstone. Many beltway pundits believed that Turner got blacklisted for his green politics. Reportedly vying for the Secretary of the Interior position, under the 2001 Bush administration, Turner was demoted to the assistant secretary for the Bureau of Oceans and International Environmental and Scientific Affairs.

As MARDY GREW FAMOUS, lecturing all over the country, more people came to visit her cabin. To pay their respects for the creation of the Arctic National Wildlife Refuge, let alone to understand the spiritual meaning behind the value of this place, wilderness lovers who couldn't make it to the Far North often came to see the Murie's seventy-seven-acre ranch instead. On the western rim of Jackson Hole, as many Arctic aficionados know, the Tetons erupt through a fault block in the earth's crust, tethered to their Brooks Range beginnings.

In the fall, cottonwood leaves colored the air and ferns rotted with a skunky musk. Some said that northern Wyoming winters are windier than and almost as cold as the sub-Arctic of Mardy's childhood. Although Wyoming lacks caribou, the other deer family members—elk, moose, and mule deer—ran freely past Grand Teton National Park headquarters, where Murie visitors turned immediately left after the Moose Post Office, then took another quick left, a half-mile down the pot-holed and muddy road.

Mardy's log cabin had been hewn in the 1920s, and its long spruce poles and rough-sawn planks looked more Alaska homestead than modern-day Wyoming. Horses hadn't grazed this ranch for decades. Out on the spacious front porch, Mardy often greeted her visitors by pointing out migrating hawks. The uninitiated who took the trouble to call before visiting found that to the day she died her number in the phone book was still listed under "Olaus Murie."

Many flew in from urban areas—including dozens of environmental lobbyists from the nation's capital—to fill their lungs with air free of nitrous oxide, to hear coyotes sing, and to be inspired by the Grandmother. Thousands came. They in turn told their friends. Many wrote stories. In a grassroots way, all those who Mardy's friends came to call "messengers" helped grow the myth. But even to those determined to drill for oil in the Arctic, Mardy became unassailable. Friends and would-be foes cherished her because she never made the battle personal, or self-righteous, and she listened respectfully to each person's opinion.

To those visitors who didn't have such an awe-inspiring backyard, time stood still on the ranch. Mardy's cabin revealed her as an anachronism, the last Pioneer Woman. She stood behind many causes, but her impact upon the collective eco-consciousness often seemed murky, if not obscured, by her humility.

Inside this log cabin of listing furniture, people came precisely because she didn't speak in the arrogant tones of the intelligentsia, and because Mrs. Margaret Elizabeth Murie—who insisted on being called "Mardy"—was much more interested in learning about her visitors than talking about herself.

Through the single-paned picture window the ancient bulwark of the Grand Teton grabbed so much light that Olaus's framed paintings looked dim in comparison.

Hung prominently on the living room's east wall was a painting of mallards floating past a refuge snowbank, next to Olaus's oil of the Arctic loons from the Sheenjek. Mardy couldn't help pointing out that the species—*Gavia arctica*—mated for life. Still, she remained the jovial storyteller, passing around the platter of caloric cookies, or playing her favorite music, the whistling ballads of Roger Whittaker, which the children loved. Anywhere else and the adult visitors would have scoffed, but in the Grandmother's temple, people worshipped her every move.

As Mardy served tea, former Secretaries of the Interior, authors, governors, schoolteachers, senators, and congressmen all looked to her for wisdom. In this, her visitors had a tendency to be disappointed, at least initially, because she always claimed that her knowledge came from other people, from the books she had read. To adults or children—students all—she let the wilderness speak for itself. She didn't infer God as the transcendentalists did, nor did she relate the death-defying adventure tales that some of her younger visitors expected to hear. She let her visitors draw their own conclusions.

One day, the founder of the Teton Science School came by and meekly pressed her about how he could be a better teacher.

"You *do* go outside?" she pointed out the window.

He nodded his head yes.

"You *do* teach your kids about animals?"

He nodded again.

"You spell the word 'pine marten,' correctly, right?"

"Always," he said.

"You ask them to take care of this environment and wilderness and remote places?"

He nodded.

"Well," Mardy smiled, "I think you're doing your fair share—you're doing great."

Urus arctos can swim, after a fashion, but not
with the grace of a polar bear.

Whale tail iceberg near the Canadian border of the refuge.

Herd of musk oxen on Arey Island, west of Kaktovik.

Fording the Hulahula River after a mid-August snowstorm.

Soft evening light in the refuge is often created by large forest fires to the south.

Storm lighting amid the nameless mountains
above the coastal plain.

Dall sheep habitat along the flooding Kongakut River.

Half-century-old grave markers of Iñupiat Eskimos in the northeastern corner of the refuge, lit by the sun sinking into the Beaufort Sea.

A lone bull begins its thousand-mile journey southward through the glaciated mountains of the refuge.

Colony of ground squirrels in a sandy riverbank.

Chapter 11

FLYING

Real freedom lies in wildness, not in civilization.
—Charles Lindbergh

On the Iñupiat island called Barter, I slid together a two-piece mast. I fitted it with a sleeved sail, then let the boom arm swing with the wind as I folded myself into the cockpit. Camera shutters clicked and my Iñupiat Eskimo audience shouted "Safe journey!" as I sheeted in the sail and the easterly wind snapped the white fabric taut. My Klepper kayak raced west faster than the children could run. It felt like flying.

My eyes teared as the bluffed shoreline raced by in a blur. Ground squirrels whistled, cloud-shaped sea jellies floated through the water below, and the coastal plain parted from the Beaufort Sea as if the Inuit goddess Sedna had combed it precisely.

A dozen miles west of Barter Island, I regained solitude and put my feet back on the ground. On the five-mile-long, eighth-of-a-mile-wide sands of the eerily green Arey Island, eight musk oxen circled protectively around a grazing calf. It seemed an unlikely refuge, until I considered that the lack of grizzlies and the copious sedges—utilizing nitrogen remnants of an ancient Iñupiat camp—made this deserted islet a musk oxen paradise.

The musk oxen couldn't swim and had nowhere to run. So,

given their hoof-stomping unease, I walked slowly and deliberately to within thirty yards of their defensive circle along the shore. The shaggy animals—more goats than oxen—bowed their heads back to the sedges, seemingly unconcerned, but probably not amused by my presence.

Of all the species that could make a case against sharing the Arctic with human beings, the travails of *Ovibos moschatus* would win in any courtroom. Musk oxen are in the family Bovidae, which also contains Dall sheep, goats, and domestic cattle. A million years ago, their oxen ancestors first crossed the Bering land bridge to North America. They grazed with wooly mammoths and wooly rhinoceroses, from the plains of the Midwest to the forested East Coast, from Europe to Asia, and across the high Arctic. As the other ice age creatures perished eighteen thousand years ago, the musk oxen evolved from their ancestors and moved to the high Arctic. While their huge coats and their ability to go months without food allowed them to withstand the subzero winters, these survivors of the Pleistocene could not survive human hunters.

By 1860, whalers had wiped the musk oxen out of Alaska. Sought after for their incredibly soft robes, rather than their acidic meat, the species was also being extirpated in Canada, until a 1917 law protected them. In 1930, the Biological Survey shipped thirty-four musk oxen from Greenland to Fairbanks, then to Nunivak Island—a thousand miles southwest of the refuge, beyond the reach of hunters in the Bering Sea. The herd flourished, and in 1969 a dozen musk oxen were airlifted to Barter Island. When they fled out onto the sea ice, the Iñupiat, who had all but forgotten the animals, gently herded them back to land. By 1985, the musk oxen had spread throughout the refuge, permit hunts were authorized, and their population stabilized at 450.

The harem here on Arey Island, along with the other herds spread around the refuge, and another forty-five hundred musk oxen throughout Alaska, were direct descendents of the thirty-four Greenland animals. In the last few years, however, a quarter of the refuge population has died off.*

Still self-conscious about talking to wild animals, I looked over my shoulders to verify that I was alone. Then I asked the musk oxen: "If you could have music here would you listen to Beethoven, Bach, or Mozart?" I lifted my arms to indicate the vast orchestra pit between us and the nameless mountains, forty miles south.

The bull snorted. From up close, the animals resembled loose, waist-high piles of hay. Their cinnamon-colored hair hung to the ground, and no doubt they would stay on their islet all winter, kicking down under the ice for sedges and laughing in their beards while shrugging their several-inch-thick cashmere robes against subzero cold. As the bull with its dangerous looking curved horns began stomping belligerently, I squeezed off one last photograph, and stood back up. Slowly.

With no warning, an adult tern protecting her brood swooped down on me and dragged its talons through my hair, screeching ratchet notes in my ear. I looked down at a crook of camouflaging driftwood and discovered a tiny chick, forty-five thousand times lighter and forty sizes smaller than the seven-hundred-pound musk oxen that first drew me here.

The round ball of gray fluff with a yellow beak and opalescent

---

*By 2002, USFWS researchers found that the musk oxen population in the refuge had shrunk to less then 350. In the 1980s, grizzlies rarely killed more than a half-dozen musk oxen per year, but by the end of 2001, the bears had learned how to kill up to fourteen musk oxen per year. During the same period, calf production declined precipitously as a potential result of decreased "fecundity" (caused by the same Artic Oscillation or global warming reducing the Porcupine caribou herd). Patricia Reynolds, Kenneth Wilson, and David Klein concluded in the USGS *Arctic Refuge Coastal Plain Terrestial Wildlife Research Summaries:* "Musk oxen in the Arctic Range are vulnerable to disturbance from activities associated with petroleum exploration and extraction because of their year-round residency, their small population numbers and their need to conserve energy for the 9 months of the winter if they are to successfully reproduce."

eyes was still flightless. But sometime in the next month, this chick would fledge on fingerling fish, grow sturdy feathers over its soft fluff, jump into the air, and spread its wings for the most amazing migration of them all.

This four-ounce subadult would join thousands more Arctic terns crossing the Atlantic. Tracing Europe down to the bulge of Africa, they would recross the Atlantic, make a brief landfall in Tierra del Fuego, then cross another frigid ocean to the Antarctic Peninsula, happily transported to another summer of continuous daylight. No animal in the world is as wired as this fork-winged tern, and no animal in the world experiences as much daylight. Their twelve-thousand-mile migration, flown twice every year, renders my 450-mile journey into a relative skylark.

I was assisted by maps and a cell-phone–sized GPS, struggling to reconnect with my abandoned instincts. The tern chick, with a brain the size of several microchips, follows electrical impulses and barely perceptible vibrations in the earth and familiar smells and bands of natural light. Like caribou, these birds are not flocking out of the refuge because of the coming cold. They're migrating for food. And to the discriminating tastes of an Arctic tern that spears tinsel-sized minnows all day long, there's no sense stopping in the relatively barren equatorial waters. Only the poles of the earth can satisfy their ravenous appetites.

I walked backward to my kayak, facing the musk oxen, just in case of an unexpected charge. I held my arm over my face. I bowed, quickly, each time the black-capped, screeching adult tern dropped out of the sky—like a flung handkerchief—trying to rake out my eyeballs.

I pushed the boat out until the sea lay an inch under my boot tops, spanned the paddle behind me across the cockpit, and levered myself in while bracing against the paddle. Then I spun sideways and slid in, twisting into a sitting position to lock my hips, like seal-ing the lid of a jar. It took another half minute to snap the water-proof spray deck on over the cockpit.

I paddled several brisk strokes westward, then realized that I had been too preoccupied to refuel on Arey Island. I holstered the paddle in the foredeck shock cord, reached under the sprayskirt, and grabbed a quarter pound of "Iñupiat power bar"—smoked Arctic char. I imagined a glass of dry white wine, and chewed in quiet inspiration, contemplating the refuge's mood.

Since filling the silence with talk and seeking definition appeased my loneliness, and since all good meals deserved a song, I pulled out the microcassette recorder from the cockpit dry bag and repeated my earlier question:"What music would describe this place?"

Several Beethoven symphonies—especially the Ninth, "Ode to Joy," that I often sang—might fit the snowy Brooks Range bursting up out of the southern horizon. Until winter rendered both air and mountains into a blank, white canvas. Otherwise, it was hard to imagine a musical accompaniment for the refuge.

Bach's intricate pianoforte and Mozart's string concertos were too polished and technically perfect for the unstable coastal plain. As my kayak bounced south through choppy water, a rainbow formed over the distant peaks, and I double-checked my position on the USGS map (wrongly labeled "William O. Douglas Wildlife Range") to verify my sense of direction in this broad seascape. When I glanced back up, the rainbow had disappeared, replaced by black and electrically barren Arctic storm clouds that rarely carried the drumbeat-rolling, symbols-clashing cacophony of thunder and lightning. To the north, the chop corduroyed the sea, but the blinding cerulean glow of the ice pack quelled the string symphony of crashing waves.

While the legendary composers of centuries past created music that evoked oceans, storms, pastoral rivers, the four seasons, animals of the Savannah, and even the majesty of the Alps, the Arctic, with its unnamed mountains and valleys of unknown origin, remained a mysterious netherworld. This extraordinary landscape had been ignored by the glacial weight of the Pleistocene, while its sea stood silently locked through the seasons by two yards of ice, as its fur-clad hunters shared wives inside snow domes, and its surreal animals became myths so convincing that all of refined Europe believed in albino bears and unicorns.* So how could a powder-wigged and cultured composer possibly put music to such a naked and untraveled world?

The dynamic, ever-changing moods of the remote refuge will continue to defy musical interpretation. To my ears, the syncopated drift was unmistakable. I had listened to grunting caribou, squeaking beluga whales, and double-larynxed songbirds. I heard exhaling tundra, hissing subzero air, and cracking sea ice. Alone up here, the ordinary music scale seemed irrelevant.

Even worse than hearing things and talking to oneself, spending too much time alone here could tempt one into misanthropy. Vilhammer Stefansson, the Arctic anthropologist and explorer, was famous for his arrogant disdain, and for denying the existence of his Eskimo children. Roald Amundsen, after becoming the first conqueror of the Northwest Passage and then the South Pole, died a lonely bachelor. To attain self-reliance and physical mastery, accomplished Arctic travelers often turn their backs on their own cultures.

Personally, as a loner, this initial move away from the approval of my peers and society at large was easy enough to attain. On

---

*Several invaluable tusks of Arctic narwhals circulated in European courts during the Middle Ages. Royalty attributed the single horn to a prodigious and magically gifted horse. The Unicorn myth began in Greece along with stories of the polar bear—whose hides had been carried south by traders. Hailed by Pliny and Aristotle, then included in the Bible, it wasn't until the seventeenth century that a European cartographer identified the narwhal as a small Arctic whale with a long tooth protruding from its forehead. The Unicorn legend persisted for another two centuries.

many days, free from boat or airplane traffic, and surrounded by utter stillness, I couldn't help wondering if the Bomb had dropped.

The greater challenge in front of me—now that I had learned how to both thrive and survive—was to completely let go of self, and to avoid the overwhelming temptation to see the refuge through the rose-tinted glasses of my own creation. At the same time, I had to open my mind to achieve empathy with the wildlife and wilderness here. To attempt anything less would have been like walking out on a brief marriage, and I would never really understand the refuge.

Over the last five weeks I had been straining my ears to try to figure out what caused the persistent humming that vibrated up from somewhere between the land and the sea. I tried to capture it with my recorder, but the low-pitched noise—like a cross between a grouse call and the chanting of Trappist monks—eluded cassette tape. I hadn't heard it in the mountains or on the rivers of the refuge and I couldn't help but wonder if this coastal hum was the same anomaly of magnetic vibrations that drew migrating animals north.

As it faded, I heard a distant chorus: *"whouk, whouk, whouk."*

I looked all around, but again I was stumped. I had to learn how to find delight in yet another mystery. After all, where is it written that we must quantify or identify all of creation?

Willing to accept whatever fate awaited me, I realized that, for the first time in my life, I was lingering, paddling slowly, happy to be alone and feeling so at peace. No one was expecting me, I had no radio, and even if I emerged from the North a month late, who would care? In Kaktovik, I mailed my wristwatch to a friend in an effort to lose the constraints imposed by time and to live in the present. The freedom of abandoning itineraries and contrived schedules, without a gun or a wristwatch, allowed me to see the natural world with a new and avid appreciation. The only challenge was, how could I ever settle for any other life after this?

THAT NIGHT, I slid the tent poles into the sleeves of my leaky tent. The tundra smelled of nutmeg. A quarter-mile north, two sandhill cranes danced in sunset light so thick and golden I had to sit down, because walking felt like swimming and the tundra appeared to be radiating nuclear heat. The maddened cranes jumped two feet into the air, snapping at insects, whooping, and beating wings against their chests. It could be just coincidence, or maybe even a mating ritual, but there was the distinct sense that the cranes felt the same pressure drop that showed up on the altimeter this afternoon and made my bones ache. A storm was coming.

Although this place receives less than six inches of precipitation a year, I fell asleep to the drumming of rain on taut nylon. Hours later, I woke to a dream of drowning and found my cheek submerged in a cold puddle. I raced naked out to my kayak and grabbed the big boat sponge from the cockpit. Then I stopped myself. *Why am I in such a big rush?*

I sniffed the air and got nothing, so I closed my eyes and listened to the raindrops snapping on dry plants, the sea sighing on sand, and the ocean rustling like silk against the breeze. This wind blew out of the south, and although the rain pelting my shoulders was not warm, I didn't feel cold. So I ran out into the icy sea, splashing in backward, and yelled in shock as the gubernacular response contracted my testicles up into my groin.

I sprinted, double speed, back to camp. My feet tore across coarse-grained sand, against prickly Lapland rosebay, overturning the furry undersides of Labrador tea leaves. Now the rain felt warm.

Inside, I dried off with my pants as towel before sponging the puddle out the door. I curled into a fetal position on the high side of the tiny tent and forced myself into a prolonged shivering bout until my toes felt warm and the strange and distant chorus— *"whouk, whouk, whouk"*—lullabyed me to sleep.

At dawn, I bit off another chunk of Iñupiat power bar, which would keep my stomach from grumbling for hours. After my morning stretch session, I rolled and smoked a cigarette, imagining the hidden sun crawling up the sky, until, in lieu of its warming rays, the embers burned my fingertips. I kicked the ashes into the sand and pocketed the unburned rolling paper.

Scanning about for polar bears, I pulled down my pants and crouched on the low-tide line of the beach and reflected. At my feet lay hundreds of miles of the inch-wide, half-centimeter-thick brown deli line of ground-up sea jelly tentacles and pulverized driftwood and ancient fish bones and annelid worms and miniature crustaceans and uncountable invertebrates. Here, amid this thin but lengthy strip of fecund refuse, the Beaufort Sea, or perhaps a hungry seal, would remove all trace of my passage. I paused, like all good mammals have paused since time immemorial, and showing the evolutionary progression of my species, I reached for the flat stones that worked better than toilet paper. Then I had the pleasure of skip-throwing these stones out toward the North Pole. A saltwater douche completed my morning ritual.

I jogged to warm up, my breath fogging the air and my arms out-flung like a kite flyer's as I lined my kayak through the shallow surf east of the Sadlerochit River. As I trotted down the beaches, hundreds of least sandpipers entertained me. I could hear their tiny muscles ticking as they repeatedly flew off and relanded, pecking out their favorite treats from the deli line, then springing back up and thickening the air with buff backs and wings and black, quivering beaks. In their coming migration to South America they would compete for the same high altitudes used by commercial airliners.

Then the sun beamed over the eastern fogbank, stopping all of us in our tracks. I sat on glassine silt washed down from the mountains and admired the light rays reddening my arms as these sparrow-sized, wind-up sandpiper toys bobbed and twittered in the lagoon, swimming in dizzy circles without feeding, lost in primeval celebration of this surreal glow.

"If people lived out here all summer," I wrote in my journal, "wouldn't we too dance for the beauty of the light?"

Through the lifting fog, the maddened chorus of *whouk*s grew louder. I pulled my kayak firmly ashore, lifted up the binoculars, and focused in on a riotous white ballet of bird wing waving across the coastal plain.

Snow geese!

Every August, a half-million lesser snow geese stage here after flying five hundred miles from Banks Island. This flock, specifically drawn to the coastal plain's kitchen, will spend three weeks amid the string-of-pearls stretch proposed for oil development. On arrival, each goose weighs in with 22 grams of fat. Several weeks later, they each depart with a paunchy 600 grams—collectively recycling eight million pounds of protein-rich cotton-grass stems—the caribou had already nipped off the cotton-ball heads. Then they would trace the fecund deli line 250 miles east to the Mackenzie Delta, join a million geese, and migrate fifteen hundred miles to the cow country of Alberta, where they would pluck and recycle corn from cow pies before continuing another thousand miles south.*

I slid back into my kayak, smiling. Within minutes, a several-hundred-pound bearded seal splashed alongside. He nudged the hull of my kayak with a whiskered and strangely canine snout. The water to the west was a blackened mirror, but the kayak ripples dis-

---

*According to the USGS *Arctic Refuge Coastal Plain Wildlife, 2002* report, "Several studies suggest that human disturbance can displace staging snow geese from feeding habitats and possibly diminish the size of juvenile fat reserves. . . . We cannot assume that snow geese would be able to locate adequate feeding habitat in other regions if they were displaced from the Arctic Refuge coastal plain [by either petroleum development or aircraft activity]."

rupting its surface now seemed part and parcel of Nature's plan. For the first time in my life, it felt as if I belonged in this wilderness, where animals and humankind are allowed to interact together during their collective migrations. As the seal continued to blow and dive at me, I tagged after him, west toward his winter home in the Bering Sea.

He repeatedly surfaced beside me in this blackened sea-sky. Each time he rose, I put down my paddle and said, "Hello again." Each time, he craned his neckless head and looked into my eyes with anxious soulfulness. The last time, he dropped away with a quick gasp and a plop. And I never saw him again.

I pulled ashore against the western bank of the Katakturuk River. As I torched up my stove to heat a pot of Earl Gray tea, warming my fingers over the open flame, several thousand caribou migrated toward camp. I shut down the sputtering MSR and stood up. This was the moment that I'd been waiting for. At first, the herd moved away at some predetermined signal, their leg ligaments clicking like castanets. I sat down and bided my time.

They stopped and bowed their heads back down, worrying the tundra. Their fur rippled as warble flies buzzed past and the wind stretched across a tundra pond. As it calmed, the grouse-chant breathing began anew. In the distance the snow geese cried "*whouk, whouk, whouk.*"

Another warm gust blew out of the south, through the herd and into my face. The caribou couldn't smell me. I was not yet animal enough to smell their steaming bodies, wet from fording the river. Several hundred calves bawled alongside maybe four thousand antler-shed cows, mixed in with a couple hundred antlered bulls. The calves must have been two months old.

I sat in the "1002 Area"—a coastal plain threatened by oil development, which the Gwich'in call *Vadzaii Googii Vi Dehk'it Gwanlii*, the Sacred Place Where Life Begins. The Native Americans who still worship these animals believe, as they were taught by their elders, that the caribou carry a piece of men in their hearts, while men carry the caribou in their hearts. According to the revered myth, we always know what the other being is up to.

Remembering a game played by Gwich'in hunters, and knowing that caribou are curious, I slowly stood up. Then I bowed my head, raised my arms in imitation of antlers, my fingers splayed out like antler tines above my ears, and began dancing, slowly, moving sideways toward the herd. The herd suddenly swelled toward me. I looked at the ground, avoiding eye contact. I crabbed sideways so that I wouldn't scare them. And suddenly I began running like a wolf, swamped by the herd racing back and forth beside me. The binoculars swayed across my chest. The herd grunted. Old warble holes grayed their backs. The calves were shaking scared, so the bigger bulls blurred past me, and I exchanged eye contact—large unblinking brown and black dilated pupils, hundreds of them, staring back into my soul.

Even at a trot, the caribou protected their calves. Although the herd may have accepted that I was not a predatory threat, the bodies of chest-high adults repeatedly blocked me from their young. From within this gentle throng, waist-high calves repeatedly bleated, "*meeeeeee!*" slowing their nursing mothers, who grunted, "*a-a-w, a-a-w, a-a-w,*" as they nose-butted their young onward.

We raced across the tussocks, my running shoes padding magically on the swaying tops as the herd—as we—splashed through green-scummed water with bugs ricocheting off our heads like hail. We cantered over a hill and raced down its far side until the caribou snorting and wet-sweater smell pulled away into the distance. Why they were still here in early August with snows approaching was a mystery that a biologist would solemnly address, but I was glad to watch them disappear—fleeing as have all the birds clacking overhead each night, chasing an urge wired into their collective cerebellums for a millennium. The herd was headed toward the rich lichen country of the boreal forests, and as their legs bent and clicked, their bodies fell from sight, until only the swaying tines of antlers floated south above undulating polygons.

I turned and sprinted back up the hill. As the herd moved en masse, like a tawny carpet shivering out over the coastal plain, a calf dropped out. Its legs bowed double-jointedly, and the calf bleated in lost confusion. Without his mother, the calf would die—caribou would not adopt stray calves. I watched through the binoculars, spellbound, until a cow broke sideways out of the herd and galloped back north, skidding to a splay-legged stop, nursing her grateful calf. After a quick minute, the cow spun a full circle, and nuzzled its calf on toward the departing herd.

OUTSIDE OF THE REFUGE BOUNDARY, my kayak journey to Prudhoe Bay suddenly went to hell. I had learned how to be alone, I could deal with the blizzards, and I could ration my food and hunker up with a book while waiting for the seas to go down. But every day that I paddled west was like descending into industrial perdition.

I tried to catch every sordid detail in my journal. All my joy at being alone in the Arctic vanished with every paddle stroke that I fought west.

Three days after leaving the refuge, as I watched a seismic oil exploration ship through my binoculars, thumping through the distances and violating the silence, the kayak leash slipped out of my hand, a half-mile offshore on a shoal. When I put the binoculars down and saw the kayak sailing away in the wind, I dove into the icy sea and swam after it—without my boat, I'd be dead. Fifty yards out, waves broke saltily into my mouth. Several more yards out, I laid a hand on the rudder, swam the boat back, reboarded with cramps in my calves, and paddled to the mainland.

I pulled out my dry bag of books and ripped out the opening pages of Patrick O'Brian's *The Wine-Dark Sea*. I was shivering so hard that when I unscrewed the canister of matches from around my neck, all but two matches spilled out. I flicked one against a tooth and forced myself—bracing my right hand with my left, like aiming a handgun—to torch the pages. The flame electrified my numbed fingers and licked over the torn book, until a gust of wind-driven snow snuffed it out. My teeth were chattering as I grabbed several pieces of dried out driftwood, doused them with my reserve white gas, snapped the last match onto a roaring bonfire, and sobbed in relief—saved by the oil industry.

I stripped off my wet clothes and hung them on an immovable spider-shaped stump next to the fire. As darkness descended I turned back and forth, warming my stomach, then my rear end, against the flickering wall of heat. My chest and leg hair were unavoidably singeing and although the smell and sound of sizzling body hair revolted me, I couldn't abandon the heat, so I continued to spin like a side of beef over a barbeque. On each rotisserie cycle facing out into the blackness I felt scared. I no longer understood the land and seascape that I had entered into.

One hundred miles west of the Canadian border, the Brooks Range swings south away from the coast and the land goes level as a pancake. Not a hill, a pingo, or even a high riverbank. An early explorer cast up on this shore would have had no trouble believing that all of the earth was indeed flat.

Rivers meander lazily through vast bird sanctuaries and count-less small ponds—summer home to millions of birds. Although scientists call this a "biologically productive" coastal plain, the oil companies have set up shop here for a half-century.

Since 1944, twelve thousand miles of seismic lines have been blasted, while 420 exploration wells, including thirty-two offshore, have been drilled in the Alaskan Arctic. Countless acres of wildlife habitat have been destroyed, forever altering the ecosystem. Most people will never visit, let alone care about this coast, but because it's flat and remote and unprotected, does this mean it should be forgotten?

I BATTLED WEST through snowstorms and freezing rain toward the eerie yellow gas flare at the artificial gravel island of Endicott. I paddled past bits of floating blue foam and coffee cups and steel rods and outboard oil cans and dead birds and clothing and soda cans and planks and pipes and comic books and oil drums and tools and huge tires and plastic bags. During nights turning noticeably colder with much of my body hair singed off, it was too chilly to read, so I shivered to sleep.

On the sixth night west of the refuge, I lay in a fetal position, angry that my tobacco was smoked up, and sheltering from another storm. Then a tent pole broke in the wind, and ripped through the nylon wall like the claw of a polar bear. I screamed, but nothing stood outside the tent. As the storm whipped snow through the hole, I staggered down to tide line, dragged back logs, and stacked them next to the tent. From behind the windbreak, using a headlamp, I patched the pole with a spare ferule, then ran stitches through the gash in the nylon with needle and thread.

Next morning, I paddled through timid sunlight. After a week alone, cold and wet from rain and snow, I felt desperate for human contact. When I spied workers up in a tower at the air force DEW line site of Bullen Point, I waved and yelled enthusiastically, but they wouldn't return my greeting. Minutes later, a burly foreman ran down to the shore and walked with me as I paddled along the beach. He was dressed in the ubiquitous Alaskan Carhardt coveralls. "I can't let you come ashore," he said, "unless you show me some ID."

"No problem," I replied. I beached, and for the first time on this trip, I dug out the small bag stuffed into the bulb of my bow and handed him my driver's license. He looked at it and asked, "What in hell you doing all the way up here from Colorado?"

"Mostly watching birds," I said but the look on his face said that he didn't believe me. I told him I had paddled more than four hundred miles from Canada's Mackenzie Delta over the past five weeks.

"You're crazy," he scratched his beard. "Hold on," he said, "I gotta sat-phone this in.

"Hey," he asked as an afterthought about leaving me unguarded on the beach, "you armed?"

"No," I laughed, and flashed him a peace sign, which only seemed to piss him off.

Twenty minutes later he found me at a rusted, overturned 42-gallon oil drum. Three herring gull chicks were peeping up at me from their nest—nature preparing to prevail soon as humankind leaves. The foreman handed back my license. "Sorry about that. Your record's clear. Have a cigar." He passed me a cellophane-wrapped Dutch Master from the collection lining his chest pocket like a scientist's pens. I thanked him.

"Hey," he said, flicking his Bic for me and trying to be friendly, "you know what you're doing wouldn't be my cup of tea?"

"Most days," I said, cupping hands around the lighter, "since I left the refuge it isn't mine either."

Several miles later, at the bustling Badami construction site, a man wearing a white hard hat with a BP decal warned me to stay in my kayak and push away from the dock. Another supervisor, an educated petroleum geologist or an engineer, judging by the grammatically correct precision of his sentences, walked the shore with me, exchanging banalities, escorting me a half-mile down the beach to the edge of the Badami oil lease, until he felt certain that I wouldn't stop.*

Outside the Sagavanirktok River Delta, a frigid wind teared my

---

*The Badami construction was finished in 1998 at a cost of $300 million. The field had been estimated to contain 115 million barrels of oil. At $30 per barrel, BP could have earned over $3 billion. But in summer 2003, the field was shut down because the oil trickled out at only 1,350 barrels per day. Environmentalists cite Badami and other expensive dry wells on the North Slope as good reasons to keep oil leasing out of the refuge.

eyes. Nasty rips buffeted my kayak. Brown river water streaked the sea like a chocolate layer cake, with shiny new snow frosting the shore.

I steered inside the giant light of the oil flare toward Endicott, the sixth-largest oil field in North America. I aimed toward a causeway that was sporadically crossed by what looked like toy trucks headed out over the Beaufort Sea to a man-made island.

Waves broke across my spray skirt and the thought of drowning alongside the BP island refinery frightened me into paddling overdrive. I pushed and pulled so hard that a ligament strained and gave way in my back, but adrenaline and fear allowed me to paddle through the pain. The splash of waves was so numbing that I couldn't feel my neoprene-gloved fingers on the paddle.

Beneath the truck-rattling causeway, the current and wind suddenly stopped. I stared back at Endicott, a self-contained oil facility, complete with seawater-distillation plant, restaurants, gas-compression facility, and yet another causeway leading to the drilling platform.*

At the south end of the causeway, a man with a gun in his unbuckled holster waited for me on the beach. The lights on his police cruiser truck were flashing, and he made violent "go-back" gestures with his arms, making it clear that I should not get out of my kayak. I paid no attention, because I had become accustomed to the wariness of oil workers who made their living on the North Slope. "You know you're not allowed here," he shouted, "so don't you come out of the water!"

Instead of bracing myself out of the kayak with the paddle, I

---

*BP, while actively promoting ANWR oil leasing, built Endicott in 1987. By 1997 the company had been accused of 104 oil spills in the American Arctic. On September 23, 1999, BP pled guilty to injecting hazardous wastes into the wells at Endicott and violating water laws from 1993 through 1995; BP Amoco (the expanded company) paid approximately $22 million in federal and civil penalties. In 2000, BP Amoco acquired ARCO and became the second largest oil company in the world.

rolled out painfully onto my side and into the shallow water. I crawled to shore. Then I stood up and pulled the gloves off with my teeth.

I was clutching my back. Normally I would paddle another ten miles to avoid this hostile-looking guard, but now I had no choice. I was tired of fighting winter along a coastline destroyed by oil development, and my back was injured.

In a friendly voice, I told the uniformed guard how far I had come, then I looked back at the white-capped bay, dangerously sloshing with current. If he couldn't read the water, surely he saw the black bags of exhaustion under my eyes. Still, he looked ready to draw his gun.

"Charley," I said, reading the nameplate pinned across from his badge, "I'm just trying to get south to Fairbanks." I smiled. My swollen fingers were white and wooden with cold, so I stuffed them up under my wet jacket and beneath the sweat-stiffened neoprene against my stomach.

Charley stepped back apprehensively, then realized that I was only reaching for the warmth under my jacket. Charley too was shivering, but to his credit, he was futuristically on guard for Alaska's first oil terrorists. "Stay where you are," his breath flew past as a white cloud in the raw wind. He ran back to his truck to warm up and get instructions for my disposal. A supervisor's voice blared omnisciently over Charley's radio: "Give him a break; he's probably hypothermic!"

"*Hypothermic!*" Charley said, "Come on!"

I began dragging my kayak up onto the road, ready to put my thumb out for the next pickup truck. Since I was leaving Endicott, he couldn't stop me unless he wanted to shoot me. "Hey, you armed?" Charley yelled defensively, hand now on his gun.

I could only giggle. It came up from my belly, a rolling laugh that made me forget my back and plop down on the kayak stern for a seat and throw my head back until tears came to my eyes. Charley looked at me like I was crazy.

Trying to talk with such men was really more about listening patiently to them. Expecting Charley to understand why I was traveling unarmed would have been unrealistic. I also laughed because I felt defeated, stung by the anticlimax of finishing on land leased by the oil companies.

I had no idea how my trip went so suddenly out of control. Still, I wanted to believe that difficult expeditions imparted humility, insight, and a disciplined ability to act on new resolutions. I could only hope that my memory would substitute what happened in the refuge, now fifty miles east, as the end of my journey.

"CIGARETTE?" The pilot tapped one out of his pack.

"No thanks," I smiled, "I just quit."

A half-mile below us, the seismic oil vehicle tracks tearing up the tundra bore an eerie resemblance to the ancient runway lines in the Peruvian desert. The Alaskan lines were cut through a plain of ten-foot-wide polygons, filled with water, and stretch as far as the eye can see. To the west, a brown haze hung above Prudhoe Bay. Then, with industrial wasteland suddenly yielding to verdancy, we flew over the vast wash of the Canning River and the eastern refuge boundary. The oil industry faded, except for a few seismic vehicle lines from the 1980s, jokingly pointed out by the pilot. When he veered north, toward the sea, he began jabbing his Marlboro pointer toward a huge column of what appeared to be red ants filing into the river. I pulled down sunglasses, clicked off the camera lens cap, and flipped up my ball-cap's visor.

The herd was strangely unaffected by the noise of our diving Cessna, and I blinked if only because seeing what had to be several thousand caribou at once blurred the land and the herd together. Flying in small planes definitely creates a bewilderment about where you are, as well as magnifying the potential for airsickness. But it also seemed as if those caribou were literally attached to the land, and with the sun glaring and one-hundred-miles-per-hour flight and herd movement disguising small calves from big bulls, I couldn't see space between hooves and tundra. As the pilot banked to circle and stall-in low over the herd, I tapped his shoulder and suggested that we leave the wildlife alone.

All the tracks and animal sign that obsessed me on the ground gained a new perspective from the air. Along the coast from a plane on a lucky day you could pick out the vapors of passing whales or the jaundice-colored blobs of polar bears blubbering across the black sea. Caribou trails spider-webbed up and down tundra, river-banks, and any mountain shy of vertical. Dall sheep paths con-toured cliffs. Bear diggings looked like hand-plowed homestead plots. My nose flattened against the window—I love flying.

Flying offers superb closure after slow travel under the relent-less pull of gravity and the weight of heavy packs and ponderous sea kayaks. While flying I can laugh at how quickly time and space fly past. Just like in my dreams. Everything that seems normal on the ground changes when you soar up into the sky and borrow the Creator's view.

Inuit shamans claimed to have flown over vast distances in order to bring back new perceptions or spirit powers to their people. The Dorset, who predated the Inuit, believed that polar bears flew. And today, anyone who spends more than a few days on the coastal plain hopping tussocks, paddling a kayak, or swatting bugs can't help fan-tasizing of a winged escape—or at least gaining some high ground.

Although small planes routinely fall from the sky in Alaska, this seems irrelevant if you sit with an experienced pilot, like the chain-smoker who was taking me back to Fairbanks. His Cessna 185 had become the accepted taxi of the Alaskan bush. We could cruise six hundred miles, or go as fast as 160 mph. As we followed the Hulahula River south into the mountains and the wings tore into a nasty headwind, the plane began to buck. Still, it seemed like nor-mal turbulence.

Through nearly three decades of flying in the North, I had only been airsick once, looking for poachers while stuffed in the rear seat of a tiny Piper Super Cub. Otherwise, I had accompanied an aerial wolf hunter plying his dirty business, made emergency landings after running out of fuel, held the controls for sleeping pilots, broken a wheel-ski during an out-of-control glacier landing, been lost in clouds while flying beneath big peaks, and breathed bottled oxygen while searching for lost climbers at high altitude.

So, as the pilot lit up another cancer stick, I reassured myself that we were crossing a low-altitude pass in the Brooks Range. The Continental, 300-horsepower engine purred under the front cowling as we climbed several hundred feet per minute into the headwind. At about two thousand feet above sea level, a strong gust popped us up a hundred feet, suspending my camera in midair, spewing cigarette butts, and triggering the stall-buzzer alarm. The plane fell, then rose. Again and again.

I'd never been so weightless before. My temples began pounding; my stomach rose up into my throat. Now, thinking like all airsick victims, it seemed certain we were going to die.

My mind raced over other crashes. As a teenager, I had found a Cessna crumpled on a high mountain ridge; body parts had been obscenely strewn across the scree field. Ten miles west of our bouncing 185, a USFWS plane had crashed and burned in similar turbulence. It was twenty-two years before the plane and its victims were found, spread as unrecognizable, charred skeletons and sheet metal across another boulder field. Several years after that, Mardy Murie's plane went down between here and the coast. The remoteness of the Brooks Range meant that rescues took a long time. The region is also known for dangerous vertical wind sheers caused by icy Arctic air colliding with warm southern weather.

We were thrown up again and again. The airspeed dropped from 90 to 60, repeatedly tripping the high-pitched stall alarm. Since

Cessna 185s had to fly at least 65 mph to maintain control, the pilot goosed the throttle. The plane started jumping so hard the wings were flexing, rattling the first-aid kit, and bringing more bile up into my throat. A quarter-mile below, the boulder fields were padded with two feet of new snow. The stall buzzer now rang continuously as the pilot—lips pursed over the smoked down to the filter butt—gripped the controls with white-knuckled fingers. He refused to look at me, and I didn't want to distract him by yelling out any stupid questions.

I swallowed hard to lose the metallic taste, closed my eyes, and reassured myself that we'd be safe once we hit the calm air on the south side of the Brooks Range. The map put the divide at seventy-two hundred feet; the altimeter read forty-six hundred feet. We had to climb higher. With any luck, as long as the engine kept purring along, we'd make it.

⌂ ⌂ ⌂

Although Mardy wore her emotions on her sleeve, she never complained about her fear of flying as she crisscrossed Alaska in small planes. She flew southwest of Anchorage to the proposed Lake Clark park five times. The seventy-two-year-old then flew around Denali to see the proposed park expansion, then back south of Anchorage to survey potential parks at the Harding Icefield and Kenai Fjords. While en route to the Arctic during summer 1975 she flew north to Fairbanks in small planes three times.

She also spent a lot of time on the ground, listening to Alaskans' opinions about the proposed federal additions and expansions. She learned that many residents opposed expanding the Arctic National Wildlife Range. She heard a lot of confused talk about "the feds taking over Alaska," and even though it was her job as a government task force member to listen, she had already decided that the state needed more legislated wilderness, regardless of what some of its citizens thought. After all, 95 percent of Alaska was uninhabited and its 300,000 residents lived in a place twice the size of Texas, population 13 million.

When Mardy flew with Ave Thayer out of Fairbanks to survey the 7.9 million acres of the proposed Gates of the Arctic National Park, they both looked down in horror at long, green sections of pipe. It was no simple "pencil mark across a sheet of paper" as the oil companies had said, but "a broad and portentous scar across an empty and innocent land." When the pipeline faded from sight, and their plane seemed swallowed by a horizon of undulating tundra, she tapped on Ave's shoulder and pointed to a blue meander below. Since the Beaver's nine-cylinder, supercharged 450-horsepower engine drowned out conversation, she passed him a note asking for the river's name. Ave kept his radio earphones on but shook his head, implying the river had no name. Mardy, swept up anew with emotions for the land, wrote him another note, from Robert Service:

> *There's a land where the mountains are nameless,*
> *And the rivers all run God knows where.*

The next day, she began surveying the Arctic National Wildlife Range. She camped with Ave at Sheenjek Lake, along with a cow moose and its calf. At dawn she strolled alone through tall fields of lupine and fireweed that caressed her open palms. She declared it "like coming home."

The next day, with the firebrand conservationist Celia Hunter, they landed on a saltwater lagoon east of Kaktovik. Mardy had learned over the last few days that while their pilot rarely spoke, his economy with words belied a fierce spirituality. Mardy had earlier assumed that since Mr. Thayer, manager of the Arctic National Wildlife Range, worked for USFWS, he would advocate development if his boss, the Secretary of the Interior, directed him to. So Mardy had already written a letter to this pilot-manager, gently expressing her wishes that the area be preserved for eternity. Mardy, as it turned out, underestimated Ave Thayer.

Here on the southern shore of Beaufort lagoon, standing in the refreshing ice-cold sea air washing over warm tundra, Ave said, "I'm a pantheist." He spoke in a soft voice that made Mardy and Celia strain to hear what they knew would be a short speech about nature being a part of who they were, and since nature and religion are almost the same thing—since God made the place—Ave waved his arm to encompass the ocean, the coastal plain, and the mountains, "I don't want to screw this up."

The mosquitoes had zeroed in on their carbon dioxide emissions as the women sucked on cubes of clean-tasting sea ice. Salt sinks out, Ave explained, as the ocean freezes. Then, following Celia's eagle-eyed gaze, they spotted three snowy owls perched like royalty on their tussock thrones.

Ave flew them back west. Mardy loathed the weightlessness and spatial disorientation of flying, but she was thrilled to be back in the Arctic. She was dismayed by all the intrusive signs of man—tire tracks, landing pads, gravel roads to drill pads, and oil drums—outside of the range, west of the Canning River. She was relieved when Ave steered back east.

They flew above the Sadlerochit River, alongside its lush western banks, fed by an underground spring. Mardy gaped at the two-thousand-foot-high sandstone hills, speckled red like the dorsal fins of grayling, fluting above the green body of the coastal plain.

They also sighted a dozen musk oxen, reintroduced six years earlier to Barter Island. As Ave circled, the herd circled three calves resting in a bed of purplish lupine. Mardy fought her fear of flying to pay attention, if only because Olaus had lobbied for these animals to be moved here before his death. Neither woman needed to tell Ave not to fly too low and scare the herd, and they continued south over Shrader Lake to camp at Peters Lake.

In the morning, Ave reminded his passengers to buckle up. He then turned the ignition key and popped the propeller into a quick-roaring breeze that sent several hundred oldsquaw ducks gabbling across the lake. Veteran flyer Celia sat next to him in the copilot's seat. Ave pushed his carburetor-mixture lever in to warm up the Pratt and Whitney engine, and after two minutes, he nudged the lever again and taxied south, gaining speed, with rooster tails of water flying behind the floats. Mardy cupped her hands over her ears. At forty miles per hour, Ave put down the flaps and they felt a muffled judder, a short bounce, a splash, then a sudden sensation of weightlessness as the floats broke suction with the lake. Ave eased off on the power and the din fell to a steady rumble; Mardy let go of her ears. As the dock tie-ropes pinged harmlessly on the floats below, Ave followed the Sadlerochit north to show Celia and Mardy the proposed extension, which would add over nine-million acres to the Arctic National Wildlife Range.

The two pilots felt secure because their DeHavilland Beaver was a flying pickup truck built for pounding about the Alaskan bush. At 110 knots top speed with a four-hundred-mile range, it didn't fly as fast or as far as most airplanes, but unlike the glut of Cessna 185s and Piper Super Cubs buzzing over the Alaska wilderness, DeHavilland had designed its planes to withstand the huge payloads and bad landings that folded up the other planes like mosquitoes in the pinchers of yellow jackets.

The previous June, Ave had been forced to set down his ski-equipped Beaver out on the coast. When he lost power to the engine, he merely aimed at a snowdrift, eased up the flaps, slowed the plane down and coasted to a stop—plane and passengers unharmed.

After ten minutes flying over the Sadlerochit, they turned up into the steep canyon of Eagle Creek to look for Dall sheep. Suddenly, a "terrific clatter" came from the Beaver's fat nose, as engine pieces inexplicably broke apart and pinged into the cowling. Black smoke poured out of the fuselage exhaust. Ave quickly spun the plane around, steering north, out of the steep mountains. Celia and Mardy couldn't help thinking of the USFWS Alaska director Clarence Rhode, whose paunchy Goose floatplane had disappeared eighteen years earlier over this same stretch of wilderness. The women looked to Ave for reassurance. Mardy later wrote:

> Even a mechanical ignoramus like me knew that something was very wrong. Ave grabbed the radio transmitter but didn't have time to say much, he was too busy with the plane, turning it immediately to get out of that steep valley and back into the Sadlerochit, wider and gentler.
> Celia said: "There's a pond over there."
> Ave said: "What do you think?"
> Celia replied: "Too small."

Not only did it look too small, but Ave knew that if the Beaver didn't reach the pond, they would crash into a boulder field. He pushed in the carburetor lever and tried more gas. Nothing happened. The prop was still spinning with only 15 percent power. He pulled back to lean it out, but this made no difference, they were in a downward glide. To make the women feel better, he pushed and pulled the lever several more times, just to infer that they still had options and that their pilot wouldn't sit helplessly. He calculated that they had about thirty-six gallons of fuel—enough to cause a blistering explosion if he landed too hard.

Ave shouted: "Grab your sleeping bags and hold 'em over your faces!" Mardy reached back to grab Celia's down parka, threw it up to her, then put her sleeping bag over her face.

Ave held the clanking, smoking plane on course for a smooth stretch of tussocks, several-hundred yards in front of the pond, before the boulders. His plane had been designed to land at slow speeds. But he had to hit those upcoming slippery-looking tussocks perfectly. If he flopped down slower than forty-five miles per hour, the rocker surface of his floats would flip the Beaver upside down; too fast, and they'd slide into the boulders. He had to go on his gut instincts, because he had never landed his floats on tundra and he had no idea how the Beaver would perform. So he leaned the gas out as he got closer to the tussocks, looking like a field of long-necked human heads. As the speedometer nicked 45, he flipped off the ignition lever to minimize the chances of an engine fire, and then leveled off his flaps.

He pushed in the nose slightly to touch down on the front part of the floats so the plane wouldn't rock over as they hit—*Bang, Bang, Bang*—past a boggy stream as Ave felt the struts bending. Celia prayed the floats would hold the fuselage fuel tanks off the ground and sparking rocks. And Mardy, unafraid, peeked with her left eye from behind the sleeping bag at the blur of passing tundra and imagined Olaus's smile brightening his blue eyes. She was ready to join him.

At exactly midday on July 10, their clattering DeHavilland Beaver skidded to a smoking halt on the tundra of the Sadlerochit. The struts had buckled, but inside, miraculously, no one was hurt. Celia and Mardy began thanking Ave for saving their lives. Ave, however, still fearing an explosion, kicked the door open and shouted at the two women: "Get out quick!"

He jumped in back, yanking out backpacks and tents, pushing it all out in an avalanche of gear, shouting to Mardy to stand back so she wouldn't get hurt. They were in the middle of a vast wilderness, surrounded by fierce clouds of mosquitoes. If Thayer's passengers had been most any other people so much older than him, he figured he would have had his hands full. But these two, he thought, "were an asset." As he began trying to raise a rescue, talking into his VHF radio—stoically using the standard instead of the emergency frequency—he was relieved to see Celia and Mardy setting up the two tents, dressed in their down jackets and shoepacs for wet tundra. Mardy kept coming over and offering him cookies; Celia fixed him hot cocoa.

While Mardy wrote in her journal about how gracefully the red phalaropes bobbed on the pond out beyond the boulders, Celia tried to read a book. They played cards. At eight o'clock, they cooked freeze-dried chicken and served it to Ave with wheat bread and jam. At ten o'clock, they fell asleep.

After midnight, Mardy heard the rescue plane's twin props lumbering over the roar of the Sadlerochit River. They shouted to Ave's tent and woke him up. Celia ran through the fog of mosquitoes—warning Mardy: "Don't you come out in all these bugs!"— to listen to the radio. A big, green C-130 was circling two miles above like a giant moth agitated by the midnight sun. They radioed down that they could see the orange rescue cloth.

At three-thirty, in the shapeless dawn of Arctic summer, they awoke again, this time to the noise of a helicopter. Since Mardy would never complain, Celia, fifty-six, bristled: "Why can't they wait until eight in the morning to rescue us?"

A "nice young man" dressed in a military jumpsuit emerged from the Huey and reached into their tent to help Mardy out. He said, "I'm sorry about this."

"Sorry?" Mardy replied. "Why sorry?" she smiled. "We're alive—you don't know how grateful we are!"

WHEN STELLER'S JAYS HOPPED into the bird feeder at Moose, and visitors sagged into the old couch, Mardy embellished the story of the naturalist, Georg Steller, who lost his life getting back to Russia because he was too busy discovering the jay that would be named after him. She told this story because punctuality had become her lifelong habit, and because naturalists, like her husband, were too preoccupied while collecting skulls and scats to afford punctuality.

"It's important," Mardy waggled her index finger, "for someone to be on time."

To the devoted Murie readership, on page 301 in their jointly authored *Wapiti Wilderness*, she and Olaus confessed their favorite time. Since their summers were too busy to celebrate their August 19 wedding anniversary, every year they waited until October 19 and picnicked with two friends who had also been married on August 19. October 19 became Mardy's tradition, and long after the other three picnickers died she imagined those midday anniversary outings with her husband on the shores of Jackson Lake.

In the bittersweet redolence of October, during the final haul before the white slate of winter, the cottonwoods and aspens reflect pupil-dilating quantities of light and color. Geese fly in chevron formation, elk trumpet their marching orders, and the mountains shine like newly polished incisors above the emerald waters of the lake. As Mardy grew older, she clutched this date as an intensely private day of celebration that signaled a journey she began with Olaus in 1924, on a northern honeymoon that she would never forget, no matter what. She never missed such an important date.

Congress however, did. Legislation to lease the wildlife refuge to oil companies, or to make it wilderness, came and went with each new administration. In 1991, a bill to develop the coastal plain was met with a filibuster and intense opposition from environmental groups and the Gwich'in, who had filed a lawsuit against the Department of the Interior.

Mardy wrote to the new president and asked him to protect the refuge. In 1995 Republicans gained control of Congress and announced a budget reconciliation that included an amendment bill to open the coastal plain. The president vetoed it.*

And the Arctic oil versus wilderness battle raged on. Regardless of each new Congress, regardless of each new executive branch, the 1.5 million acres have been neither leased nor protected as the permafrost continues to melt. The diminishing Porcupine caribou herd continues its own embattled journey in and out of the Sacred Place Where Life Begins each year, along with millions of snow geese, ducks, sandpipers, terns, swans, cranes, whales, and seals.

To CELEBRATE THE great Grandmother's one-hundredth birthday, Mardy's friends put on a hootenanny. A five-foot-long Paystreak Cake—layered with mocha, like the seams of gold streaking a Fairbanks streambed—sat under a large white tent that served as a theater. A troupe of actors from Tennessee put on a play, *Evening of Enchantment,* based on the romance described in *Wapiti Wilderness.*

Over two hundred locals showed up, while a band played bluegrass music in the meadow. The crowd danced like Olaus and Mardy used to: their hands up by their ears, mimicking caribou antlers, in the old-fashioned and forgotten Arctic jitterbug, the altered Hesitation Waltz that had become Mardy Murie's ritual. Goldenrod, bitterbrush, fireweed, and lupine swayed in the breeze. Someone sighted snow geese passing over the Snake River.

After the party, the ranch stayed lively with the Murie Center's "conversation" seminars, started by Mardy and Olaus a half-century

---

*The 1995 legislation had been proposed by the Alaska delegation of Don Young, Frank Murkowski, and Ted Stevens. They held office consecutively for twenty-two years, longer than any state's delegation in Congress. The three Republicans all held influential chairmanships for the development of their states'—and the whole nation's—natural resources.

On January 17, 1998, President Clinton awarded Mardy the Presidential Medal of Freedom. As the president bent over and put the medal around her neck, Mardy, who could now barely speak, whispered into his ear, "We still have work to do."

earlier. The center carried on the education traditions of the family. Although Mardy began slipping into a silent battle with Parkinson's, and was no longer able to fully articulate her goals, every month or two she'd make a pronouncement that left everyone stunned. Naturally, they began recirculating Mardy's thoughts.

Even though she could no longer hit the bully pulpit, as the so-called Grandmother of the Conservation Movement, the power of her presence and her bequest of caring for wild lands and animals began to take on a momentum and meaning all its own. If she remained silent, her confederacy of believers and acquaintances often spoke for her.

Her oldest son, Martin, joked good naturedly, about the widely told story of how Mardy perceived an elk walking around the ranch as Olaus. Some locals and at least one family member couldn't help questioning this sort of veneration, arguing that the Murie Center might be exploiting Mardy for its own ends. Others suggested that the matriarch might have inadvertently stirred up resentment from her family by lavishing too much attention on conservation matters. She had adopted and been adopted by a community of fiercely loyal, sentimental, anthropomorphizing tree-huggers who studied her books and correspondence and interpreted her infrequent whisperings.

Beyond all of Mardy's reckoning, the legend grew.

Chapter 12

FINAL DUET

Cream together sugar, shortening, salt and spices. Add beaten egg. Add the molasses and blend well. Gradually mix in the flour. Then add the water and vinegar. Bake at 350 degrees for 10–12 minutes. Place on cooling rack. While still warm, dab tops of cookies with icing.

  —"Cry-Baby Cookies,"
    from white tin recipe box in Mardy Murie's kitchen

Several miles below the Sheenjek headwaters, I kneeled to measure the strange tracks next to some shed moose antlers gnawed by tiny lemming teeth and covered with moss. The prints were neatly embossed in the mud, ten and a half inches long, showing the thirty-inch stride of a biped in Vibram soles. Shadowing the backpacker's prints were the four-toed and distinctive triangular pads of a male wolf's five-inch-long feet.

A mile upstream, I found sign of the backpacker's vanished feces dug out of a shallow hole in the sand by a hungry rodent. Toilet paper, which should have been burned, or carried out, bannered the willows. In the past, I had discovered browned paper fluttering like prayer flags below Everest, frozen into the snowy summit of Denali, and littering pristine beaches from the Sea of Cortez to the Gulf of Boothia. But finding toilet paper in the refuge was a first for me.

As I continued upriver, mosquitoes flew into my mouth and nose and eyes. By striding at a fast four miles per hour, the light-winged bugs were sucked into the wake of my slipstream. I preferred this technique to the usual bug-proofing options—until I had to stop and wait for the group; freeing the mosquito cloud to zoom around onto my face. My five companions wore sunglasses and headnets and the lethal DEET. But I had long suspected that my allergies and rashes and baldness derived from using too much bug spray when I first started coming to the Arctic. Nor could I tolerate claustrophobic items blocking my face. I needed the freedom and space to sense bears and wolves and all else that might wander our way.

While traveling in the North, I had stumbled upon a way of perceiving hidden wildlife and the often-indiscernible sublimities of the natural world. Instinct—for lack of a better word—allowed me to understand the wilderness, the wildlife, and even the weather. By combining all five senses with an alert open-mindedness, I suddenly knew of a presence on the nameless mountain above. I didn't see or smell anything, but quick as a falling star, an intense and prickly awareness washed over me.

They ambled a mile away. Initially, in this broad, treeless valley of deceiving distances, they appeared to be ground squirrels. Then I locked onto the blonde grizzly and her cub. I ripped out a handful of sedges and threw them up: the wind was blowing from us toward the bears. They were moving unpredictably and quickly downhill, so I encouraged everyone to speed up into a mosquito-shedding pace. Since I had been coming here for twenty years now, and since I had already talked these clients out of packing a bear gun, they followed quickly.

Nomadic Inuit and our hunting ancestors relied on a similar "sixth sense," and as a species, people haven't yet lost the ability to reconnect with these instincts. It takes concentration, along with depth perception, familiarity with a place, and a constant awareness of movement mixed with colors. In this fashion, I had learned how to listen to the refuge as a whale reads its sonar in the ocean.

To wit: the mountainside above supported a knee-high forest of dwarf trees below steely gray, disintegrating shale cliffs. By sweeping my eyes around, I could use peripheral vision that didn't require focusing on the bears, and showed their blonde coats in moving contrast against the green and gray. If they were Dall sheep, I would've locked on white blurring against rock.

Forget the binoculars.

It helped that I had been expecting bears. The valley was rife with pea vine and tundra diggings. From previous time spent here, I had anticipated the broad and deep sense of scale. Combining this with color impressions and animal sign, I was able to perceive the bears, preoccupied with roots, before they got wind of us.

In this broad and glacially virgin topography that lacks the edges and visual cues of our more southern biosphere, Iñupiat Eskimo and Gwich'in people still innately know wildlife. They still travel without maps and discern direction without compasses. Like bears and wolves, they have learned how to *feel* their way through this landscape by analyzing and combining complex bits of information about game trails, snow texture, depth perception, scat piles, stray hairs, pawed tundra, color, smells, and wind.

In Inuktitut, for instance, it was not necessary to point or use gestures to show wildlife. The People's understanding of this place had grown so complete that single words could be whispered to indicate "below the sun," "along the horizon," "in the distant water," or "at the tip of the ridge."

As I cinched my shoulder straps and speed-walked toward the headwaters where Mardy Murie tried to cure her husband's cancer, I felt delighted to have found a sanctuary where we could reconnect with our remnant genes, where we could experience wildlife and wilderness in a visceral and sensory way—unlike the flat experience of zoos, game preserves, or micromanaged parks. These gut-level experiences, or "intangible spiritual values" showed what the Muries had in mind by creating the refuge. And now that I had discovered, mined, and exploited these innate pleasures within myself and the Arctic, I had found enough of my own reasons— gleaned from the Muries—to stop coming.

It wasn't just the propeller drone of sheep hunters in Super Cubs, finding toilet paper in the willows, or discovering fresh Vibram prints in the headwaters. And it had little to do with the iridescent clouds of mosquitoes.

My pregnant wife, June, was waiting for me to come back home to Colorado.

ALONG A RIVER not far from here, at the end of mosquito season many years ago, Olaus and Mardy Murie slept out in the open. In the rosy dawn, they were awakened by monotonic howls from across the river. Mardy believed the wolves were serenading them. Olaus believed the wolves' territory had been intruded upon.

Two wolves sat silhouetted against the sky, howling back and forth. As the male finally ran past the Muries to join its mate and continue their duet, Mardy felt a sudden sense of rapture, a harmony with the natural world. Olaus called it "the voice of the wilderness."

As we pitched camp along a burbling brook close to the Sheen-jek, close to the Murie's camps and above the valley filled with wolf sign, I kept thinking about that wolf encounter. The Muries wrote and talked about the howling wolves repeatedly, and their experi-ence represented the culmination of an essential wilderness outing. Wild spaces without wolves—the signature predators—were no longer ecologically intact places. No wolves meant no ground squirrels, no snowshoe hares, no mice, and no caribou. In other words, no wilderness.

The renowned philosopher Joseph Campbell once said that we created our own Gods; while the writer Barry Lopez added that we also created our own Animals. In the Arctic, seen through the eyes of both white and northern cultures, the wolf and the bear sat atop the food chain—practically, spiritually, and mythically.

More than the bear, the wolf had proved a talisman and a guide for my time in the North. It began with the blonde huntress in 1983, calling her pups away, and allowing me to observe the familial complexities of wolves. It continued in fleeting glimpses and distant howls. More recently, on the tip of Canada's Cape Bathurst—at 70° 35' North, the northernmost point for me—a wolf stalked me from two miles away. I had been trapped by a gale at the end of a long sandy peninsula with my kayak. I hadn't seen or spoken to another person for ten days and felt overextended, miserably secluded. As I watched the wolf approach through my binoculars, I deliberately pushed my pistol-grip Mossberg away. The remarkable wolf, also unafraid, sniffed me, smiled in that sidelong yet friendly way of canines, and with a quick turn, ran back into the tundra with his tail held high and the Beaufort Sea glowing in his eyes. That wolf and I were not altogether different. My state of depression vanished, and I slept soundly that night for the first time in a week.

Later, I described the encounter to an Inuit guide and his bear hunter client—a boastful car salesman from Pennsylvania who had shot his grizzly trophy from a snowmobile. The client laughed the wolf experience off, saying that the animal must have been rabid. Away from his client, the guide later told me that my encounter was a sign. He said that the wolf would bring me luck. He said that we should always pay attention to wild animals.

Through admiring the wolf, and fortuitously modeling myself after him, I had found mastery, independence, and a physical sense of belonging in wilderness. I had also substituted a sense of wonder for the prevailing trend of skepticism, although my old-fashioned behavior was as much about responding to the wolf's primeval landscape. Finally, like *Canis lupus* entering the den, I had discovered the need to raise a family.

Standing near the divide of the Kongakut and the Sheenjek, pretending to be a wilderness guide, I cleaned out my bowl of soupy freeze-dried pasta, supplemented with the unavoidable and crunchy bodies of countless drowned insects. Then I set my sodden boots beside the tent door.

Although I couldn't be blamed for the mosquitoes, I was being held responsible for making everyone walk in the river, rather than in ankle-spraining tussocks, disintegrating the stitching in our boots. I had also packed calorie-barren freeze-dried food because it kept our packs light, and its odorless packages helped keep bears away. I would have been blind to miss the baleful stares coming from my hungry companions, but as Olaus Murie once said, "in the evolution of human spirit, something much worse than hunger can happen to a people." By the time we finished crossing the range, these clients and climbers might feel thankful. Even if we never saw the caribou migration, most of the group would be glad to shrink a size, temporarily forget about their high-pressure careers, or revel in the new, well-earned tautness in their legs.

Before I could escape the pestilential whining, a bull caribou trotted past. His sides flinched with mosquitoes, his hooves sucked against soft tussocks while his mouth held the wind. Downstream, he stopped to catch his breath and plow his nostrils through wet mud to escape the delirium of bloodthirsty mosquitoes.

I jumped into the tent, spent ten minutes squashing the accompanying horde of insects, then lay back on my malleable moss bed. Like most nights after carrying a heavy pack through tussocks and innumerable river crossings, no longer afraid of bears, I fell asleep within minutes.

Until the howling woke me up.

Along the creek nothing moved. No color, no sound, no smell. I looked up through the haze of mosquitoes toward the skyline and spied a flash of brown and black against boulders the color of storm clouds. The wolf ran a bit longer, then sat back on his haunches, lifted his muzzle to the starless sky, and again let loose: *"Owwwwwwwwwwwwwwwww."*

His body was patchworked but dark, in the way that Iñupiat Eskimos believed signified a great hunter. He stood too far away to accurately size, but I guessed his large tracks were those shadowing the backpacker's Vibram prints. I guessed the wolf had had enough of our kind here.

Through the binoculars, I could see the wolf shaking and pacing. He held his tail low, showing his agitation. He leapt through another sweep of boulders, bounced straight up and down, then stopped by straightening all four legs. He barked. He yelped. Then his voice approached a scream as he hit a crescendo of mournful, long-held high notes—unlike any wolf I had ever heard.

In all three tents, flesh crawled on everyone's backs. The wolf was asking us to go, to leave the refuge alone.

Long after he disappeared over the ridgetop, I could still hear his scream.

───────

After passing the century barrier, Mardy's face lengthened and paled. It was about this time that the pine martens and the Steller's jays moved away.

Pooto the hunter stayed close that last year, confining his kills to whatever small rodents unwisely entered the cabin. Pooto, like his Eskimo namesake, was exceedingly affectionate and cheerful. It took an effort to lift the paunchy cat off the couch.

A member of Mardy's family had recently petitioned to move

her into a retirement home. Since most of her friends and family objected to the plan, and a generous neighbor continued to pay for round-the-clock nurses, she stayed. But as the Grandmother's star brightened, her body went the way of all flesh.

Mardy often sat in a wheelchair next to the couch, still following her admirers, family, and friends carefully across the room with her eyes. Although they appeared faded glacier-gray with cataracts, she liked to sit in front of the large picture window, where she could see the light burnishing the Grand Teton and cock her head for bird voices.

In spring 2003, as the woods filled with the liquid cries of returning thrush and western tanagers, the director of the Murie Center read a letter to Mardy from an old colleague who helped establish ANWR five decades ago. The letter writer—yet another Washington, D.C., lobbyist—windily praised Olaus, knowing what Mardy wanted to hear.

Mardy unexpectedly spoke: "I can see the white light," she looked up, "but I'm not ready to go yet." By this remark, everyone now felt certain that she had a date in mind.

She had already been diagnosed with dementia. But her recent remark, along with discreet glances at the calendar, winks, and an attentiveness to the details and dates of the week told everyone around her that perhaps Mardy had a plan.

The doctor continued pronouncing her heart and lungs healthy, but he had no idea why she was still alive. When he heard the idea that Mardy was hanging on to make sure that nothing happened to the Arctic National Wildlife Refuge, he laughed. Still, the doctor thought it strange that such an elderly person would request ear cleaning so that she could better hear the owls.

In mid-August, Mardy's nurse wheeled her out onto the big concrete porch next to round chairs laced with translucent elk-skin seats. A crowd of long-skirted and patched-pants people danced in front of the cabin in honor of her 101st birthday, while platters of cookies made the rounds. Swallows performed great spiraling dives, plucking mosquitoes from the air.

After an hour, the musicians—playing fiddle, cello, guitar, banjo, and a dobro—lugged their instruments onto the porch, next to Mardy. The dobro player bent to take a request, nodded his head to Mardy, and then broke into the old Jimmy Davis tune that she and Olaus would listen to:

You are my sunshine, my only sunshine.
You make me happy when skies are gray.
You'll never know dear, how much I love you.
Please don't take my sunshine away.

Mardy wore a lavender shirt and clenched her jaw as she concentrated on the words. Wildflowers colored an upended log on the porch; ice cream melted next to the two cakes. Her cheeks were flushed as she annunciated over the music, "This is *wonder-full.*"

Swallows chirped, and the fiddler closed his eyes while the dobro player and the guitarist sang in a final duet:

The other night dear, as I lay sleeping,
I dreamt I held you in my arms.
When I awoke dear, I was mistaken,
So I hung my head down and cried.

ON SUNDAY MORNING, October 19, 2003, Mardy's friend Mike drove from his home alongside the Snake upriver toward Moose. He felt unnerved that a couple of years had flown by since his last visit with Mardy and he would never forget the speech she made at his high-school graduation three decades earlier. Like most of Mardy's intimates, he figured there was still time: two days remained until the anniversary of her husband's death.

Mike represented one of many Murie associates: Republicans and Democrats, Independents and Greenies, politicians and ranchers, writers and plumbers. Anyone with an open mind and a love of the outdoors found themselves welcomed on the ranch. Mike happened to be a half-century younger, a former high-ranking USFWS official who served along the beltway in patent-leather shoes, rather than the cowboy boots he grew up wearing in Jackson. He now had a family and a busy career as an environmental attorney, specializing in showing corporate clients—mining or oil and gas operators—how to respect endangered species and the Clean Water Act.

After turning left past the post office, it came as a shock that the park service had widened and graded the half-mile road into the ranch. The sagebrush meadows rattled with larkspur and lupine seedpods.

Water and electric lines had just been buried beneath newly planted grass. The recently completed bathhouse appeared a bit precious, with Olaus and Mardy's photographs denoting the Men's and Women's entrances. The attorney noticed that the moldy, tilting outhouses were still fertilizing the forest behind the eighteen cabins—resting on new concrete foundations and now declared a National Historic Landmark.

He walked across the front porch and pulled open the storm door into Mardy's cabin. A smiling photograph of Olaus sat on the piano, in the living room where the attorney had spent so many evenings drinking tea, with the caribou poster over the foyer and the Eskimo ivory collection in the far corner. He winced at the blast of heat rising out of the stoked-up fireplace and gas stove.

The morning nurse said Mardy was resting in the east bedroom. She had been given another shot of morphine just before dawn.

The cabin smelled of molasses. Pine boards creaked beneath his weight. Inside the bedroom doorway was the hand-tinted photograph of the green-gabled seaside houses of Frimansled, Norway, that belonged to Olaus's forebears. The attorney could have been entering another time zone, like coming into a far-off Arctic temple where all is hushed and everyone removes their shoes.

Mike felt shocked to see how weary Mardy looked in front of the oxygen bottle and behind the nasal canula, her face bluing from hypoxia. Since she stared up at him with familiarity, he sat down and took her hand and talked about his wife and their kids—now eleven and fourteen—who loved the outdoors.

Immediately he sensed Mardy slipping away, and even though he had been trained in a judicial system of irrefutable logic, nothing in life, he told himself, happened as coincidence. He kept talking, reassuring Mardy about how important she was to him, how many friends she had, how she really made a difference in the world. "You aren't going to leave this earth alone," he said.

He believed that his mentor, although unresponsive, would understand every word. He cleared his throat and continued his monologue.

"The country's getting ready for winter with all the leaves in the air," he said. "The coyotes are howling, the elk are bugling, and the geese are flying overhead." Then Mardy closed her eyes and stopped breathing.

He looked at his watch: 1:14, October 19, 2003: the day that she and Olaus celebrated their wedding. On this day each year, during what they called the benediction of October, they walked the shores of the big lake holding each other's hands, watching birds soar past, keying out the footprints of the animals, and listening to the music of the wilderness.

She had picked a wonderful day to die.

EPILOGUE

The director of the Murie Center steps up to the podium, taps the microphone, and pauses in front of five hundred people. It is an odd gathering—young and old, conservative and liberal, people dressed in both T-shirts and ties.

The woman then reads from the last sentences of *Wapiti Wilderness*:

> Nature was to him in October, and not in spring, poignantly suggestive, deeply mysterious, in her intense and visible occupation. She was enormously busy, but she was serenely busy. She was stripping her house of its deckings, dismantling her habitation to the last and uttermost leaf; but she stripped, dismantled, extinguished, broke away, not in despair, defeat, but in ordered preparation and with exquisite certitude of glory anew.

Outside the ski-lodge auditorium, the snows are so deep in northern Wyoming this winter that workers, fearful that the Murie Ranch will be crushed, have to shovel off every roof.

Several other locals, obviously unaccustomed to public speaking, yet so moved that they feel an obligation, make their way to the podium to share remembrances about weather, birds, and lessons learned from the Muries. Three different speakers stand up straight and keep talking as tears course down their cheeks, but most of the eulogists cause peals of laughter. Just the way Mardy and Olaus would've wanted it.

The ceremony goes on for what seems like hours. Writers and a retired senator and officials from Washington, D.C., stand up and expound, carefully, on politics and wildlife and wilderness.

The superintendent of Grand Teton National Park abashedly concedes to trapping park wildlife in the 1960s to help feed Mardy's pine martens. Then, while studying Arabic at the American University in Cairo, Egypt, four levels beneath the ground, as far as you could get from the Tetons, the superintendent met the only other student in his class for the next five years: a man who also lived in Moose and was a devotee of the Muries. His father wrote the Wilderness Act.

"You can't get away from Mardy," the superintendent concludes.

Clearly, the crowd has come to celebrate rather than to mourn. A schoolteacher who had been married on the Murie Ranch implores the crowd to: "go home and write your congressmen about how important the Arctic National Wildlife Refuge is." Others repeatedly invoke the refuge, calling it Mardy's second home. A deputy director of the USFWS (and former manager of ANWR), steps up to the podium and reminds everyone that her life spans the one hundred years of the national wildlife refuge system.

Young children play and laugh near the microphone. Hundreds of cookies sit ready to be eaten, and while schoolchildren sing "the Teton Waltz" into the microphone, the Snake River Band pulls out their instruments. In a closing public summation, a filmmaker reminds the crowd that Mardy had a knack of making a joke or telling a silly anecdote whenever things threatened to go too serious. And the mood here, at least to an outsider, seems strangely jubilant for a memorial service, but this crowd knows how Mardy appreciated a good party. It's high time to start dancing.

As the fiddler begins sawing, kids dart for the cookies, and skirts twirl out on the dance floor. Among the laughter and handshaking and talk of making trips north, the Muries would have been pleased to hear the private words of a high-ranking official from the pro-oil administration. He is an earnest yet relaxed man, dressed in an earth-colored sports coat and checkered shirt with no tie, and since he is no stranger to northeastern Alaska, his colleague leans close and listens intently to the whisper.

"They'll never drill the Arctic refuge. It just won't happen."

ACKNOWLEDGMENTS

My debts stretch wider than those 19.6-million-acres.

Jeff Long—a talented novelist and my advisor for two decades—critiqued initial proposals and commiserated with me throughout the publishing process. Although I always followed a sense of direction in the refuge, I repeatedly lost my way trying to tell this story properly. Many friends came to my rescue. Chip Brown, David Stevenson, Steve Chase, Ryan Rich, Gary Kofinas, Ralph Bovard, Duane Raleigh, Mark Herndon, Jared Ogden, Liz King, Steve Roper, George Schaller, Cam Burns, Jim Gilchrist, Peter Nichols, Richard Compton, and Susan Townsend all read and helpfully commented on various sections or drafts.

The Murie family too were incredibly helpful and generous. However, any mistakes I may have made interpreting the complex lives of these people are my own. Although the written record is extensive, memories are often faulty, and in some cases I have been forced to rely on journals and correspondence to lift the veil on the Muries' private lives.

Nonetheless. I have treasured Olaus's *Animal Tracks* since puberty. Mardy first caught my attention with a round of tea and cookies in 1989. Her children, Don, Joanne, and Martin, and her grandson, Thomas, gracefully attended to my questions and even my presence when it was least expected. During my fifth visit to the ranch, in mid-October 2003, Mardy unexpectedly passed away.

I'm thankful to the filmmakers Charlie Craighead and Bonnie

Kreps for making the romantic documentary, *Arctic Dance: The Mardy Murie Story*, that originally inspired my book. Gregory Kendrick's scholarly work "An Environmental Spokesman: Olaus J. Murie and a Democratic Defense of Wilderness" helped put Olaus's life in perspective. Timothy Rawson's *Changing Tracks: Predators and Politics in Mt. McKinley National Park* and his interview transcript of Louise Murie brilliantly illuminated Adolph Murie. *The Sibley Guide to Birds* and Olaus's writings allowed me to accurately write voice descriptions for a dozen haunting birdcalls that I heard while traveling through the North. Adolph, Olaus, and Mardy's books—*A Naturalist in Alaska, Wolves of Mt. McKinley, Two in the Far North, Journeys to the Far North* (the only title out of print), *Wapiti Wilderness*, and *Field Guide to Animal Tracks*—were essential for understanding the Murie quest.

I could not have detailed their epoch without the following people consenting to interviews: Mardy, Martin, Louise, Jan, and Donald Murie; George Schaller, Brina Kessel, and Bob Krear—who shed new light on the 1956 Sheenjek River Survey; Chuck Clusen of the National Resource Defense Council and Bill Reffalt, formerly USFWS director for the Alaska Lands Bill—who explained the intricacies of ANILCA and subsequent Congressional actions and inactions; Doug Scott of the Wilderness Society, who shared his knowledge of how the Eisenhower administration created the range; present and past USFWS employees David Payer, Roger Kaye, Patricia Reynolds, Fran Mauer, Pam Miller, and Ave Thayer, who spoke of his near disaster while piloting Mardy; Ginny Wood and Celia Hunter—who were an inspiration every time we met; Debbie Miller, who shared the insight that also informs her thoughtful *Midnight Wilderness*; Laurie Kutchins, who granted permission to use part of her poem that appeared in *Arctic Refuge: A Circle of Testimony*; Dr. Bruce Hayes, a friend of the Muries, who spoke candidly about Mardy's health; Dr. Norman Levine, who helped me uncover the origin of the word *permafrost*; Mark Herndon, again, who patiently tutored me in petroleum geology; Dr. Nancy Shea, Amy Brennan, Toni Archibald, Jamie Reilly, and all the dedicated staff of the Murie Center—the world's finest institution for carrying on the grassroots ideals of the Muries; Charlie Craighead, who shared minutiae about the Muries; Ed Zahniser, who reminisced about Olaus; Inger Koedt, who remembered how Olaus and Mardy acted as a couple; Lois Crisler, head nurse–cum–Mardy confidant; and Mike Brennan, who shared the remarkable tale of his twenty-nine-year friendship with Mardy.

The Iñupiat Eskimos of Kaktovik, on the northern edge of the refuge, were always kind to me. One of my few regrets, over the two decades that I have been journeying North, is that I have not been able to spend as much time with the Gwich'in people, on the southern edge of the refuge.

To others—Randy Udall, Karen Barkley, Mark Madison, David Backes, Don Congdon, Alison Murie, Carol Duell, and Christian Boissonnas—and any others I may have forgotten to mention, thank you. To dozens of friends who accompanied me on adventures to the Arctic—infusing this narrative in whole or in spirit, from 1983 to 2002—your companionship acted as true North.

To all the people who consented to interviews or rolled out the red carpet in Fairbanks, Deadhorse, and Kaktovik, your courtesies and graciousness will not be forgotten. To the staff and students of the Oil Versus Wilderness course, thank you for indulging my version of the story, which, no doubt, would be presented in two dozen divergent versions if every participant had the opportunity to write it down.

The psychological support, sustenance, and artistic recognition offered by the Colorado State Council of the Arts in 2003 and the National Endowment for the Arts in 2004 are deeply appreciated.

Both fellowships came to me as life preservers, when I began submerging under the weight of a heavy narrative.

My research into the lives of the Muries and Arctic history was enhanced by studying the holdings at several libraries. In particular, the Murie papers in the Conservation Collection at the Denver Public Library proved invaluable. Also, my trips to archives at the University of Alaska, Fairbanks, the University of Wyoming, Laramie, and the National Conservation Training Center in Shepherdstown, West Virginia, helped elucidate the Muries' lives. Hundreds of pages of congressional testimony and various letters found at the USFWS offices in Fairbanks proved to be revealing glimpses of the Muries' and the refuge's past.

Martin Murie of North Bangor, New York, deserves further mention. As a true "varmentalist," he fed me at his farmhouse, tracked elk with me in Moose, and shared hundreds of pages of correspondence between Olaus and Adolph Murie. Martin became a confidant who answered scores of questions and told nuanced stories. It would be remiss not to mention Martin's little-known books: *Red Tree Mouse Chronicles, Burt's Way, Windswept,* and *Seriously Insistent.*

I believe that several other publishing houses rejected this book because of its controversial and potentially negative environmentalist slant. While New York is the red-hot center of publishers that bank on controversy, many of these corporate-owned houses owe their financial stability to big oil. Yet Roby Harrington, my editor at W. W. Norton, last of the great independent publishing houses, seemed oddly cool about jumping into America's heated battle of corporate oil against simple wilderness. He showed patience and support from this project's ponderous inception, onto a half-cooked draft, until the book's final creation. I'm also grateful to our mutual friend, Dr. Ralph Bovard, who introduced us.

To all the other editors at W. W. Norton who watched over these pages, including Andrea Haver, John Barstow, Aaron Javsicas, and Susan Sanfrey, and to copy editor Kristin Camp Sperber with her keen birding ear—thank you.

And finally, to June Waterman, whose support and insight are the foundations of my earth. My debt to her and our son is a life-long pleasure.

—JONATHAN WATERMAN
January 2005

APPENDIX A:
LOCATIONS/QUANTITIES OF ARCTIC OIL

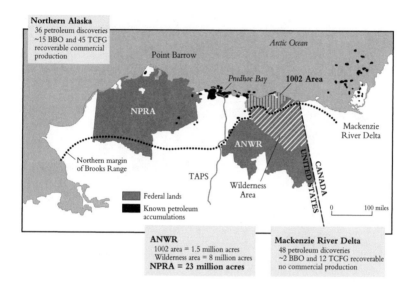

Northern Alaska
36 petroleum discoveries
~15 BBO and 45 TCFG
recoverable commercial
production

Arctic Ocean

Point Barrow

Prudhoe Bay   **1002 Area**

NPRA

Mackenzie
River Delta

ANWR

Northern margin
of Brooks Range

TAPS

Wilderness
Area

Federal lands

Known petroleum
accumulations

0   100 miles

UNITED STATES / CANADA

ANWR
1002 area = 1.5 million acres
Wilderness area = 8 million acres
NPRA = 23 million acres

Mackenzie River Delta
48 petroleum dicoveries
~2 BBO and 12 TCFG recoverable
no commercial production

National Petroleum Reserve-Alaska (NPRA). Locations of known petroleum accumulations and the Trans-Alaska Pipeline System (TAPS) are shown, along with summaries of known petroleum volumes in northern Alaska and the Mackenzie River Delta of Canada. BBO—billion barrels of oil (includes cumulative production plus recoverable resources); TCFG—trillion cubic feet of gas, recoverable resources.
(Source: United States Geological Survey)

APPENDIX B:
ANWR 1002 AREA

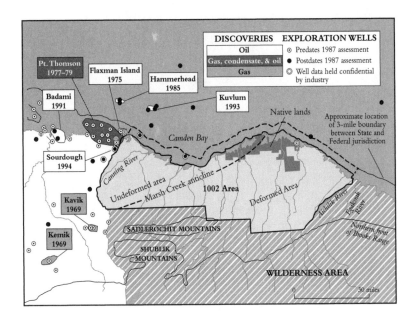

Map of the ANWR 1002 area. Dashed line labeled Marsh Creek anticline marks approximate boundary between undeformed area (where rocks are generally horizontal) and deformed area (where rocks are folded and faulted). Boundary is defined by Marsh Creek anticline along western half of the dashed line and by other geologic elements along eastern half of the dashed line. Exploration wells are coded to show whether information from them was available for the 1987 USGS assessment of in-place petroleum resources. Northernmost dashed line shows the offshore extent of the entire assessment area.

(Source: United States Geological Survey)

APPENDIX C:
SUMMARY OF AGES, NAMES, AND ROCK TYPES PRESENT IN THE ANWR 1002 AREA

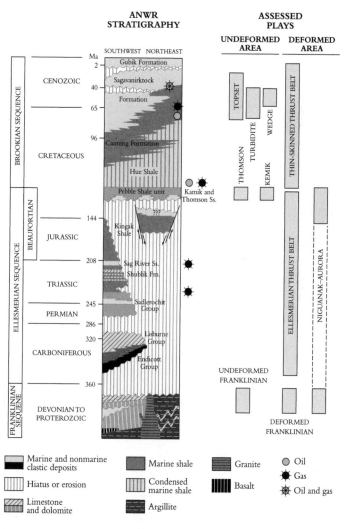

(Source: United States Geological Survey)

APPENDIX D:
GASOLINE CONSUMPTION
AND OIL PRODUCTION

Annual Gasoline Consumption: Gallons per Person

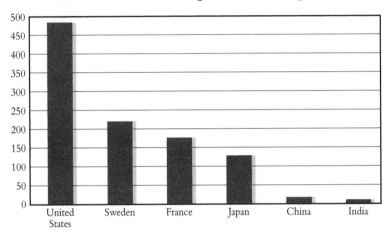

U.S. Oil Production 1900 to 2050

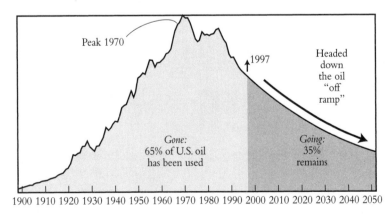

(Courtesy of Community Office of Renewable Energy)

APPENDIX E:
HOW MUCH OIL IS LEFT?

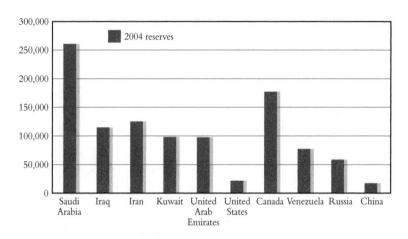

All figures in billions of barrels.

(Source: derived from information in Oil and Gas Journal)

BIBLIOGRAPHY

Alaska Conservation Foundation, "Super Profits Keep Oil in the Pipeline," *Dispatch,* Winter 1993.

Alaska Oil & Gas Reporter, "BP Says Horizontal Well in Disappointing Alaska Oil Field Shows Promise," August 4, 2003.

———, "Viscous Oil Begins to Flow at Orion Field in Alaska," September 17, 2003.

Anchorage Daily News, "ANWR Video Sparks Outcry," April 12, 2002.

———, "Arctic National Wildlife Refuge Holds Promise of Light, Sweet Crude-Oil Yield," February 18, 2003.

———, "Size Estimate of BP Oil Spill in Prudhoe Bay, Alaska, Increases Dramatically," May 31, 2003.

———, "BP, Partners Hope to Recover 200 Million Gallons from Prudhoe, Alaska, Field," September 9, 2003.

Appenzeller, Tim. "The End of Cheap Oil," *National Geographic,* June 2004.

Backes, David. *A Wilderness Within: The Life of Sigurd F. Olson.* Minneapolis, MN: University of Minnesota Press, 1997.

Bailey, Holly. "Pictures of Controversy," *Newsweek,* May 5, 2003.

Banerjee, Neela. "Oil Industry Hesitates over Moving into Arctic Refuge," *New York Times,* March 10, 2002.

Banerjee, Subhankar. *Arctic National Wildlife Refuge: Seasons of Life and Land.* Seattle, WA: The Mountaineers Books, 2003.

Banfield, A. W. F. Review of *Never Cry Wolf* by Farley Mowat. *Canadian Field Naturalist* 78, 1964.

Bartholet, Jeffery. "Alaska: Oil's Ground Zero," *Newsweek,* August 13, 2001.

Bartimus, Tad. "Nature's Helpmate: Mardy Murie Carries On with Her Wilderness Fight," *Seattle Times,* December 26, 1982.

Berton, Pierre. *The Arctic Grail: The Quest for the Northwest Passage and the North Pole 1818–1909.* Toronto: McClelland & Stewart, 1988.

Bishop, Sam. "Murkowski, Young Oppose ANWR Compromise," *Fairbanks Daily News Miner,* February 27, 2002.

Borneman, Walter R. *Alaska: Saga of a Bold Land.* New York: Harper Collins, 2003.

Boyd, Greg. "Saturday Night Vs. Farley Mowat," *Eye,* May 16, 1996.

Brody, Hugh. *Living Arctic: Hunters of the Canadian North.* London: Faber and Faber Limited, 1987.

Burch, Ernest S. "Muskox and Man in the Central Canadian Subarctic," *Arctic,* September 1977.

Byrd, Jo Anne. Interview of Mardy Murie, Wyoming Council of Arts, March 3, 1978.

Caro, Robert A. *The Years of Lyndon Johnson: Master of the Senate.* New York: Alfred A. Knopf, 2002.

Cassidy, John. "Beneath the Sand," *New Yorker,* July 14–21, 2003.

Campbell, Colin J., and Jean H. Laherrère. "The End of Cheap Oil," *Scientific American,* March 1998.

Campbell, Duncan. "Bush Plan to Exploit Alaskan Oil Thwarted," *The Guardian,* March 21, 2003.

Chandler, Lynn. "Warmer and Wetter Winters in Europe and Western North America Linked to Increasing Greenhouse Gases," *NASA News,* June 2, 1999.

Craighead, Charles, and Bonnie Kreps. *Arctic Dance: The Mardy Murie Story.* Portland, OR: Graphic Arts Center Publishing, 2002.

Curry, Peggy Simson. "Portrait of a Naturalist," *Audubon Magazine,* November–December 1963.

Dobbyn, Paula. "Visitors Queue to Visit ANWR," *Anchorage Daily News,* May 10, 2001.

Douglas, William O. *My Wilderness: The Pacific West.* New York: Doubleday, 1960.

Engel, Matthew. "Senate Vetoes Oil Drilling in Alaska Refuge," *The Guardian,* April 19, 2002.

Faulk, Diana. "Portrait of a Conservationist: Mardy Murie," *Master Network,* Summer 1996.

Firestone, David. "Both Sides Confident as Senate Nears Vote on Alaska Drilling," *New York Times,* March 14, 2003.

Floyd, Timothy. "Bear-inflicted human injury and fatality," *Wilderness and Environmental Medicine* 10, 1999.

Gamarekian, Barbara. "Guarding the Wilderness: A Lifetime Job," *New York Times,* April 15, 1985.

Gendlin, Frances. "The Reasons for Things: A Conversation with Mardie Murie," *Sierra Magazine,* July–August 1979.

Glover, James M. "Thinking Like a Wolverine: The Ecological Evolution of Olaus Murie," *Environmental Review,* Fall/Winter 1989.

———. "Sweet Days of a Naturalist," *Forest and Conservation History* 36, July 1992.

———. "Olaus Murie's Spiritual Connection with the Wilderness," *International Journal of Wilderness* 9, April 2002.

Goddard, John. "A Real Whopper [Farley Mowat]," *Saturday Night* (Canada), May 1996.

Goldstein, Edward. "Defending the Wild Places," *Reed Magazine,* November 1998.

Hagemoen, Rolf, and Eigil Reimers. "Reindeer Summer Activity Pattern in Relation to Weather and Insect Harassment," *Journal of Animal Ecology* 71, 2002.

Hall, Sam. *The Fourth World.* New York: Alfred A. Knopf, 1987.

Harris, John F. "Clinton Signs Oil, Gas Royalty Bill to Simplify and Boost Collection," *Washington Post,* August 14, 1996.

Haugen, Geneen Marie. "Conservation's 'Grande Dame,' " *Denver Post,* October 12, 2003.

Heilprin, John. "Scientists Find Mounting Effects from Oil Drilling in North Alaska," *Aspen Times,* March 10, 2003.

Hebert, Josef. "Is Drilling ANWR Worth It?" *Associated Press,* March 20, 2004.

Herndon, Mark. "The Last Frontier," *Forum for Applied Research and Public Policy,* Summer 2002.

Herrero, Stephen. *Bear Attacks: Their Causes and Avoidance.* Guilford, CT: Lyons Press, 1988.

Hulse, Carl. "Pet Projects Flood Energy Bill Before Crucial Wednesday Session," *New York Times,* October 15, 2003.

Hutchinson, A. S. M. *If Winter Comes.* Boston: Little Brown & Co., 1921.

Jalonik, Mary Clare. "Alaska's Lightning Rod," *CQ Weekly,* September 27, 2002.

Jettmar, Karen. "A Meeting of Generations," *Fairbanks Daily News Miner,* November 2, 1997.

Kaufmann, John M. *Alaska's Brooks Range.* Seattle, WA: The Mountaineers Books, 1992.

Kaye, Roger. "Alaska and Beyond: The Wilderness Legacy of Robert Marshall," *Wild Earth,* Winter 2000–2001.

Keim, Frank J. "In Memory of Mardy Murie," *Fairbanks Daily News Miner,* October 26, 2003.

Kendrick, Gregory D. "An Environmental Spokesman: Olaus J. Murie and a Democratic Defense of Wilderness," *Annals of Wyoming* 50, Fall 1978.

King, Robert P. "The Long Haul North to Alaska's Arctic Shore," *Aspen Times,* March 10, 2003.

Klinkenborg, Verlyn. "Mardy Murie's Vision," op-ed page, *New York Times,* October 24, 2003.

Kofinas, Gary. "Porcupine Caribou, Environmental Impact Assessment and Political Agendas," unpublished paper, 1992.

Kosova, Weston. "What's Gale Norton Trying to Hide?" *Outside Magazine,* June 2002.

Kristof, Nicholas D. "Cool to Arctic Oil," op-ed page, *New York Times,* September 10, 2003.

Krugman, Paul. "Two Thousand Acres," op-ed page, *New York Times,* March 1, 2002.

Kumins, Larry. "Alaska Oil Exports," *CRS Report for Congress,* April 5, 2000.

Lavelle, Marianne. "Living Without Oil," *U.S. News & World Report,* February 17, 2003.

Lavietes, Stuart. "Margaret Murie, 101, Who Helped Save Wilderness, Dies," *New York Times,* October 23, 2003.

Lentfer, Hank, and Carolyn Servid, eds. *Arctic Refuge: A Circle of Testimony.* Minneapolis, MN: Milkweed Editions, 2001.

Lentfer, Jack. "Agreement on the Conservation of Polar Bears," *Polar Record* 17, 1974: 327–30.

Looney, Ralph. " 'Mother of American Conservation' Still Going Strong at 89," *Rocky Mountain News,* September 21, 1991.

Lopez, Barry. *Of Wolves and Men.* New York: Charles Scribner's Sons, 1978.

———. *Arctic Dreams.* New York: Charles Scribner's Sons, 1986.

Lovins, Amory B., and Hunter L. Lovins. "Energy: the Avoidable Crisis," *The Atlantic,* December 1987.

Masiel, David. "Crude Reality," *Outside,* February 2004.

Marshall, Robert. *Arctic Village.* New York: Literary Guild of America, 1933.

McCart, Peter. "Fisheries Investigations Along the North Slope and Beaufort Sea Coast in Alaska with Emphasis on Arctic Char," *Arctic Gas Biological Report Series* 41, February 1977.

McPhee, John. *Coming Into the Country.* New York: Farrar, Straus and Giroux, 1976.

———. *Annals of the Former World*. New York: Farrar, Straus and Giroux, 1998.

Miller, Debbie S. "Finding Clarence Rhode's Plane," *Alaska,* January 1980.

———. *Midnight Wilderness: Journeys in Alaska's Arctic National Wildlife Refuge*. Portland, OR: Alaska Northwest Publishing Co., 2000.

Milton, John P. *Nameless Valleys, Shining Mountains: The Record of an Expedition into the Vanishing Wilderness of Alaska's Brooks Range*. New York: Walker and Co., 1969.

Moran, Tom. "Increasing Revenue," *Fairbanks Daily News Miner,* October 26, 2003.

Murie, Adolph. *A Naturalist in Alaska*. New York: Doubleday, 1963.

———. *The Wolves of Mt. McKinley*. Seattle, WA: University of Washington Press, 1985.

Murie, Margaret E. *Island Between*. Fairbanks, AK: University of Alaska Press, 1977.

———. "A Fairbanks Girl in Prince William Sound," *The Alaska Journal,* Winter 1980.

———. *Two in the Far North*. New York: Alfred A. Knopf, 1957. Reprint Portland, OR: Northwest Publishing Co, 1981.

———. "Summer on the Sheenjek," *Defenders of Wildlife,* September–October 1987.

Murie, Margaret E. and Olaus Murie. *Wapiti Wilderness*. New York: Alfred A. Knopf, 1966. Reprint Niwot, CO: University Press of Colorado, 1985.

Murie, Olaus. *Alaska-Yukon Caribou. See* U.S. Department of Agriculture.

———. *The Elk of North America*. Harrisburg, PA: Stackpole, 1951.

———. *A Field Guide to Animal Tracks*. Boston: Houghton Mifflin Co, 1954.

———. "Wolf," *Audubon Magazine,* September–October, 1957.

———. *Journeys to the Far North*. Palo Alto, CA: American West Publishing Co. & The Wilderness Society, 1973.

Nash, Roderick. *Wilderness and the American Mind*. New Haven, CT: Yale University Press, 1982.

Nelson, Richard K. *Shadow of the Hunter: Stories of Eskimo Life*. Chicago: University of Chicago Press, 1980.

Neubauser, Chuck, and Richard T. Cooper. "Senator's Way to Wealth Was Paved with Favors," *L.A. Times,* December 17, 2003.

New York Times, "White House Refutes Arctic Oil Report," March 29, 2002.

O'Hara, Doug. "Researchers Track Crude's Wandering Trail," *Anchorage Daily News,* May 13, 1999.

Outdoor Life, "Grizzly Shot in Hotel," April 2003.

Pielou, E. C. *A Naturalist's Guide to the Arctic*. Chicago: University of Chicago Press, 1994.

Pimlott, Douglas H. Review of *Never Cry Wolf*, by Farley Mowat. *Journal of Wildlife Management* 30, 1966.

Postman, David. "Inside Deal: the Untold Story of Oil in Alaska;" a week-long series in the *Anchorage Daily News,* February 7–11, 1990.

Prouty, Dick. "Memorial Award Recipient Praises Late Conservationist," *Denver Post,* February 10, 1974.

Rawson, Timothy. *Changing Tracks: Predators and Politics in Mt. McKinley National Park*. Fairbanks, AK: University of Alaska Press: 2001.

Reardon, Jim. "Clarence Rhode," *Alaska,* January 1980.

———. "Fairy Tales and Wolves," *Alaska,* January 1985.

Revkin, Andrew C. "Debating Whether Oil Wells and Wilderness Mix," *New York Times,* March 11, 2003.

Roderick, Jack. *Crude Dreams: A Personal History of Oil and Politics in Alaska*. Fairbanks, AK: Epicenter Press, 1997.

Rosen, Yereth. "Family Ties Boost and Burden New Alaskan Senator," *Reuters,* September 12, 2003.

Ruskin, Liz. "ANWR Campaign Comes to America's Living Rooms," *Anchorage Daily News,* April 19, 2001.

——. "Murkowski: Poll Gives ANWR legs," *Anchorage Daily News,* December 15, 2001.

——. "Poll Finds Majority Against ANWR," *Anchorage Daily News,* February 1, 2003.

Schaller, George B. "Arctic Valley: A Report on the 1956 Murie Brooks Range, Alaska Expedition." April 1957.

——. "New Area for Hunters," *Outdoor Life,* March 1958.

Scheffer, Victor B. *Adventures of a Zoologist.* New York: Charles Scribner's Sons, 1980.

Schlickeisen, Rodger. "Quiet Zealot at Interior," *Defenders of Wildlife,* Summer 2002.

Selley, Richard C. *Elements of Petroleum Geology.* New York: W. H. Freeman and Co., 1985.

Service, Robert. *The Spell of the Yukon: and other Verses.* New York: Barse and Hopkins, 1907.

Sibley, David Allen. *The Sibley Guide to Birds.* New York: Alfred A. Knopf, 2000.

Spielman, Andrew, and D'Antonia Spielman. *Mosquito: The Story of Man's Deadliest Foe.* New York: Hyperion, 2001.

Stranahan, Susan Q. "The Valdez Crud," *Mother Jones News,* March/April 2003.

Strohmeyer, John. *Extreme Conditions: Big Oil and the Transformation of Alaska.* New York: Simon & Schuster, 1993.

Strum, Matthew, Donald K. Perovich, and Mark C. Serreze. "Meltdown in the North," *Scientific American* 289, October 2003.

Tener, J. S. "The Distribution of Muskoxen in Canada," *Journal of Mammalogy,* August 1958.

Terres, John K. *The Audubon Society Encyclopedia of North American Birds.* Avenel, NJ: Wings Books, 1991.

Udall, Morris. *Too Funny to Be President*. New York: Henry Holt & Co., 1988.

United Nations Press Report, "Melting Permafrost May Accelerate Global Warming," February 7, 2001.

U.S. Department of Agriculture. Biological Survey. *Alaska-Yukon Caribou*, by Olaus Murie. Washington, D.C.: U.S. Government Printing Office, 1935.

U.S. Department of the Interior. Geological Survey. *Arctic National Wildlife Refuge, 1002 Area, Petroleum Assessment, 1998, Including Economic Analysis*. Washington, D.C.: U.S. Government Printing Office, 1998.

U.S. Department of the Interior. Geological Survey. *Arctic Refuge Coastal Plain Terrestrial Wildlife Research Summaries*, edited by D. C. Douglas, P. E. Reynolds, and E. B. Rhode. Washington, D.C.: U.S. Government Printing Office, 2002.

Verhovek, Sam Howe. "Mention Drilling, and Tourists Rush to Alaska," *New York Times*, June 10, 2001.

———. "Talk of New Drilling Raises Doubts on Alaskan Pipeline," *New York Times*, March 11, 2002.

———. "Drilling Could Hurt Wildlife, Federal Study of Arctic Says," *New York Times*, March 29, 2002.

Vickery, Jim Dale. *Wilderness Visonaries*. Minocqua, WI: Northword Press, 1986.

Waller, Douglas. "Some Shaky Figures on ANWR Drilling," *Time*, August 13, 2001.

Wall Street Journal editorial, "Kerry vs. Caribou," April 11, 2002.

Washington Post, "Mixed Verdict Offered on Alaska Oil Drilling," March 5, 2003.

———, "Mechanical Problems Pinch Oil Production at Alaska Facilities," December 4, 2003.

Waterman, Jonathan. *Arctic Crossing: One Man's 2,200-mile Journey Among the Inuit*. Guilford, CT: Lyons Press, 2002.

Watkins, T. H. *Vanishing Arctic: Alaska's National Wildlife Refuge.* New York: Aperture, 1988.

Weidensaul, Scott. *Living on the Wing: Across the Hemisphere with Migratory Birds.* New York: North Point Press, 1999.

Whitney, David. "Big Voice for Alaska," *Anchorage Daily News,* August 7, 1994.

————. "Seeking Statehood Stevens Bent Rules to Bring Alaska into the Union," *Anchorage Daily News,* August 10, 1994.

Wild, Peter. *Pioneer Conservationists of Western America.* Missoula, MT: Mountain Press Publishing, 1979. Pp. 113–29.

Williams, Terry Tempest. *An Unspoken Hunger.* New York: Pantheon Books, 1994.

Yergin, Daniel. *The Prize: Epic Quest for Oil, Money, and Power.* New York: Simon & Schuster, 1991.

Young, Steven B. *To the Arctic: An Introduction to the Far Northern World.* New York: Wiley Press, 1989.

Younge, Gary. "America Is a Class Act," *The Guardian,* January 27, 2003.

INDEX